PENNY ELLIS

BIG BROTHER 2

Meet Me at the Mirror

Coping with reality.

First Edition. First published 2023

Published by:
Morgan Lawrence Publishing Services Limited
Ridge House Annexe
16 Main Ridge West
Boston
Lincolnshire
PE21 6QQ
www.morganlawrence.co.uk
email: info@morganlawrence.co.uk
Company number: 12910264

ISBN: 9781739296902

Photographs courtesy of: Channel 4/Shutterstock, Ken McKay/Shutterstock, PA
Images/Alamy Stock Photo, Photoshot / TopFoto and author's collection.

Cover design by LCgrapix. Cover photos by Channel 4/Shuterstock, Ken McKay/
Shutterstock.

Edited by Amy Memory.

Printed and bound in Bulgaria by Pulsio Print

Contents

Acknowledgements

My special thanks to all who have journeyed with me.

For those who witnessed my highs and lows through my days in the house and beyond.

To *Big Brother* devotees who have given their enthusiasm and support.

To my good friend Paul Bedsprings for encouraging me to write this book in the first place.

To everyone at Morgan Lawrence Publishers: Mathew Mann, Barrie Pierpoint, Lee Clark, Amy Memory and Harry Worgan.

To my husband Mark for giving me the confidence to finally write the book and for reading every single draft. His feedback to "go deeper and tell your whole story" was invaluable.

Much love and kindness to everyone x

FOREWORD

Who is Penny Ellis?

A flutter of fabric, cheers from the crowd, intense sunshine and rain all at once – and the storm on the horizon!

I didn't know Penny in the *Big Brother* days. I'm writing this foreword from a completely different perspective – the way I know her, some years away from the spotlight yet still strangely relevant today.

Big Brother was (and will continue to be) a cultural phenomenon. The incredible insight into a group of housemates living in close quarters and sharing their confined lives. I've been told that one can pass countless hours viewing the chosen contestants who have been permanently housed and broadcast on television twenty four hours a day, seven days a week. Over the years, millions of fans (and super fans) have been enthralled by the most engaging programme of its time.

Beyond being thrust into relative stardom and, of course, the tabloid press, one must constantly attempt to carry on with some semblance of life. Working hard to establish themselves aside from the brief reality star they were isn't always easy if this is shaken, damaged, or stolen totally.

In July 2009, while out with some friends at Harris', a tapas bar in Hastings, I met Penny Ellis, a naively wonderful, gregarious, but emotional, extrovert. She was serving thirty covers while gliding between the tables and chatting and laughing with the regulars who frequently came to enjoy the cosy ambience, and her warm, welcoming hospitality. Most of her customers assumed she had opened the business following her success, while others made reservations just for the entertainment!

Penny has always been true to herself, though. She was immediately enamoured with the experience from the minute she accidentally dialled the contestant line and left a panicked message that was picked up.

Before I went to pay our bill, we had hardly communicated at all. As she handed me the receipt, she asked, "Do you like jellybeans?"

"Of course, who doesn't?" I replied.

Suddenly, as if from nowhere, my right hand found itself holding a massive bunch of beans, and Penny was gleefully stuffing handfuls into my mouth. That was THE moment I will never forget!

Several months passed, but I found myself back in the old town in January. Since it was lunchtime, I decided to stop by Harris' once again. Penny appeared out of nowhere, arms outstretched wide to give me the warmest hug conceivable! I was parked at table fourteen, which was close to the bar, so we could talk between service. Ever since she has always been a part of my life, and I have always known her as Lisa, not Penny. On 17 January 2011, a year to the day before we first met, we got married.

Navigating our shared transition out of her past and into our shared future has been a challenging journey. There have been a lot of setbacks for us along the way. I originally found it challenging to get used to people stopping us (Penny) in the street to talk about the *Big Brother* days, but that was just the beginning.

I still have no idea what it must be like to be suddenly propelled into relative fame after years of anonymity. The blight of negative internet comments and tabloid exposure never seem to leave your side. Columnist comments, expert analysis, and endless pages of rumours with drawn-out tales of this and that grind into everyday existence.

These were even earlier than the era of social media, in which a tale is out the door before the truth has a chance to put on trousers! I hope people will be kind while I scroll through social media, but inevitably they aren't. The saying "yesterday's news is tomorrow's fish and chip paper" is long gone.

Coping with the past in the context of today's reality has been one challenging component. Google never sleeps, so many permanent teaching job applications are rejected, and you wait for the phone to ring for the occasional day of supply teaching on zero hours before the inevitable happens: "Weren't you Penny from *Big Brother*?" from a student or staff member. Expect fast contract cancellations and, on occasion, being escorted out of the premises.

Then the slander and demolition begin once again. . .

Since *Big Brother* Series 2 in 2001, Penny's life has been increasingly challenging, as evidenced by her story. The highs, lows, and never-ending struggle to reconstruct her life after her life-changing fifteen days in the house have taken almost two decades to rebuild.

So, 2020 arrives along with the effects of lockdown. No longer teaching an ad-hoc contract in Rye, Eastbourne (or anywhere else), and like all of us, plunged into uncertainty and worry for loved ones.

Time away from the classroom hysteria gave her the opportunity to reflect and re-evaluate life, which is how this book came to be.

Penny's memoirs, thoughts, and insights surrounding reality TV from the days before, during, and after her stint in *Big Brother 2* offer an idea of what this crazy life was all about before the smartphone was even invented!

We now look forward to the re-launch of the *Big Brother* house and wish the best to the new housemates. Penny's book offers insight into how a simple reality TV series may not be as it would seem for those of us looking in.

You may be asking yourself if I ever watched *Big Brother*.

The answer is no, but I'm looking forward to reading about it – and I know you will be too.

Best wishes & much love.

Mark.
(Aka Mr Penny Ellis) x

ACT 1:
Squeezing into the Blueprint Jeans of Jesus.

SCENE 1:
The phone call I didn't know I had made.

I shall start by trying to answer the questions in most people's heads as so many years have passed:
Why write this now?
Who are you?
What were you famous for?

I have divided my story into Acts and Scenes because as contestants on *Big Brother*, we were put into what was, in 2001, an experimental brand new concept of a reality TV show. *Big Brother* aired for the first time ever in 2000, and I would have loved to have sat in on those meetings where producers and all those creating the show were discussing ideas of how to make another *Big Brother* TV reality show in 2001. I don't think anyone knew if the concept would work again or what would actually make a Reality Show a success. I was asked by the producers, when I met with them after being accepted as a contestant but before I went into the *Big Brother* house, to "play a motherly role". I think, in my opinion, they were trying to figure out how a completely new idea for a show like this would work. There was no guarantee that the ordinary people they chose this time would be watched by an audience, so perhaps they thought that if I was "motherly" (as an actor plays a character), certain scenes and dialogues that take place during the days in the house would develop, as well as conversations and reactions that would make it more interesting for viewers.

During my auditions, I had to improvise scenes in groups of everyday situations; perhaps they chose me because I had theatre training, who knows? This is the time before the creation of reality shows, which have become our normal viewing in 2023. To be at the start of something that has now grown beyond anyone's wildest dreams is difficult to fully comprehend, let alone the impact having my own reality constantly interrupted by my *Big Brother* "reality" for twenty years has taken its toll on my mental health and the events of my life. I love helping and taking care of people and loved being "in the kitchen, out the kitchen" in the house, as I did most of the cooking during my time in there. Despite the producers' request, I was just myself. I didn't play any role. I have always cooked for friends and hugged my friends, thinking nothing of it. I think I would have liked the stories written about me in the newspapers to have been about me doing the cooking, feeding the chickens, and being a caring and kind person. But I suppose those sorts of stories wouldn't have been very interesting. They wouldn't have sold newspapers.

My mother calls me "Alice in Wonderland," as she says I am so trusting and naïve and I always think the best of people. I had no idea of the stories in all the newspapers or whatever opinion had been formed about me on radio and TV as I walked out of the *Big Brother* house on my eviction night 8 June 2001. I was interviewed by Davina McCall live on Channel 4 and then there was a huge press conference with hundreds of journalists throwing questions at me. It was overwhelming. It was then that I found out how the media had portrayed me.

I couldn't really cope with the stories that were told about me in 2001 and in the years that followed, and instead of facing my feelings, I just kept burying my emotions deeper inside myself. This allowed my manic depression and OCD to control my erratic life. Over the next two decades my life spiralled out of control and it took all my strength mentally to finally write my story.

I had no idea, on 8 June 2001, as I gave my interviews, that I was in danger of being sacked by the school I worked at as a teacher because I had become the first *Big Brother* contestant to appear naked on the show.

I had no idea that the public (and my employers) believed that I actually wanted sex on live TV after stories about me hugging Paul, one of my fellow contestants, dominated the tabloid headlines.

I had no idea that a whopping four million people had seen my naked body or that everyone thought I had deliberately dropped my towel and consciously flashed my breasts and vagina to the world.

I had no idea that the headlines about that infamous towel-dropping incident had completely destroyed my character and would follow me around for the next twenty years.

I think, in my opinion, the producers had stumbled upon a format for future shows as hundreds of stories and thousands of emails from people watching flooded their offices and the ratings shot up. Sex sells.

The word "titillation" used in many of the headlines about me means "to excite someone's imagination, especially in a sexual way." The media portrayal of me, linking my name to sex and nakedness – especially as I was a Christian school teacher – is something that would make any reality show gripping and cause audience figures to shoot through the roof.

Watching my "best bits" on YouTube for the first time in 2021 made me feel self-conscious. The way the show had been edited made it look as though I wanted to have sex with one of my fellow contestants. No wonder the teachers and students I have worked with over the past two decades have reacted the way they did when they realised that I was Penny from *Big Brother* teaching in their school. My employers would have thought about the reputation of their school and the moral implications of me teaching their students. I have no idea what my old bible group and various friends must have thought. I didn't see a lot of people I used to know for ages after the show because I became caught up in the celebrity circuit.

Looking back now, I wish I had met with them and discussed all my concerns in 2001. I would say to anyone reading my story that it is so important to ask for help and not hide from things, hoping they just go away. I didn't know in 2001 what to do or what I could have done about the stories written about me. I was so naïve. After my eviction I accepted an offer from *OK! Magazine* to give an exclusive interview, a decision I deeply regret. By accepting their offer, I wasn't allowed to talk to the press for two weeks, so I couldn't challenge any of the stories I saw written about me. I just hoped it would all go away.

Hindsight is a wonderful thing. We can all look back and recognise what we'd do differently, and I am no different. If I had my time again I would have handled my reputation and online personality at the time. I didn't, but this is my opportunity to tell the truth. I can finally say to the world, "I didn't deliberately drop my towel at all. I would never want to flash my bits for fame and fortune." I honestly didn't imagine that anyone would be filming me showering or drying myself off. Yet that "Dragon of Fame," as I call it, has never lost its breath from 2001 – until now.

Ironically, I have an article from 2001 that I cut out and put in one of my scrapbooks, which a friend Donna started for me while I was in the house. I thank her and her partner Steve for making me that scrapbook (Peter and Ted also made me one – thank you both). It is called: *Big Brother* your questions answered. One question asked: "Why didn't you censor Penny dropping her towel?"

Big Brother's answer is: "While the team watch everything carefully and there is a delay of about ten minutes to help us make sure nothing too bad gets through, this one did slip through the net. It was an honest accident, just like Penny dropping her towel was an accident."

Another question is asked: "Why didn't you show Penny dropping her towel on the main show?"

Big Brother's answer is: "The Channel 4 shows are trying to tell a story of that day's events, and we didn't feel that the Penny dropping the towel incident was a crucial enough moment that day to warrant including it in the show. We are editing down hours and hours of key footage to show how the relationships are developing between the contestants, and that shot wasn't important."

Imagine what that has done to my mental health. Not only did they "accidentally" broadcast my towel drop and my naked body, but nobody has ever apologised to me personally. Not the producers or creators of the show. They may have put an apology on screen and in a paper, but not to me personally. To read that my towel drop wasn't even "important" and wasn't a "crucial enough moment" (*Big Brother*'s own words), when in fact it shot up the ratings for the show and has caused me incredible shame, mental stress, and multiple job losses for over twenty years, is really hard to cope with. With all their power, surely, they could have said something, and then maybe the whole story could have disappeared in 2001 and I could have moved on with my life.

Another question asked in this article is: "Why does the live coverage keep going silent on E4?

Big Brother's answer was: "E4 has to follow the rules of the TV regulators. We have a system designed to make sure the coverage meets the normal TV regulations on language, nudity, and other adult material. So, for instance, if at 2 p.m. the contestants start swearing, the editing team here will dip the sound to make sure that the swearing is removed by the time the coverage goes to air".

My own head screams *So why didn't my towel drop get edited out? Why is it being called "towel drop" when I didn't even do it? Why am I living a life sentence for something I never did in the first place?"*

In my scrapbook, I have a booklet that explains how the show worked in 2001, as this was TV before social media really took off. It has one page that reads: "*Big Brother* on Channel 4." It then lists:

Monday, 28 May, 9 p.m.: *Big Brother* starts.

Tuesday 10 p.m.: nomination night.

Wednesday 10 p.m.: Nominations revealed.

Thursday 10 p.m.: Daily show.

Friday 8.30 and 10.30 p.m. Eviction night.

Saturday 9 p.m.: Omnibus.

The second page reads: "*Big Brother* on E4." Then says, "*Big Brother* Live direct from the house through the night and the following day." (That must have been where they showed me drying myself.)

It is funny how it has always been: "Penny who dropped her towel," when in fact I am holding it as I am drying my back, not realising the whole world is watching me do so and my private parts are all on display. I remember the producers telling me there was always a fifteen minute delay in filming, so I never imagined my body would be flashed to the world while I took a shower (I found a huge double-page naked spread photo of me in the actual shower in one of the tabloids) or while I, like anyone else, naturally dried myself off, as the producers would have time to edit it out?

The other things listed were the *Big Brother Magazine* show that was on at 7 p.m. and 11:10 p.m. on a Monday, and 7 p.m. and 10:30 p.m. Tuesday to Thursday, bringing all the news and gossip from the house. There was also an interactive TV option where you could use your remote to choose the camera view, catch up on what you missed, play along and test your knowledge, and vote by remote control.

The next page reads, "*Big Brother* on the Web. Live action from the house streamed to your computer twenty-four hours uncut!" This included Fave Cam, which allowed you to follow the most popular person in the house at all times; Pan Cam, where you could control the three-hundred and sixty degree camera view from the dining room table; and Email updates, to keep you posted on information from *Big Brother*.

The last page reads, "*Big Brother* on your mobile." It says: "There is no excuse for not knowing what is happening in the house. Access on SMS: breaking news, nomination and eviction results, sent directly to your mobile. WAP users will receive exclusive news, games, polls, and other special features of the house."

In 2001, those were the most updated media: SMS, WAP, and the Web. It flabbergasts me that this story of my "towel drop" has run on for twenty years. We are all much more aware of how social media works now, but in 2001, unless you had studied media studies at university, why would you even have any idea of how media manipulation works?

I was utterly shocked in 2002, as I had a journalist say they would pay me a huge sum of money for "Tit and Bum" shots. I was aghast. But it seems that if you are famous enough and stumble out of a car after a night out and flash your breasts or bum, you can earn money for those photos. I was too ordinary to be famous, and thanks to *Big Brother* I am too famous to be ordinary. When an actor finishes a role in a play, they hang up the costume and go home. I haven't been able to do that. Despite trying to go back to my life before *Big Brother*, and not telling anyone who I was, or even having social media accounts, I have been met with stories and reactions, both wonderful and truly horrendous, that have forced me to rethink and change direction in my life many times over. I didn't ever use Penny Ellis as my name in my teaching roles.

Trying to live my reality inside another reality is a very strange experience. In 2001, you just expected to go back to your normal life as there was no platform for reality TV stars, and I was fine with that. I had a super time after coming out of the house – nearly two years of amazing times where I met so many famous people. That was fabulous, but I never imagined it would go any further than that. I expected it all to be forgotten about after a couple of years at the most.

When I was asked to host *Big Brother's Little Brother* alongside Dermot O'Leary on 3 August 2001, I was invited to creep through the galleries built behind the walls of the *Big Brother* house. They reminded me of being backstage in a theatre. They were huge compared to the space we had in the house. The mirrors that the contestants looked into from inside the house were actual windows through which the cameras filmed. So many cameramen were filming, and I was careful not to make a sound as the housemates were all really close up to these windows/mirrors, and I was trying not to trip up on all the cables and squeeze past the cameramen I could walk all around the whole of the house inside the galleries. It was a really surreal experience just like the end of series 2 when we were invited to tour the house. There were various hidden doors open so you could access the galleries. The cameras were all gone, and the house was so empty. It was evening time, and it was so quiet. I picked up a little stone from the garden and whispered goodbye to the house. I truly believed that was the final act of a wonderful experience that had now come to an end. It was like looking into scenes from a play, so I decided to call Act 1 "Squeezing into the Blueprint Jeans of Jesus." We all deserve to be able to return to the blueprint of who we truly are. I liken it to a pair of jeans, as we all have those moments of trying to get into an old pair of jeans that used to fit us. I hoped to get back to my faith in God and to who I really am. I tried to get back to me over the years but had to keep leaving teaching jobs in shame, fear, and humiliation.

There have been close to forty reality star suicides over the years. We all need to talk more, share more, and ask for help. It has taken me twenty years to finally fit into those "pair of jeans" that my title suggests and be happy in my skin. It has taken until now for me to finally realise that life didn't have to be such a struggle and that I just needed to tell my story. We need to face the things that frighten us the most and have the courage to know that we can defeat them.

I am always interested in what might have happened on the same day hundreds of years before. I found an app that is called On this Day, so I thought I would write three lots of On this day into the start of my story.

The first On This Day is 25 May 2001, the day I entered the house and *Big Brother 2* began to air its first show. I have said that I am the eleventh reality star in the world just to try to give a perspective on what life was like before social media or reality shows even existed. Imagine being one of the very first reality stars ever on planet Earth!

The second On This Day is 25 May 2020, when a box arrived at my house full of my first published book, *A River through My Desert*, and I finally faced up to using social media. I set up my Twitter, Instagram, and Facebook accounts as Penny Ellis only because an American Christian TV station wanted to interview me about my book and publish my social media sites on a TV advertisement. I quickly created them, as I didn't have any! I had no idea how to use them or how to use hashtags. I was totally ignorant. My husband had suggested I put my author's name as Penny Ellis, and I did so at the very last minute before my first book went off to be printed. That absolutely terrified me, as I was still teaching at the time, in February 2020. However, the supply teaching stopped due to lockdown on 23 March 2020, and I never went back to teaching. I couldn't believe anyone would remember me in the media world in 2020 or want me to give interviews, but they did.

My first book is a Christian prayer book. I had massive responses from the Christian media, which involved going back on TV for an hour-long interview, "TBN meets Penny Ellis." I also had a live radio interview for UCCB on 9 July 2020, on their show called "This is My Story." I had an article about myself in *Christianity Premier Magazine* in January 2021, telling my story. It was at that time that I realised how many stories were still being written about me. I hadn't dared to look and had spent so many years just getting by, hoping no one in the schools mentioned *Big Brother*. I lived like a coiled spring and was stressed out of my head for years. Suddenly I was free of teaching and the incessant reactions on a daily basis about having been on *Big Brother*.

No more condemnation; no more having to explain myself.

No more dread and shame.

My relationship with the media has been a troubled one over the years.

On 13 May 2020, Davina McCall was in the newspapers, and the stories were all about the twentieth anniversary of *Big Brother*. "Penny the teacher who dropped her towel on live telly and shot to fame showering naked" was the story under the anniversary headline about twenty years celebrating *Big Brother*, along with a photo of Davina, Rylan, and me alongside them. I couldn't believe that my story was the one featured. I'm also featured in the twentieth Anniversary highlights of every *Big Brother* show from 2000 to 2018! I am also in two of the three episodes of Best Bits of *Big Brother 2*.

My voice is heard first in the very final credit roll at the end of the last TV episode of *Big Brother* in 2001. Even Rylan posted on his Twitter page in 2020 a photo of me and said, "Let's not forget Dame Penny." I was astounded by how many times my photo and the story about dropping my towel were used. One of the replies to his tweet read, and I quote, "Never mind the towel slip; it is the deliberate application of ice-blue eye shadow that has shaken me to the core." It made me realise how powerful social media is today that words grow on these social media sites and can ruin someone's character or cause untold mental stress. Another said: "Looking back, she was so ahead of her time; what a character she was." A couple of other people tweeted: "OBSESSED with her. I would love to see a series of all the people who were voted out first; that would be amazing," and "Ah, another iconic housemate gone too soon." It did upset me a lot that one former *Big Brother* housemate tweeted, "The teacher that got her knockers out, lol." In reply, someone kindly tweeted, "Poor woman got the sack for that as well."

I find stories about my supposed towel drop all over social media, dating from 2001 to 2022, and I realise how easily the students in the schools I taught at would have found them. On 18 August 2022, I was mentioned again in the newspapers, linked to an article about the launch of *Big Brother*'s return in 2023. I headlined that specific article to commemorate *Big Brother*'s most iconic moments. Since 2022, learning how to use Tiktok, Instagram, Twitter, and Facebook Reels has been a revelation for me. One of my posts has had fourteen thousand views!

I am so grateful to Scott. He started social media accounts on Tiktok, Instagram, Facebook, and Twitter. He asked me for a video about myself in March 2022. When I sent Scott a video of me talking about *Big Brother* after twenty years of not going on any media sites or saying anything about *Big Brother* to his @bbitv2tt account, it got one thousand four hundred views and six likes. I find it amazing how people have followed me on my social media platforms, been so kind, and liked my posts. Thank you to all of you. I made the video for Scott on the beach in Hastings, saying hello to anyone watching and reminiscing about being "in the kitchen, out the kitchen" in the *Big Brother* house. I was so nervous and sent it off to him again, wondering if anyone would watch me or even remember me. I was so grateful for the positive responses.

The media has always had such a huge influence on public opinion, even twenty years ago when there were just newspapers and magazines. In November 2001, an article said, "For two fleeting weeks, her name, Penny, and face became the most famous in Britain. She was the talk of every office, she bumped Posh Spice off page one, and even made it on prime-time TV news." I really had no idea how famous I was or how to look after myself, as I had no management to steer me.

In 2004, an article read, "The critics may snipe, but Penny can't help but radiate genuine warmth with pantomime goers who will be on the receiving end in Porthcawl this year."

In 2002, the headline of a newspaper article read, "Penny, six months on, and with the notoriety of being an inmate in the *Big Brother* Channel 4 copyright spy-cam house."

Today, all sorts of photos and comments can be shared instantly and across different social media platforms. Just by typing on Google "Penny *Big Brother*," so much information and so many photos of me come up on all social media platforms. It is quite incredible and terrifying, especially as every student in school seems to have a phone. Another contestant from a reality show said in an article: "It destroyed me for a very long time." I can relate to that. Anything that is said about you can be read so easily and believed.

In 2000, Google was the default search engine. By 2003, the word "Google" was added to the dictionary as a verb with the meaning: to obtain information on the web. People and students will search for me (if you tell them my name) as Penny BB2, and hey, they have distorted opinions and facts to form their own opinions about me. By 2011, Google was handling three billion searches a day. I didn't use a computer at all, only to make lesson plans and PowerPoints for school. All these years so much has been written about me online that I could have put my voice and truth to, which I hope is heard with kindness now. In 2011, Google's monthly unique visitors surpassed one billion for the first time. In 2014, the "right to be forgotten" meant people could request stories and photos about themselves be deleted by Google. In 2022, Google accepted requests for the removal of phone numbers, addresses, and emails. However, it won't remove content that is "broadly useful or part of public record."

In 2021, a teacher taking part as a contestant on *Love Island* was having a conversation on the reality show, and the media took hold of it. In the tabloids and online news, it was reported that "he might not be able to go back to teaching after raunchy sex admissions, it is not necessarily the first time this has happened as *Big Brother* fans will remember the English teacher, Penny." It is mortifying that I am linked to so many stories twenty years later.

In *The Daily Mail* on 9 June 2001, I am meant to have said that the "camera crew wanted to catch the female housemates in the nude or a sexy situation." I was supposed to have said in an interview I never gave, "We could hear the cameraman grunting as he tried to film us," and again about the cameraman "he made me look like a man-hungry slapper determined to bed someone."

It is heart-breaking to remember Sophie Gradon, who died in 2018 at age thirty-two. Also, Mike Thalassitis' death in 2021; he was just twenty-six. His death sparked calls for improved aftercare for people who take part in a reality TV show.

The Jeremy Kyle Show was axed after the death of a contestant in 2019. One contestant on the first reality TV show, *Castaway*, said, "I didn't want to leave my house" once he was home after being a contestant. He even said in the article: "It is heart-breaking now seeing the reality shows and how contestants suffer after participating in the shows that followed on from *Castaway*: *Big Brother*, *X Factor*, and *Love Island*."

In 2020, in *The Daily Mail*, the headline said: "Fear for our jobs", and "Housemates have created a kind of pressure group to stop more embarrassing moments being shown for *Big Brother* Anniversary." Again, I am mentioned as a significant event of *Big Brother* 2.

On 16 June 2021, I read, ITV announced its Duty of Care Protocols following previous criticism of *Love Island* and other reality shows. "*Love Island* contestants taking part in the latest season will be offered a minimum of eight therapy sessions following the show. Psychological consultants will look after the contestants pre-filming. Before filming, psychological and medical checks, including those of the contestants' GP, will be done. There will be proactive contact with contestants for fourteen months after the show ends. There will be bespoke training on the impact of social media, how to handle potential negativity, and help with financial management. Also, help to secure representation for the media and public appearances, and encouragement to get management. The team on *Love Island* will have training in mental health and first aid."

When Adam Collard left the villa, an article on 20 March 2019, reads, "he was informed of the public reaction to him by the press team so he could be prepared for every possible situation." In an article on 29 March 2019, ITV said: "*Love Island* aftercare can't be forever." Aftercare, according to Josh Denzel, should also be in place once the fame fades. He said, "How do I transition to going back to the guy or girl I was before?"

Dr Alex George said in an article on 23 May 2019, that therapy wasn't compulsory when he appeared on the show in 2018. It is a huge change in your life to deal with social media. If you're going on the show to become famous, you will be disappointed.

I decided to write my memoirs about my experiences in *Big Brother* in 2021. I only wrote this book initially to get it out of my head as a project and to try to make sense of my life as I pieced all the bits together. I just couldn't understand how people continued to recognise me from 2001 to 2020. I couldn't understand why I kept losing teaching posts. I was emotionally and mentally exhausted. It is good sometimes to take a step back and see how your life is going, what destructive cycles you have let go of, and what you have healed from. I was amazed when Morgan Lawrence said they would like to publish it! I didn't know what to do, as I didn't think anyone would want to read it. But in 2021, @BBSuperfan did a poll on his Twitter page that ran for a week, and forty-eight per cent of people said they would buy it. Again, I am amazed by the support and encouragement that I have found on these media platforms since 2020. I had been rejected for so many years in the teaching profession that I was used to feeling like a failure. I was overwhelmed by the response from people in 2022, as I got the courage to make Tiktok videos regularly from June 2022 onwards, telling my story of *Big Brother*. I have gradually gotten used to using all my social media platforms in 2022 and posting things, and I have gained such lovely comments from @bigblagger, Vincent, who sent me articles that I hadn't found on the internet, Jon Moses, Julian LeBlanc, and Simon Meets, who takes thousands of amazing photos of celebrities. I get such lovely messages from people through social media, which is a completely new experience for me, saying "this book sounds just what we need to read about" and "the early years are truly the golden years." Some students I have taught over the years have found me on social media and have gotten in touch, which has really healed my heart. To get messages saying what a great teacher I was and how grateful they are fills my heart with joy and lifts away the years of heaviness. I have even been asked to go into a book reading group in a prison; this is such a good opportunity to share my story, which is a message of rebuilding your life, and if I can go and talk and, more importantly, listen to people, it would be just wonderful. We all need to reach out to others. It has meant so much to me and is a complete revelation to be accepted and free to be me again. Freedom of mind and spirit is something you can't buy.

Finally, after more than two decades, I am in control of my narrative.

I now work at my local Morrisons, where I started as a key worker during lockdown in March 2020. In my first month, some ghastly students came in and hurled abuse and mockery at me. They attempted to throw tins at me while I was picking groceries for online shoppers. As they yelled horrifying things and laughed hysterically about me being naked on TV, I felt the dread I had felt in schools over the years flood back to me. I was amazed by the support of the security guard and Claire, the people manager, who is wonderful and caring. They marched these students off the premises and threatened them with the police. After that, no students came into the store to mock me or throw things at me. I love my Morrisons' family. They are so kind and have overcome so many things. I cannot believe their resilience in the face of the devastating sadness that they have endured. They hold a special place in my heart. Beverley wrote this for the book: "I have known Penny for a few years and love being in her presence. She is a very high-energy person with a big heart and will help anybody in any situation. I work with Penny at Morrisons and know that she gives her best, even if it takes a little longer because her best is always given. I have had many laughs and heartfelt chats with this lady, and I truly wish the best for her in this book."

I miss Claire, who now works at another store, and her son Jim; Mandie, Jeanette, Milky Michelle, Mark, Carol, Paula (Nanny McPhee), Debbie, Katie, Sam, Stuart, Barry, Davina, Chris, Tessa, and Stefan; the managers, Jack and Martin; my kind boss, Paul, who is a fair person you want to work for; and all in the café, Pat and Carla; beautiful customers Sharon and Chris, who listened to me and told me I can get this book finished. Finally, my lovely Claire, the people manager, who has gone above and beyond to encourage me these last two years. She wrote these words for my book: "Penny joined Morrisons in Hastings during the COVID pandemic in March 2020. She was exactly what we were looking for in a colleague; she's enthusiastic and a very genuine and loyal member of our team. Penny was a key colleague due to working through the pandemic; her commitment to Morrisons and our customers for the last two years has made her a popular and valued colleague. Since working with Penny, I have been made aware that she appeared in the second series of *Big Brother*. I have watched various clips of the show and am aware that her career in teaching was ruined after her appearance. I personally feel it is a shame that the media surrounding the TV programme had such an effect on Penny's life so many years ago and that it continues to affect her now, over twenty years later. Penny is a very conscientious colleague, and it is a pleasure to work with her." I thank everyone who works there for their acceptance. Lovely, kind, and beautiful people; because of people's kindness since 2020, their generosity of spirit, and what we have all had to overcome since lockdown, because of such kindness, our hearts can be healed, and our lives can begin again. We can renew our hope, rise up into a new world and a new place, and find the strength to begin again.

My third On This Day is 25 May 1977, when *Star Wars* opened in American theatres. I chose it as an analogy because going into the *Big Brother* house was like entering a new galaxy. Decisions made in one day can cause sadness, madness, and chaos and send you to a very faraway galaxy, which you try to get back from. I hope you might agree with me that it takes a long time even twenty years to rebuild and find a life worth living after a day in your life when you made a decision that took away your blueprint. It was like entering a new galaxy because reality TV was just being discovered. I was as raw and genuine in the *Big Brother* house as I had been in the outside world. I was a bit of a broken mess when I went into the house, as I was trying to deal with my anxieties. If your life has been consumed by low self-esteem, the need to please others, nervous breakdowns, severe OCD, destructive habits, fluctuating weight, chronic debt, childhood abuse, abusive and violent relationships, or irrational fears, then maybe you will be kind in accepting this story twenty years later. We all face challenges that we can sink into or rise above. In December 2021, just two days before Christmas, my mother was in the most horrendous car crash. I didn't know if she was alive or dead for over twenty-four hours, as I couldn't get through to the hospitals in Spain where she lives. I mention this as I had been writing up my own family history into a story for my mummy, and Morgan Lawrence had kindly published it for my family to read. My mummy had lost part of her memory due to swelling as her head had been smashed. She has been able to read her story and regain memories that she lost due to the car crash. It is amazing how time and events link together.

I didn't know *Big Brother* was returning in 2023, and I never imagined being free from teaching, helping to bring so much joy to my mummy with her book, and picking up memories that I had hidden away to write my story *Meet me at the Mirror*, or that I would get to publish my story. I can now enjoy looking forward to *Big Brother* 2023, enjoy telling my story, and enjoy piecing together my memories, the joy, wonder, and sadness. I scatter poems through my story and hope you might glance at them. I wrote this poem when I was fifty, in 2017, wondering where along the way I had lost my dreams, knowing if I searched hard enough, I might find them again one day.

50-year timeline (A poem)
For all of us who believe in a second chance
to get up and live again.

Where did the years go?
> *Like lightning flashes suddenly swallowed in a black hole gasp gulp. I now count in 5s.*
> *For 5x4 will be 70. Only 4x5 years left.*
> *Four 5 years then old is the label in my clothes and the scent on my skin.*
> *5 lots of 4 are parents crumpled paper parchments, Dead Sea scrolls creased and fragile. Were they once the crispy birthday wrapping paper, the daily newspaper freshness, and the rolls of excited Christmas wrappings?*
> *Now on a conveyor belt, once gone I am the next one: never again in heels or able to make love hard as joints too stiff in all the wrong places.*
> *Oh, the joy of flat shoes. Everything I am flat just flat. Mother and Father have become the grandma. I still remember too vividly , time too quick like boiling milk for coffee has turned around: their faces the same age as time has layered life lived into one , they all look the same more like the old were every day . Old has a breath that is bitter and smells of leeks.*
> *The child within stretches it cannot get out.*
> *All the comfort blankets, lullabies and sky-blue wholeness of protection given for year's mother's milk of goodness torn in two. It is finished indeed, turned into scars as the vultures came for me. Robin red breast flew willingly onto the thorn and just sang.*
> *The vanilla smell of comfort blanket full of milk warmth, happy stains of ice-cream and ketchup the smell of mother's song corners shredded from wear, knotted into hands full of hope and cartoon Disney dreams.*
> *Fed and watered like a lily rooted. Where did my petals go falling into a cloak of shame where blood razor drops fell all over it and I only had five loaves and two fishes left after all these years. Why did I pick stars from the sky did I think they would never run out?*

I placed them in a box calling it my moonlight it is my comfort. How did my blanket get so small?

I don't think I thought how I was to build it, this life I am in.

I didn't cement the edges together. It just came at me like a slot machine win, like that fairy-tale a shower of gold coins as I walked under belly deep laughter, in velvet coated dinner parties, lights of the city dancing in my hair in late night out. Calling my parents only once a month. A never-ending lottery win flying on wings angels had rented me. A price was paid. Death calls, it is a sound you have never heard before. Like a dog calling whistle sharp and cold, ears prick up and my face now holds sadness in rain cloud heaviness.

The mirror holds friends. Some have changed like rainfall overnight, like dye added to a wash cycle. Some has outdone death and mediocrity; they are the surprise. When I have stopped still in time they have flown. Some are doing what I did, unpicking the vital seams of their tapestry it will fall at their feet in pieces but they do not heed my shriek "It is a mistake "These all best friends know without it being said the road led these fifty years together, signposted so carefully, they slide into the comfort of this warm log fire assurance of a certainty.

But we all hear the sound, the dog whistle warning and who will go first who will be last, one alone when all are gone snowflake melted and a thick fog of nostalgia too heavy to wear is lain at one of our feet. Friends die. Alone becomes a reality like an envelope labelled but unfilled. Photo albums full of those super special moments that defined and shaped life. We cannot re-enter but press our faces against them to intake that breath of then.

If I listed my deepest regrets like waves in the sea, they would call in their ocean voice: "Oh hindsight." "Oh, if I knew then." "Oh, if only." "Oh indeed." Years boil down like jam one word equalling twenty. That word lead weighted at the bottom of the sea. I put on the red shoes from the story book they ran away with me.

Why didn't I save like squirrels in the park, pay off the mortgage. Because youth was impulsive, naïve and optimistic and goblins tricked me and pulled my hair. A time where fun was the silliest things, life looked through a brighter lens. Films that made me cry were popular as pain hadn't lain me down or wrapped its coil spring round my heart. It took meeting me at the mirror to be free. It takes a long time to find the mirror that you can see yourself in.

Lines like naughty children draw on bedroom walls have lined my face. There is a sense that settles cat lap into an acceptance as being alive means hope glimmers that you haven't become who you were meant to be yet. Not just yet.

Now the things that belong to my peace are in my heart and home. I have such memories that live in pods and hang off twisted trees of wrong decisions closer to rainbow colours of joys.

I find them like coins in a muddy puddle.

I can still touch my toes and only need glasses for reading.

But I can't remember already when that moment in time actually happened like breath from a runner at the end of a race. Life changing moments have vanished into Angel's hair.

I had a dream I wrapped it in yellow ribbons and waited. Then there was time twenty years of time to be able to finally unwrap it. It would be the touch of peace that is now my bone marrow. I waited on my dreams and found my reflection in the mirror.

I open my box of moonlight.

The End.

I wanted to include my profession of faith in my story because it is what I believe in my heart.

Some of you may skip ahead to my days in the *Big Brother* house, and I hope that once you've read my story, you'll return to read this section. I have finally let God have my whole life. I hope he will use it to bring hope and healing. Once we cut the puppet strings, it has no more power, but it is really about getting your mind to believe that it is over.

There are two quotes that resonate in my life: "Hope deferred maketh the heart sick" (Proverbs 13v12), and "My heart is restless till it finds it rests in you."(St. Augustine). In the Bible, Jesus asks a man who has been sitting at a pool for thirty-eight years, " Do you want to get well? Get up".

It was a simple question, but I think it reveals how we can make excuses, believe ingrained perceptions of ourselves, and not recognise learned behaviour. We may not be the elephant who believes the gossamer thread on his leg is still the metal chain, or the fleas who have been trained not to jump any higher even when the jar lid is removed, or the dog who, after years in a cage, can only go round in circles when set free. Sometimes, the only definition we have of ourselves is a pity one or a stoic one. But we continue to suffer and believe that those cul-de-sacs are where we are coping with life. If we change the pattern of our thinking that this is how we must live (like changing a piece of clothing), we realise just how small we have made our lives or opportunities. Courage is in completely changing one's mind in the face of overwhelming emotions and circumstances. We can sit down in the same manky bath water one too many times with excuses for our weight, debts, jobs, and relationships, and keep going back into that cycle of problems. I have found my freedom in Christ, who says, "Get up," and who, I believe, possesses the ability to renew my mind, stabilise it so that it does not wobble around like jelly, and transform it. We all love a bit of clear thinking. I can have this realisation, but if I don't use it, what is the point? It has taken me twenty years to realise this and live free. It takes time; look at the pearl made in an oyster's shell only because of the grit that got into that lovely shell. I hope to inspire you to use the grit in your life and change it into a pearl. A lot of our stuff we don't really want to surrender; we seem to accept it without stepping back and looking at it closely, like we do with our reflection in the mirror: our lives and habits, our stresses, thoughts, and feelings. I had a fabulous life, and apart from deep-rooted insecurities, I functioned well. But if something is going to change, it must be cut out. That means pain. Why hurt yourself deliberately? God doesn't want you to hurt yourself; he just wants you to know who you are without that "thing." I believed what people told me. I trusted people. I now trust God with everything.

I had to Google the word "gravity." It said, "An attraction that exists between all objects everywhere in the universe." We are meant to be in balance and harmony. I looked up the first law of motion: an object at rest, stays at rest, and an object in motion, stays in motion with the same speed and in the same direction unless acted upon by an unbalanced force. That sums up your lovely evening until you get that dreaded phone call or some other shocking or unexpectedly horrible surprise. There are numerous examples of things that unbalance us unexpectedly throughout the day. I don't know A-level physics, but I do know that I have "Got up," and I know God is looking after me. I don't know about gravity, but when I go for a walk, I know I won't float in the air! I wear clothes I don't know how to make. I eat food I don't know how to cook. I do the majority of my daily activities without fully comprehending how they occur. People are marvellous. They live a brilliant life, not knowing how that plane flies, but they enjoy the experience. There is so much more we could learn and understand about ourselves. We don't think about breathing, but we do it; we don't think about walking, and we just do that. Some of us can learn the piano easily, understand math, or pick up several languages, and no one else in our family has ever done it. There is a drive for creativity and talent in all of us that has come from somewhere. When you shine from that spot, you're at your happiest at the centre of your life, and you know you're whole and sane. That is my journey over these twenty years. To meet myself at the mirror as the person I am truly meant to be—the person I always was.

I lived on wisps of beauty and had so many beautiful moments despite making some really bad decisions after I left home and the umbrella of wisdom and Christian faith of my mother. If only I had listened to her guidance in my twenties. I am sure a lot of us think like that now that we are in our fifties. The intensity of the media stories about me pushed me back into what I hoped to escape: back into chaos. Nietzsche said, "He must have chaos within him who would give birth to a dancing star." This story is based on what I remember and my recollections of events. It is my own point of view and opinion. The constant hysteria and focus, which were both positive and negative aspects of the entire experience, threw me off balance mentally and emotionally for years. I know now that I wasn't strong enough to face it and build on the opportunity in 2001. The dragon of "fame," as I have said, has never lost its breath these twenty years (that is why I am writing this, as it has never gone away), with the recognition, reactions, and some ridicule being almost unbearable. As I wrote this book in 2021, everyone had a phone and was immersed in social media. The name "reality star" has consumed a generation. So, let me take you on a journey to the very beginnings of this frontier land, a long time ago in a galaxy before MSN Messenger and before new "planets" were known of: Myspace created in 2003, Facebook created in 2004, and You Tube created in 2005. Let me take you back to the creation of *Big Brother* Series 2 (2001) over two decades ago. . .

The moment I made that phone call, everything changed.

I worked as an English teacher at the Sarah Bonnell School for Girls in Stratford, East London. I had been there for over eleven years. During that time, I had built myself into the students' lives as a form tutor and a teacher, and I had taken time to help them develop skills and hobbies. I was close to their families and would invite parents to come into my classroom to work alongside the students and watch the way I taught so they could help their daughters at home with their studies. I had passed all the threshold requirements in 2000 and was on the upper pay scale for a teacher. I had a BA with honours from London University. Reading University awarded me a PGCE in Drama and Contextual Studies. It was a real success to pass the threshold. My mother always said if I had stayed at Sarah Bonnell, I would have become a senior-level teacher. But she also said that I missed my calling by not seizing opportunities after university, and that if I had, I would have been a theatre director. I threw myself wholeheartedly into Sarah Bonnell and the girls I taught, getting involved in changing their lives and using my own money and time to help them find their way.

I made a real difference to their lives too. A letter to the *Sun* newspaper on 4 June 2001, reads: "My friend's daughter is a pupil at Sarah Bonnell School for girls, where *Big Brother* contestant Penny Ellis works. It is outrageous that the headmistress is considering sacking her. She is a hard-working, well-respected teacher whom all the girls adore. With teaching in the UK in such crisis, we should be trying to hold onto such gems."

Even to this day, I have a wonderful, deep friendship with eight of the girls I taught at Sarah Bonnell School. I see them as "family." We are so close, and they are now older than I was when I taught them. They are all grown up and hugely successful. One of the girls, Zainab, is an athlete; she trained for the Olympics as well as being a brilliant businesswoman. She is beautiful and talented. Lizzie, who travelled extensively and learned many languages, is training to be a vet where she lives in Norway, and Emma, who works in finance, is retraining as a dog groomer. Heena is a writer with her own English school who lives in Singapore but is coming back to London. Kuljeet is a teacher in London. Suky is a CEO. Kerri and Kathleen were in Kinderwein, my theatre group. They have so many skills, and it always amazes me what they have done and are achieving. I remember my mum saying to me once, as I retold tales in wonder at their achievements, "What happened to you?" I didn't think about or realise the opportunities that were available to me then. They always say hindsight is a great thing, and it is true. I had a lot of opportunities to buy property with my mum in London, travel and work abroad as a teacher, or move into a completely different job in London. I think I was just broken by things that had happened to me and didn't deal with the root cause. I just lived with the things around me as they were, without building them any higher or planning my future. I lived quite erratically, manically, and spontaneously. I invested in my students and my friends. I was constantly doing something with my drama group at school, so I got to make up my own title at work by 2000 and was given two permanent days a week off teaching to promote and develop creative projects. It was a fantastic opportunity. The title I made up for myself was Initiative and Creative Projects Coordinator. When you walked into the foyer, there were hundreds of framed achievements and awards in speech, debates, poetry, and drama that I had initiated with the girls, and I had great plans for what to achieve with the girls and my drama group in the year to come in 2001 in my newfound role. Life was quite magical in lots of ways. It was in pieces, I must admit, but each piece was a good piece not like a smashed-up cup or glass, but more like complete miniature paintings. Each piece of my life was its own rock pool, completely full of life, and just now and again a huge wave of disappointment, heartbreak, or insecurity would wash over it, spilling the contents. I would make huge, spontaneous decisions that would cause me unnecessary stress and debt. I could see myself self-destructing in areas of my life, but I just couldn't break the cycle.

My day would begin with my walk down to Angel Tube from Essex Road. I loved living in Islington. Everyone who worked on Essex Road was friendly and always said hello. I would pass the vegetable store with its glittering display of shiny vegetables. Then the Laundrette, where the blind Cypriot man would kick his legs in the air for exercise over the stair banister while the clothes dried. Then a cappuccino from the tiniest coffee van you have ever seen, and a chat with Jack, who owned it, always about cleaning our teeth (funny what you remember)—he had a beautiful Persian girlfriend and made the best cappuccinos I have ever tasted. I'm not sure if you've ever taken the central line from Bank to Stratford; you become accustomed to your commute: the wait, the cramping as we all crammed on, the time it takes, and how far underground it actually is. The only difference over those years was reflected in my clothing and hair. I wore mini dresses and stilettos. I skewered a few toes in the jolt on the tube, and I apologise. I even went to work once in my pyjamas when I was depressed. All the highs and lows of my life were really dramatic, but not one part of my life had become complete as I suffered silently from depression and anxiety.

But I had 7A, my form, and what a form it was. They were brimming with energy and talent. We kept a scrapbook each year crammed full of achievements: Raising money for charity in all sorts of ways, including the traditional sponsored silence. We also held talent shows where the girls expressed themselves through dance, poetry, physical theatre in school, and some street theatre too. We built a strong debating society that won lots of awards, even being invited to make a speech in front of Baroness Jay at Westminster Hall. Poems were published in the Young Writers Book that was sold in WHSmith every year. We became part of International Newspaper Day every year, in which we made a whole newspaper in a day and competed with groups around Europe, running to the post office to post it on time. We were part of the magistrate court events, where everyone played a specific role in a real takeover of a court for the day. We had trips around London, some with the school, some just with me and the students and their parents. We did marathons. We went to the theatre and stayed at the after-parties. There were violins learned, corsage horse training, gymnastic feats, and the Bar National Mock Trial Competition. Every birthday was celebrated in style, and every Friday we had a "kangaroo court" to discuss the behaviour of some girls who had misbehaved and, as a group, make a joint decision on how to help them, along with answering anonymous questions from our question box. At the end of every year, we arranged our classroom for our "Oscars." There would be a show of talent (singing, violin playing, dancers) combined with my end-of-year speech reflecting on all that had happened, from braces being removed to naming those who had done good things for the form and the community, and those girls who had overcome illness and problems; changed their ways and found a new confidence. I called out the list of all the charities we had raised money for, and all the awards we had won throughout the year. I would make up specific awards for those who had overcome challenging obstacles in their life. The girls would then come forward to receive their "scroll," which was tied in a red ribbon as a reminder of everything they had done that year to help themselves and each other. I included a personal letter from me telling them how proud I was of what they had achieved and overcome and how I wanted them to embrace their uniqueness. I would take a photo where they held their scroll across their chest like Americans do at graduation. I had found little Oscar statues in a shop in Covent Garden. We would have cake and food and laugh and sing together. We were also one of the first schools to be part of the "Shining Through Awards" in Newham. I was always on the lookout for anything "theatre," and I just entered girls into the competition without realising its enormity. The school then realised what an amazing opportunity it was for the students, and lots of other teachers started entering their students. It reminds me of one of my favourite films, *Shawshank Redemption*, and the quote (if you have seen the film as many times as I have): "They all remembered their tax returns the next year."

I had a theatre company called "Kinderwein" (meaning in English: the voice of the child), and we were working with the community and also ended up working with the police at their conferences, producing physical theatre productions that showed drug use, violence, and domestic struggles. I had such a good relationship with my theatre company; they would embrace my ideas and add theirs so brilliantly. We created a lot of physical and visual drama. At one conference, we were all showing the effects of drug use and acting out scenes that were really shocking. There was fake blood on the stage, needles, and desperate situations. The police came from all over Newham and beyond. It was a massive conference. I had no idea if it would work. There were hundreds of police there, and at the end of our physical theatre production, there was silence. They then went into groups for some sort of group discussion. I found out at the end that they used our "scenes" "as the focal point of their discussion scenarios for the conference day. We were invited back again the next year. We also held weekend drama workshops in the community, which were lovely for parents and students. I just loved seeing people's confidence building. We were the only school to take part in the Royal Festival Poetry Event. It was massive, and I had been liaising for over a year and a half with famous poets and the Royal Festival Hall. St. Martin's Art students created a mini pink windmill with each girl's poem on it for her to keep. We walked into the Royal Festival Hall and gasped as all the girls' poems were hung up on huge plastic swirls twisting around from the ceiling of the Royal Festival Hall. Everyone could see and read them. The girls shone on that stage. They got to read their poems with all sorts of famous creative people; it was magical. Afterwards, we ran across Waterloo Bridge in the dusk of the day with all our mini pink windmills swirling in the breeze.

Why am I telling you all this? Well, the morning I made the phone call that would change my life, I had seen an advert on the *Big Breakfast* on TV before I left for work that morning about a poetry competition they were holding. I thought how much fun it would be for the girls in my theatre company and my form (after all their achievements) to get a chance to go on television and read out their poems. So after setting the class a writing task, I ran out of my first lesson that morning and up the steps to our English staff room. It was a little quirky room right at the top of the beautiful old Victorian building that was my school. I was not supposed to leave my class, so I had to hurry. I wanted to call the *Big Breakfast* and ask them to send me an entry form for the poetry competition.

Before I could even speak into the landline phone, there was an automated voice saying, "This is the *Big Brother* hotline; leave your name and number." I stepped back and looked at the phone. I had never seen *Big Brother* or even heard about it. I hardly watched any TV. In 2001, it was, in my opinion, really hard to get your head around watching normal people doing their normal things as an actual TV programme. I didn't even own a computer or use one. I didn't understand the computer; it was a completely new concept to me. I was a bit perplexed by the automated voice message as maybe I heard wrong because I was in a rush, so I actually left my details, thinking genuinely that it must have said "*Big Breakfast*," and I really wanted the girls to get on to read their poems. That was my phone call. I didn't think anything else about it. It was a complete accident, and I had no idea I had left my name and details on the *Big Brother* application phone line.

SCENE 2:
The *Big Brother* Auditions.

My mum used to say that once I get something in my head, however self-destructive, I have this vice-grip mentality about it, and I just won't let it go. I should have and could have sat down with wise friends and wonderful church friends, but I let the enormity of getting an audition to go on *Big Brother* re-adjust my perspective. I really thought I would just take a creative break from school, get my theatre company some contacts, and have a bit of a laugh doing something to entertain my friends. Having a theatre background, the thought of going to an audition excited me.

The letter, when it did arrive by post, said: "Thank you for calling the *Big Brother* Hotline. Please find enclosed all the details you need to be considered for the first round of auditions. Read all the sections carefully and take time to answer all the questions on the ten-page application form. Try to be creative and original, and please be honest."

The letter also had suggestions to ask family and friends if you were struggling with a question and to read the pages that answered the most commonly asked questions. The letter said they expected a large number of applications but promised to read all the forms and watch all the three-minute VHS videos that you had to send alongside the application form. It ended by saying, "This is stage one in a very thorough audition process, but it is important that we get as much detail as possible from the start Thank you for applying for *Big Brother*, and we hope to see you soon." It was signed by *Big Brother*.

I immediately thought that I wouldn't be able to do it, as I didn't know how I was supposed to make a VHS video. I had that same feeling in 1997 when I was offered the opportunity of having my own radio studio at a Christian radio company in London, creating create radio dramas. I walked away from that offer feeling too scared to take the opportunity. I remember standing in the doorway of the staffroom at school, and one of my English teaching colleagues, whom I had told about the letter, said, "If you don't do it, you will never know." We were a very close staff; everyone had been there for years, and we all met up socially as well.

We had lost one of our colleagues to cancer; she had been my Head of Yellow House and had been incredible over the years dealing with my emotional breakdown, eating disorder, and the massive fallout with another member of Yellow House I was a part of. I thought about her and her wonderful positivity. The last time I saw my Head of House before she died, she smiled at me and told me to "get busy living." I thought maybe I should just take this opportunity. I felt really scared and hesitant again. I thought about Mel, the member of the Yellow House, with whom I had fallen out over a misunderstanding. She had come to live in my living room when things went a bit nuts with her boyfriend in the 1990s. I couldn't believe all the rails of clothes she brought up the stairs that evening. When he found out where she was (a few days later), he stood in the street outside my flat. He seemed, in my opinion, to be a completely controlling and manipulative man. He convinced her to go outside my flat to talk. At that time, he convinced her that I was the cause of all their disputes. She believed him, took all her clothes, and left that same evening. Her story took a new beginning when, pregnant, happy, and one of my best friends again, she moved back into my living room and painted it blue in May 2001, just as I went into the *Big Brother* house.

This is what she said about me: "I have known Lisa since 1993 when we met at Sarah Bonnell School. We struck up a friendship immediately and are still friends today. Lisa is the kindest, most courageous, fun-loving, supportive, and most amazing friend, and we have shared the most awesome times together, both happy and sad. From dancing at the Hippodrome, having meals out at Giraffe at Angel, watching dance performances at Sadler's Wells, helping move house, doing the church Alpha Course, doing many great races (was that what they were called?) with teachers from school, and dressing up like surgeons and the Statue of Liberty. Lisa is a fantastic teacher who has touched the lives of many students. Her enthusiasm for theatre and literature shone through in her lessons, with her animated English voiceovers and fun-loving personality making her a favourite teacher among many students.

What *Big Brother* did to Lisa was, in my opinion, highly shocking and uncalled for. I truly believe it was done to sell papers and draw viewers to the show. Who would not sell a paper if they were exposing a teacher in this light? (I'm referring to the towel incident!) Lisa is not the person she was made out to be on the show; in fact, she is the opposite. I lived in Lisa's flat when she was on the show and was hounded (outside the flat and via numerous phone calls) by the press. I refused to sell a story, as my trust in them was zero after the stories and photos about the towel incident. I truly felt they would twist the reality of my story.

I had the experience and pleasure of meeting Davina at the studio when Lisa came out of the house and met the rest of the contestants and a few celebrities at Lisa's birthday party in Soho.

Lisa is my friend for life; she is genuine and loyal. We continue our friendship even though I now live on the other side of the world. We regularly check in with calls, texts, and voicemails. Lisa can always make me laugh, and I know she will be there any time she is needed.

I frigging think she is a warrior after her *Big Brother* ordeal.

Go, Lisa! You are truly loved.

Your friend, Mel xxxx"

***

I thought to myself that so many people spend their final days looking through an empty photo album of a life they never dared to live or were never given the chance to live. We have a life, and I dare to live it. Why not? I hoped I could dream my fears away by taking this leap. You see, after my own completely disastrous manipulative relationship breakup in 1994, I was trying to find myself and peel off the layers that still stank of sadness and loss. I hadn't got over it years later as I was still grieving in 2001.

Time to Look up and try to see (A Poem).
For my friend Mel and all who have
overcome destructive relationships.

I find myself amongst sounds and circumstances where nothing is consistent except my undoing.

I could end it all inside this fear. I have locked myself into a coded safe and can't remember the numbers.

Yet I still smell the sweetly cut grass of friendships.

The chance and delight as three people call at once.

Locked into a mind of tasteless habits and fears I created that now exist.

This madness cannot find a definition in a day or night routine this breakdown this OCD this terror is a question mark that meets a question mark.

When the light comes in it is so dim a slight chip in the armour.

I bend over the tinniest speck to capture the truth and I try to unlock my mind in this web fine light.

Can I trust myself not to end it all?

I see a raven fly from my window I see blossoms on a square cut tree.

I must cut myself free from this despair and walk away letting the question marks erase each other.

Only in the walking away will my life unlock the meaning of hope and that will overtake time.

The end.

I will continue to incorporate poems into my story because some things can only be expressed in verse: "I'm like one of those test tubes on a science desk with mixtures in each. I am explored but not complete. I am half an equation—mixture of experiments of half-filled tubes of liquid and green smoke. They say it is harder to find than to lose. If I lose myself completely in this unknown surely, I will find or at least I will know what I have lost."

It was at that moment in my life that my form engineered my audition. They convinced me to enter, as they thought it was a brilliant idea. They borrowed the drama department's VHS tape recorder and just pressed record. We were all laughing and chatting in my classroom. I chatted away about the things I did with my form and drama group. We didn't take it at all seriously; one of the girls was holding the VHS video recorder at a slant, and the whole video was jumping. We just said whatever we felt and didn't plan a script or anything. They loved it in all its messy, noisy silliness. They had all stayed on at the end of the school day to get the VHS video done. We didn't retake or edit anything and simply sent the first recording we had made. The application form was like a book; there were so many pages to fill in. I scrunched it up in my school bag and took it out on the tube or in a lesson when the students were working quietly on an independent task. It was really hard to fill in, and I had to go back and forth, adding bits, usually finding a different coloured pen on different days. The whole application form was quite a mess, just covered in messy writing. I thought they would never read this, and it had been scrunched so many times in my school bag that it looked ragged. I was glad it was done once I posted it off, although I never expected to hear from *Big Brother.*

How wrong I was.

On the application form, they said, "We will contact people we are interested in meeting; please do not try to ring the production office." Basically, they said, "Don't call us; we will call you!" And call they did! They phoned and phoned; my phone was red hot! I have never had so many phone calls in my life! They wanted me to go for an audition. Looking back, the amount of planning that must have gone into organising the auditions is quite impressive. Having to phone everyone separately, post things out, wait for the post to return, and play all those VHS video tapes—the time it would have taken *Big Brother* to get back to everyone!

The auditions happened mainly around Holborn in London. I used to love going into the centre of London after work once I had done my marking. I would regularly listen to poetry on Level 5 of the Royal Festival Hall and also listen to writers reading out loud from their new books. In those days, I would pay around £5.00 to stand at a theatre production. I saw so many over the years I lived in London. One such production was Antony Hopkins and Judi Dench in *Antony and Cleopatra.* I absolutely loved it and didn't even think anything of standing for four hours. There were so many creative things to see back then, and they were both accessible and affordable. I am probably just being nostalgic. I would always go and get a bagel from Ian bagel (well, I called him that) at the bagel shop in Covent Garden and then get a good coffee from the then lovely Seattle coffee house. I told Ian I might be going on *Big Brother* when I got through the rounds of auditions. He looked at me, and I remember wondering if he believed me. But he was there in the audience when I was later evicted, smiling and cheering me on.

After one of my bagel moments, I walked up to Holborn for the first audition. It was around 6 p.m., and I suppose a lot of people had to come from work like me. It was really bright, and there were lots of cameramen holding VHS videos on their shoulders. They were so bulky and heavy back then. They seemed to be filming everything in that first audition. There was a huge group of us all standing around looking at each other. The task seemed to be how we got along as a group, as we had to link ourselves together. We all did this so politely. No one was showing off, being really loud, or trying to be funny. Looking back, no one would have thought of playing up to the cameras or even comprehended what they might look like on film. We all knotted ourselves together, twisting around and going under people's arms. We were told to knot the group together like a ball of string. Then they told us to try to untie ourselves without breaking the chain. So again, there was lots of twisting and sliding under arms and legs, and politely asking if someone would be OK to go under our arms. It was civilised. I had hoped for more of a theatre audition where I could blast out a song or quote some lines. When that task ended, we did get a chance to act out a scenario. It was a chance to create an improvisation, which I loved doing with my drama group. What happens, for example, if you are waiting for a bus and someone appears? I found it all very enjoyable. Nobody tried to upstage anyone because they wanted us to be ourselves. Then we all went home and waited to see if we would get through.

In the later auditions, it was instilled in us to not let anyone know what we were doing or where we were to meet *Big Brother*. I guess they didn't want the press to suddenly turn up at the auditions, or maybe they just wanted to create an air of suspense. Coming out of those meetings in secret locations, I felt I was training for a job as a secret agent! We were asked to just be ourselves and to create scenes of everyday events in groups. I was called a few days before and given the location. I realised I was getting through each audition and felt a mixture of surprise and excitement. I loved drama. I took my A-level drama while teaching at Sarah Bonnell School and got an A*. I also went to a weekend drama school with Mel, my friend whom I mentioned earlier, and studied there for three years. I had studied drama at Royal Holloway and Bedford New College in 1987 and had been the only student in my year to be given an unconditional place. I had contacts when I left university in 1990 to join the Royal Shakespeare Company. I really don't know how, in my last year at university, with so many hopes and dreams coming true, I allowed myself to be utterly controlled.

I met Adam in my final year as I worked in the university canteen, and he came through my till one day. For some reason, I gave up on my dreams, and when I left university, I worked in a video shop in Ashford to support his studies. We lived in a room the size of a cupboard that I rented at the back of my landlord's house. It wasn't even a separate room, as there was a curtain that divided what seemed to be his kitchen from our living space. Through the curtain, you could see an oven full of used matchsticks. It was so surreal. I had a permanent red line up my left side as the bed was too small to hold two people properly. I wonder what possessed me to be completely subdued by someone. How did they lock into me and make me feel like I had to do whatever they asked? I think that was the first time I lost who I was. My family couldn't talk any sense into me. That was a vice-grip moment where I really thought it was right. I only then went into teaching to be with him and thank God I got my first teaching post at Sarah Bonnell School. Those were the most amazing days of my teaching life. It was the most amazing eleven years of my life. It took a lot of years to finally overcome that very damaging, violent, and nasty relationship with Adam.

Dig Deeper (A Poem)
For my Form 10A.

I have thrown myself into oncoming paintings, just letting myself awake in the immediate surround.
To be part of all that mis en scene possesses.
I have lost my mind.
I unstick and scrape myself clean and go in search of the whitest screen onto which I paint.
For my life is worth living, framing, placing on a wall.
I step out as me, come and be part of my picture I invite you.
The End.

The final auditions were one-on-one. I had to get to the secret location and sit on a chair. It was a very plain room, with a black curtain hanging behind me. The VHS video interviews were quite chatty and fun. The producers wanted to hear some exciting stories. When they asked, all I could think of was my Australian friend Veronica, whom I met at the bottom of the escalator in Maida Vale in 1991, and by the time we got to the top, we had become best friends for life. Anyway, for no reason, we decided to run around SOHO and see who could touch as many cars as possible with their bottom. I know it doesn't sound funny at all, but that was the only funny story I could think of, so I told them that! It was the only thing that came to my mind. I remember leaving there and thinking what a lame response I had given. What I did say was that I was still struggling with the breakup of my relationship with Adam.

For several years, I had been heartbroken, and I had suffered from chronic OCD and was emotionally unstable. I told the producers who were interviewing me that I thought going on *Big Brother* might be the thing that jolted me into new thinking. I hoped it would be something lovely that allowed me to put all my messed-up jigsaw pieces together and make a whole without Adam in my head. I was just honest about what I was feeling. My advice for anyone auditioning is to be ready mentally. If you go into the *Big Brother* house with unresolved issues, they will be exposed.

Can you face what people might say about you?

Can you face who you really are in the light of what you become?

You will never be the same again. I will probably say it a few times, but to me, fame is like holding a boiling bowl of water over your head without spilling a drop. Be ready for the duality of the unbelievable experience of *Big Brother*.

A couple of weeks after that audition, I got a phone call saying that someone had lost my VHS tape from that audition. They didn't have time to redo the tape, so they couldn't consider me for the show as the main bosses were viewing the VHS video tapes at that moment. I was a bit disappointed, but I accepted that it was over. I had enjoyed all the auditions. So, I got back to my normal routine at school, at church, and with friends. The girls at school were a bit more disappointed than me, as they loved sending the first VHS video of their teacher, and we had had such fun making it. Suddenly, I got another phone call. This producer was adamant that he redid my last interview VHS tape. It was all so odd. He told me where we should meet. I was quite apprehensive and didn't feel right, but I went along to a hotel in Holborn, and it felt weird. The producer insisted he had convinced them to see my VHS video. I remember saying to him, "I don't know if I should thank you." The room was tiny. There was a black drape over the wardrobe and plastic rolled out on the carpet. I remember saying, as a rather bad joke as I was so nervous, "I hope this isn't a snuff movie." I felt strange; no one knew I was in this hotel room. I did start to realise I didn't really want fame or attention like this. I was a broken mess if I am being honest. I sat there and just spilled my guts out. I said, "Doing this has made me realise how much I have been grieving the last seven years over my ex-boyfriend." I just felt, in my opinion, so lost and had such little self-respect. It seemed to me that I had lost the person I used to be before Adam invaded my life. Since he had gone, I felt such acute loneliness. I lived in my flat but just didn't have the home I had longed for. I just felt so afraid all the time. I love paperweights that hold a complete image in them that seems so beautiful and perfect but so out of reach.

Maybe I thought that by being on TV, I'd finally be inside a magical paperweight. In hindsight, I think I really should have gone for counselling and on some form of anti-depressants instead of going on one of the newest experimental shows on TV in 2001 that would continue till 2018. I think I should have just gone home.

Home (A Poem)
For My Mummy.

Home is Truth, Consistency, Cereals, Communication and Kindness.

Quiet togetherness, unspoken connections, laughter phone calls, bread making and cake baking smells.

Books well-read left lopsided as the telephone rings.

Music sheets.

Layered cream crisp beds flowers, photo frames notice boards of activities and menus and calendar photos.

A white piano.

Hot baths. White fluffy bath towels.

Jokes. Traditions. Celebrations.

Moments so intimate mother, son father. Reading Sunday papers.

The End.

I would silently and painfully observe and ponder at other people's homes. I had no envy or jealousy at all. I have always been happy for others' success and happiness. But I would reach out and turn this "something I hadn't found yet" paperweight down and back again. I didn't understand why I was in such turmoil inside. I was holding down my work, had great friends, and had a lovely flat; I don't know why I kept doing so many things so wrong.

So, we did the audition and then I received a letter from Conrad Green, the executive producer of *Big Brother*. It read:

Congratulations on being chosen to join the very small list of contestants who are eligible to enter the Big Brother house. Out of fifty thousand applicants, you are one of the few we feel would be fantastic for the house. We are sending the same letter and the enclosed agreement to the very few people who will either enter the house on day one or be a standby (to enter the house to replace housemates in the event of a voluntary or enforced walkout). We are currently finalising the first group to enter the house. We should let you know whether or not you will be entering the house as one of the initial group no later than 8 p.m. on Monday 21 May 2001. You should be aware that you may not have very long once you hear to pack your bags and order your affairs before entering the house. As you know, in every country in which Big Brother has been broadcast, there have been either voluntary or enforced walkouts, so even if you're not chosen to be included from day one, you do still have a very strong chance of entering the house as a replacement. You now have a period of six days from receipt of this letter to read through the enclosed contract and rules and return it to us. We would advise you to take independent advice on the contents of the agreement. If you have any questions, contact (and they give you the phone numbers of two producers and say that the legal team will answer any questions.) Please return the signed contracts to us in the envelopes provided as soon as you are happy with the contents and no later than Wednesday 23 May 2001. Once again, we can't emphasise enough how important it is for you to keep the fact of your selection confidential. If your identity is revealed, then we reserve the right to withdraw our offer of taking part from you. Congratulations, we look forward to hearing from you soon."

Already "expect the unexpected" was in the tone of this letter. Thoughts streaming through my head:

Will I be chosen to go in on day one?

What should I do if I have to wait weeks for a replacement?

Should I continue to work at school while I wait?

I can't believe they actually want me. What do I do?

My whole form at school knows I'm getting through the auditions, but what if they tell someone?

Actually, a lot of people know, so what if I leave school and then can't go on the show because my identity is revealed?

I got myself all worked up instead of going through the contract with my lawyer friends. I should have talked to the leaders at my church. I should have gone with the union into a meeting with my headmistress and planned and signed various possible outcomes to secure my job. I didn't ask for advice from any of my friends. I never thought I was in danger of losing my job, so I never asked the Teachers Union to clarify how they might support me. Silly me, I didn't do any of that. I just didn't ask for any help or advice from anyone. Like my mummy always said, once I get a vice grip on something, no one can help me. I'm only saying it because I hope someone reading my book will go and ask for help if they need it.

A film crew arrived at my flat to make my introduction video. I was a bit surprised, as I was supposed to keep it a secret that I was going to be on *Big Brother*. They wanted to film in the kitchen and the bedroom. They came out to film me meeting friends on the street. Filming then continued in a pub along the High Street. Everyone turned up; the place was jam-packed. I had told absolutely everyone I was going on *Big Brother*, even though I was not supposed to tell anyone. Strangely, they thought it was one of my pranks and didn't believe me. "Well, you're in something in the making," Peter said. I really did not know how I felt. The film crew used my conversation on my bed as their only introduction to me. I don't know if the other footage was used anywhere. I remember looking around at all these friends and all we had been through. How they loved me whether I was in a state, like a pressed garlic crusher, or if I smelt of rose petals. Everyone was full of joy in that pub. I love making people happy but sometimes, I felt like a slide everyone slides down. I do not know how to stop my chaos and now I had a dreaded feeling it was going to pick up speed. I will have exposed myself, i.e., my identity, to the world. I felt like it was some sort of destiny that, for a reason unknown to me, I was meant to do this. It will force me to untie a few very tight knots whose ends I can't find. I need to lose some haunting memories and some old echoes. I didn't know what my answer is if someone asked, "Why are you going on TV?"

I remember *Charlie and the Chocolate Factory*. Mike Teevee, one of the characters, leaps into the television. Later, I guess I can say I have been down the chocolate river, and I know what a has been room is like. I need to believe it with a good attitude. I really wasn't going into it for fame; it will be weird to know what that feeling is supposed to feel like. How will I actually wear it? Will the challenge destroy me? How will I act in it? Respond to it? React to it? I hope I don't go to deplorable depths to find new sensations like Dorian Gray in the attic. I know I can go off on one, and I think that is why they chose me. I know it is in me to divert to crazy.

I know as a teacher I was just living out a bit of myself, and I was feeling restricted and caught in such a confined space. So far, my life has been spent living on the edge and looking in. I want to live fully, but it always seems out of reach. I keep being caught in cycles of heartbreak, debt, and fears. Maybe this will break the cycle. I want to dance, swim, jump, splash, and laugh. All I seem to do is pull in the strings like a corset, tighter and tighter. I want to finally cut them, and who knows what will happen? The irony is in letting go, and then the next thing can come. I am on the brink of being inside and outside of fame and TV for a new experience like a birth, and the feeling sways from powerful to powerless. It's that combination of elation and terror. By hiding away feelings, I have lived in a bit of a fantasy world, letting real life pull the rug from under me. People think of me as scatty, as I am not sure sometimes what is real and what isn't. I have allowed myself so far to wander through a dangerous maze, taking turns at random, and against all probability, here I am now doing this. I hope I will be warm, funny, and light-hearted; who knows what I will look like coming out the other end? I guess when I get out and cautiously watch it, I will know whether it is safe to believe in it as a reality meant for me. The night at the pub ended in laughter, and we all left with shouts of "Good Luck" and "We don't believe you're going on TV; it's you winding us up." The film crew also stayed until the end. I think they really enjoyed themselves.

Five Reasons to be friends: Paul.

We met at seventeen years of age at a creative Christian event and became best friends.

When I was homeless, he helped me get a place at the Whitechapel Mission.

After writing multiple letters, he was able to reinstate my teaching qualification after the General Teaching Council created a file on me in response to Big Brother. They advised me that working with children would be inappropriate and that I would lose my teaching certificate owing to my nudity. It took nearly two years for me to receive my teaching qualification back.

We frequently cross paths because he lives in Hastings with his partner, Alvaro.

When I was at my lowest point in 2002, he assisted me with selling my apartment and determining a course for my life.

***

Paul said to the best of his recollection and based on his opinion: "Not before and not after did any teaching structure realise the enormity of the impact being on TV would have in causing disruption. Minus the nudity, it is this incredible flutter of trepidation, wonder, jealousy, and confusion. Everyone was naive; this was a completely new experience for everyone. Before them, was a teacher; now, a celebrity. These two things really do not go together. No one really knew what to do. So, they treated my friend like hot coals. Putting her on some offenders' register, preventing her from teaching, and the threat of dismissal."

I think it is apt to put in Paul's response here as he mentions when the *Big Brother* film crew came over to my flat and filmed me in my flat and walking with about fifteen friends to a pub to celebrate my acceptance into the *Big Brother* house! It is odd reading Conrad Green's letter where I was meant to "keep the fact of my selection confidential." Yet a *Big Brother* film crew asked me to make a promotional video for *Big Brother 2* before I went into the house! That contrasts with what the letter demanded. Anyway, my friends kept it a secret because they are loyal, and I am so lucky to have them. I have asked my friends to write their honest accounts of how they felt about it all. I had no idea how they must have felt until I read some of their accounts.

Having met Paul at the age of seventeen, he has been such a loyal friend on so many levels. We have our faith and have been able to help each other look to Jesus when we have been confused and disappointed with life. It is a special friendship because if only more Christians would talk honestly, guide each other, and show each other how we all fall down and lose sight of our beliefs, Paul has shown me the way back to my faith many times. He has ironically been there for me at the most desperate times of my life, showing up like a guardian angel. Here is his account of events, and I thank him for his honesty and insight. It is his opinion and recollections based on what he remembers.

PENNY ELLIS

***Some of my memories and observations about Penny Ellis'
participation in*** Big Brother***:***

"Making a big life change is scary, but living with regret is always
scarier. This (unattributed) saying sums up my feelings when Penny
told me she had been selected as a house member in BB II. Penny
had a successful career as a teacher in a fine girl's secondary school.
I knew how hard Penny had worked to pursue teaching. Her zany,
bubbly, and frequently outrageously funny personality worked well
when she taught and directed drama. I had witnessed one or two
dramatic performances by students Penny had taught, coached, and
directed, and her talent for inspiring others was clear to see. The first
Big Brother television show was a huge success, capturing the public's
imagination. So, upon hearing about Penny's application to join the
new reality show phenomenon that was BB and then hearing she had
been chosen, I knew she was taking a risk by appearing on live TV.
But Penny was the life and soul of any gathering or party we had been
at, and I felt sure she could be a potential star of the show.

I met the frequently "outrageously funny and zany" Penny when
she was only seventeen and she accompanied a friend to a church
event in south London. I was a little older, and she immediately struck
me as "out of the ordinary." She had a real Christian faith, and was
poetic with an artistic flair, but was witty and didn't take herself too
seriously. I had known Penny for about fourteen years, or so, before
Big Brother 2. We had been through a few life adventures together. So,
when Penny said she was a contestant and asked me to join her, along
with other chosen friends, to be filmed and potentially interviewed as
part of the *Big Brother 2* launch, I nervously agreed. My instincts told
me the "new" reality TV shows craved participants with a quirky and
bubbly personality. Penny told me to meet her, the small film crew,
and her other friends being filmed at her flat in Islington, London,
one weekday evening. I turned up, not knowing what we were in for.
I was a little out of my comfort zone. I was pulled into the living room
with Penny, and we both stood with a camera thrust in our faces. We
were asked how we knew each other and what Penny was like. I cringe
when I remember myself trying to appear light-hearted and jovial in
front of the camera. I hadn't been told I was going to be asked any
questions or what type of questions. I instantly thought, *how do I
come up with a suitable, entertaining anecdote that doesn't potentially
embarrass Penny?* So, like a rabbit in the headlights, I laughingly trotted

out a few toe-curling inane generalities about Penny being "fun and bubbly." Well, the interview lasted about one or two minutes before I was ejected from the room. This was my first ever "inside" experience of the television industry, and I felt as though I had "reject" stamped on my forehead. After that, I seem to remember everyone decamping to Islington High Street. We were told to walk along the road smilingly, making light-hearted small talk in a line with Penny in the middle. To be perfectly frank, I felt rather foolish, and it all felt very phoney and contrived. The same routine continued at a bar further up the road. My personality is more introverted, so trying to appear jovial and laugh sociably in front of strangers whose only connection to me was our shared friendship with Penny felt awkward. I was relieved when it was over and judging by its exclusion from the *Big Brother 2* launch show, so were the show's producers. The "Islington introduction" sat firmly in the film can and never saw the light of day again.

Penny's enthusiasm and excitement as she anticipated being cast into the *Big Brother 2* house were boundless. I could understand why. The hard grind of working "in the trenches" as a high school teacher was about to be replaced by an uncertain but exciting life in the spotlight. A new career in the dramatic arts could be on the horizon. But I feared the effect the dynamic of the "pressure cooker" nature of constant media scrutiny in the BB house would have on Penny. The first BB show was entertaining precisely because of the conflicts and alliances between people in the house. The lack of privacy also made me worry Penny would find no respite or relaxation, something I felt was particularly vital to Penny's well-being. I was also worried for Penny because we were both teachers. I knew the conservative nature of the school's personnel management. Their primary focus is on their school's reputation as well as child safety. I feared the negative publicity from events arising in the BB house could damage Penny's teaching career. My concerns were realised when the "towel drop" incident occurred and Penny was thrust into the limelight of a media scandal. Penny's accident with a bath towel certainly earned her what Andy Warhol termed her "fifteen minutes of fame," but it would cost her dearly.

Shortly after the incident, I had a knock on my door from a journalist. I have no idea how a newspaper reporter even knew I was Penny's friend. I gave the game away that I knew Penny when I stupidly replied to his introduction with the words, "How did you know I was her friend?" It did occur to me briefly that I was being Machiavellian. I momentarily thought I could haggle for money and serve up some juicy stories based on gossip about Penny's life. But I didn't want to lose a friend for whom I had genuine feelings and a shared history. But it showed me how money and fame can so easily corrupt a person. It then crossed my mind that other reporters might come. I feared they might uncover relationships I wanted to forget in my own life. I then acted less than honourably. I said, "I am only an acquaintance. Penny's family lives in Sussex; ask them," before shutting the front door. I should have just politely shut the door without saying a word. But I feared my own life would come under some kind of scrutiny. As a teacher, I feared any publicity, and, in hindsight, I needlessly deflected his inquiries.

I remember watching Penny inside the BB house, and I felt protective towards her. I could see one of the housemates was bullying Penny, and I seethed with resentment towards him. When he was eventually voted out a little while after Penny's eviction, I cheered with delight. It was a well-deserved payback. I decided not to attend Penny's eviction "celebration." I had come to despise the shallow glitz and the "here today, gone tomorrow" attitude of the public and the media's attention span. I hoped Penny would find something good out of the experience but felt certain we would rekindle our friendship once the glare of the BB media circus had subsided.

Penny was kind enough to invite me to a promotional party held in a club in Soho, and we met up on another occasion in Green Park for a chat and catch-up. But it was still a period of upheaval for her as she sought contacts and opportunities in quest of a new career. Penny had been censured by her school for the "towel drop accident." She was no longer working for them when Penny received a letter from the General Teaching Council for England (GTC). It is their responsibility to issue qualified teaching status to allow a person to teach professionally. They can also remove a person's professional teaching status following a school's censure for capability or disciplinary reasons. Penny was informed she was subject to their scrutiny and could have her status as a qualified teacher removed. They said Penny had been charged with bringing the profession into disrepute when she dropped her towel on live TV. She contacted me; calm but upset, and she was concerned that an accident exploited by the media for sensational reasons had put into jeopardy all her hard work building a teaching career. I immediately sprang into action. I drafted a letter explaining the accidental nature of Penny dropping her towel. I then explained how much embarrassment and grief the incident, and its exploitation by the media, had caused. I informed them that Penny was seeking legal advice over their threat of a tribunal. I stated that they were adding insult to injury. The letter was written in the first person, and Penny signed it as though she had written it. As I thought they would, the GTC acted with prudence and compassion and dropped the proceedings against Penny, much to her relief, by the end of 2002. I was overjoyed that I could assist her in her hour of need.

The Christian lawyer and speaker Bob Goff famously stated, "The shallow end of hope is usually the deep end of grace." In hindsight, I think this applies to Penny's BB experience. It seemed to me that it was undoubtedly exciting and offered the opportunities that celebrity brings, namely opening doors and bringing us to the attention of the public and influential people. Unfortunately, public attention can be short-lived, and the media swiftly move on to the next sensation. Penny enjoyed the notoriety of the "sensational incident" on reality TV. But she paid a heavy price professionally. I was glad I could help her save her professional qualifications and help her sell her flat in London quickly when Penny sought greener pastures. I also feel Penny learned to swim in the "deep end of grace" through the experiences surrounding her time inside the BB house and the events that followed. It seems to me that Penny has grown in wisdom and faith and has learned invaluable life lessons by continuing to seek the value of life rather than just its price."

***

Thank you, Paul. Your perception and care have been a lifeline. I now recognise that seeking the life that God gives me and just how much we should value it is so important.

Free from for (A Poem).
For Paul.
It isn't until I freefall do I realise that a structure restricted by a formula doesn't work.

It is a risk; I pull the chord -to be more.

To cry in the winds, face and things that look so unreal like a Lego land become the real I've been looking for.

As it now rushes up to greet me.

I am landing in a new place and roll and cut free.

I can stand in the truth.

For I am one of the few people who flew through the sky, that handbag clicks around me, and my pockets bulge with the parts of the clouds that held my dreams.

The End.

I went over to my friend's, Ted and Peter, for dinner when I made my decision to go on the show. I felt I had arrived on a new shore. I summed it up as: "I am apart, not alone, but now a silent observer of all that was until now." I was worried about money, and they offered to buy my antique furniture from my living room at my flat. The money would cover at least my mortgage and bills for a month. I don't know why I was in a sort of manic state. I couldn't really think straight.

There were more calls after that. My cousin, Rika, from Japan, called. She was coming to work in London for six months and wondered if she could live with me. I had never met her. My mother has six sisters, and they all live all over the world. Two of her sisters married Japanese men. Anyway, for some crazy reason, I said she could move into my flat. I actually offered her my bedroom, and I don't remember asking for any rent. I can't really explain my rash decisions. Then my teacher friend at work, Mel, was desperate for a place to stay. All my furniture was gone from my living room, and I said she could move in there. I didn't know if they would get along, as Rika might be a workaholic and allergic to housework, I didn't know her, but Mel was heavily pregnant and nesting. I don't know why I agreed to this just before going into *Big Brother*. I was acting quite manically. It felt to me like letting go of the past and all that had happened in my flat. Give it a new identity with them in there. I didn't think through the fact that I would actually be homeless when I came out of the *Big Brother* house. I wrote Adam a letter I would take to New York just before I went into the *Big Brother* house. Adam had moved to New York. I would walk to his street in New York and leave memories there, then have a cocktail at Grand Central Station and finally release the letter in Central Park that I had written him, and then fly home the same day. I was acting manic and irrational.

The letter for Adam:

I went past your house today and emptied a seed of each year I mourned you. I had to let go and see now that if I come back, I will see all manner of colours growing up strong that can dance in the wind, and I will know a spirit of truth can never be conquered. You see, the first few years after you left me, I buried myself in the soil of your garden. You didn't notice. So, one day, I got up, very damp and earthy, and left. Even though I can still smell the earth in my pores, I don't smell of sadness anymore as I now know seeds are growing.

I have this dream for a stage production of one of my plays where the actress rolls out a roll of grass and the grass suddenly bursts into bloom all around her. After that, I did see a counsellor. But it was the *Big Brother* counsellor. It was a meeting before I went into the *Big Brother* house. It was quite a musty office, possibly another secret location. He was fascinated by my application form that I had posted back once I had completed it. He started to analyse all the swirls and notes in my handwriting. The way I had written the application was a mixture of very neat and completely messy. The fact that I had written up the margin piqued his interest. Basically, it was all over the place. I told him the truth. I had written it on the tube to work, in my breaks, and in boring staff meetings. I had written up the margin because there wasn't enough room, and some of it was my afterthoughts. Some of the questions on the application form, which was ten pages long, included having to draw a picture of ourselves, which, according to psychology, is supposed to reveal a lot about someone. Some of the questions are quite difficult to reread as I write this book. For example: Write the headline you would least like to see about yourself if you were in the house. Describe your perfect day. Have you ever had your heart broken? What happened and when? Where would you like to be in ten years' time? Who do you get along better with—imaginative people or realistic people? When did you last lose your temper, and why? He then laid out all these newspaper front pages and asked me what it feels like to walk over them. "Remember that news today will be fish and chips on paper tomorrow," he said.

The day's news in 2001 was tomorrow's fish and chips paper. A story in the newspaper would be forgotten the next day. Newspapers would be fish and chip wrappers. Magazines would be thrown away or end up in a doctor's waiting room at their surgery for people with appointments to flick through. I began rambling on about my life to him, saying things like, for as long as I could remember, my life has been erratic, so I wasn't afraid; I just saw it as another experience. I may dip into it like the journalist dips his pen in that ink. I would try to swim in that "ink," letting myself be caught by the currents and whirlpools. I stated that I saw everything as very hopeful. I told him I had been so deeply pulled under in life that I was hurt and traumatised. I just thought, "I feel at sea." I told him I am not sinking like I used to but am floating, and I can breathe.

In those days, I really had no understanding of the way newspapers and news organisations created their stories. I didn't watch, look up on a computer, or read anything about *Big Brother* 2000. I didn't realise or even imagine that any magazine or newspaper would want to write about me. In those days, in 2001, it seemed that as a teacher, you were held in high regards, like a doctor or lawyer. In those days, the students would stand when I came in the room and call me "madam." In those days, there were letters and postcards, and there was a phone line you answered at home. You would call your friend on a Tuesday and plan to meet up on Friday. You went to Boots to pick up your photos, as you had taken them on a camera and had to wait a few days for them to be developed. In 2001, life seemed very small and simple to me. The counsellor then asked me about my breakup, and I said, "I saw my heart float away; it was at the same time I tasted oxygen for the first time."

"Oh," he exclaimed. That was the session.

SCENE 3:
Friendship.

I must focus on friendship, as I really do have the best friends in the world. When I had my interview with Davina the night of the eviction, my friends filled the stands, and the producers said they had never seen anyone with that many friends. I value my friendships so much. It's funny how some of the friends you thought you'd have for life vanish as you get older. It's incredible when you look around at your friends and see the ones that have stayed and the ones you never thought you would be that close to.

My mother instilled in me the importance of friendships. As a child and teenager at church, I would always shake the old people's hands, ask them how they were, and listen to their stories. My mother had hairdressing salons, and as her Saturday girl, I would do the manicures and talk to women of all ages. My mother always opened her home to anyone who needed help. Our house was always full of people. She gave them homemade food, company, and even money. As Christians, we learn to look out for and care for others above ourselves. If someone needs help, then reach out the hand of friendship. I have always lived like that, so Rika and Mel moved into my flat, and I moved into the *Big Brother* house.

Five reasons to be friends: Mel.

I helped her finally leave that horrible boyfriend.

We went to drama school together on weekends.

We were both in the Yellow House at school under the guidance of our head of house, who died of cancer.

We kept in touch when she went to Thailand, got that tattoo, and fell in love with a man by the river.

When I went into the BB house and she moved into my flat, I was more worried about leaving her with my cousin, whom I had never met, than I was about going on TV. I just didn't really think that far, and I was just so pleased to help them both. I really believed this was a time for me to be free of my sadness from the past few years. It would be big enough to take away that deep, lonely sadness that I couldn't shrug off.

I used to walk down Villiers Street to catch the tube and overhear snippets of conversations on the way. I wondered what people would be chatting about as they walked down the street—what they were saying about me.

Villiers Street (A Poem)
For Mel.

"She never got over it "
   "It was while she was scrubbing her steps "
   "And if you think I believe you "
   "Come on it's only a laugh"
   "Why not try to give him up you never try"
   "Don't come near me again"
   "I said to him is that it "
   "Hello, fancy a drink"
   "But to merge would be a disaster for our company"
   "I didn't get it let's get drunk"
   "I don't know I think it is three days for a test"
   "Cauliflower that is all I need it starts at 8 p.m."
   "Get that cab, Harry, quick"
   "No"
   "Yes"
   "Oh really "
   "That's incredible "
   "And then it's Egypt after that who knows "
                    The End.

Mel said to me, "Gosh, there will be conversations about you. Complete strangers will sit in coffee shops and talk about you. I think you might be meeting your destiny head-on. You're still rushing, but it seems you're finally rushing somewhere, not just anywhere."

In my opinion, and based on what I remember and recall, I would face a massive media frenzy that has wafted in and out of my days dramatically for the past twenty years. I was an emotional mess. I hadn't dealt with things emotionally. I was acting as crazy as if I was looking into empty plastic bags as if I would find something. If I may attempt to explain it, once you're in something—a manic outpouring of emotion—you're at the centre of it, so the inside is now invisible, and you must find the strength to be that thing you seek.

I did also have amazing moments in the *Big Brother* house and after where it felt like rain was running into my pores and making my heart burst into bloom.

Reasons to be friends: Emma Neville Towle.

Letters and cards that spill out of files and notebooks to this day; she must have written to me at least once a week for years.

I found Emma at the first church I went to after my breakup with Adam and joined one of the best fellowship groups. We would be there for each other for picnics; we created the perfect hen night for one of our group; we became flatmates with the brothers from our group when I was homeless for two years in the 1990s after I left the Mission in Whitechapel, where Paul had got me a room. Even after flying to Australia and meeting up with some of the fellowship group, life changed and we all moved on.

Sitting in the deer park in Richmond.

Lunch at Emma's new house after she got well for the first time from cancer.

Her voice on the phone a few hours before she died told me to "shine and be beautiful."

Snatches of events before I went into the house are so real yet so out of reach, as that was when reality was the norm before I became "Penny from *Big Brother*." Before I went into the house, I had promised to do the flowers at my church, All Souls Church in Oxford Street, for my friend David's wedding. I had made the promise before I thought through how I would do it. I had never done flower arranging in my life. I turned up in a taxi from Islington, where I had bought most of the flowers in massive, long rectangle boxes from Angel Station Flower Market (about £200 worth) and bags of ribbons from John Lewis. David turned up in a total panic, realising that maybe my enthusiasm outweighed my capabilities. Also, the orchids were not going to arrive until an hour before the wedding (all the way from Singapore), which was the very next day. But Emma arrived along with Carolyn and Claire, whom I had met while doing the Wednesday kitchens at All Souls. I mourned the loss of our Wednesday kitchen time for years; it was such a fantastic time with the variety of conversations and meals at each other's homes. I recommend the unity that comes from such friendships when you all happen to volunteer for something. Best friends still to this day. Emma had done tonnes of flower arranging, so she got straight to work. We went completely over the top, hanging vines and twirls of ribbon all over the bannisters. It was fun and scary—a mix of elation and terror. David was so impressed that they carried the massive two flower stands that stood on either side of the altar into the lift and up to the reception in the hotel just by All Souls Church to decorate the reception after the service. Emma had decorated them, and they were stunning.

The next stop before entering the house became two. I flew back to New York to be a bridesmaid. I had been honoured to have been asked, and then I got the bill for the bridesmaid dress, which I didn't have – 200 dollars. It was the most enormous wedding I had ever been to. There was an ice bridge with a river and a boat floating through the centre. There were ice statues everywhere, and the men were all dressed up, heralding the bride and groom with trumpets. There were ten bridesmaids and ten groomsmen in attendance.

I decided to organise the stag do the night before the wedding instead of sitting in a hot tub with the girls I didn't know. I took the groom and all the men, some of whom were in my fellowship group from my church, All Souls, around New York. It was so much fun, and we missed the train back to Long Island, so we got back at 4 a.m., where an almighty row between the bride and groom commenced. I felt erratic, like one of those multicoloured kaleidoscope handheld toys from your childhood. All these colours were bursting out of control. I sat in Central Park after the wedding, and then crossed the Brooklyn Bridge, but couldn't face walking down the street where Adam lived. Everyone was flying back on different planes; I felt so lost and alone. When I finally got to the airport, I sat down and met a friend of a friend who invited me to see Rome with him and his boyfriend, where they lived. So, I got back to my flat, repacked, and flew to Rome. We get sand in our eyes when we are tired, but I had felt clogged up with the heaviness of sadness for so long.

I remember part of the conversation I had with Emma Neville Towle. It is funny what you remember in life.

Emma: "That's what Pen is like; she creates dates and tonnes of memories. You can see her trying to undo that pain in her heart by living to the extreme, but once you have done that, it is so much harder as there are just more extremes."

Penny: "What drives us?"

Emma: "We crave contentment yet demand variety."

Penny: "We define our space, then allow chaos."

Emma: "We escape into things when we should be relaxing and checking things off lists."

Penny: "What point are we trying to make?"

Emma: "Who is cutting out our pattern and sewing us up and dressing us in it?"

She died in 2011. The day before my last day at school, before I was to go into the *Big Brother* house, I was shocked and horrified, and a heartstring snapped.

Reasons to be friends: Tristan (Not).

He was part of my teenage years in Tunbridge Wells. I attended the Girls' Grammar School to complete my A levels. I hadn't passed O-Level maths, but after the headmistress interviewed me, she immediately offered me a place in the sixth form. It's funny because the same thing happened when I called to request an interview at Royal Holloway, Bedford, and New College London. I didn't think I would get my grades as it was such a prestigious college, and after my interview, she immediately gave me an unconditional place.

I think back in the 1990s, you had to get a B or an A in A levels to get into that college; now, I think you have to get straight A's to get on the course I did, which was a BA Honours in Drama and Theatre Studies. When I came out of the *Big Brother* house, I got so many offers of work for nearly two years, just by meeting really famous and influential people by chance, and it was only through conversations with them that I got asked to do massive events, as I had no management looking after me.

Anyway, I met the most creative and lovely girls at the grammar school and got to know some decent boys, Tristan and Henry, from the boy's grammar school, which was just over the road from Tunbridge

Wells Girls' Grammar. I call it a nostalgic memory of those teenage years. Tristan was a close friend of Henry. I even helped Tristan when I was homeless in 1995 and let him live on my floor in my room at the Whitechapel Mission because he needed to crash somewhere when he got a job in London and needed a place to live.

On the day before my last day at Sarah Bonnell, he phoned me in the middle of an English lesson. He told me that Henry died in a fire trying to save his little child. She died as well. His wife and the two boys, aged two and seven months, got out. So sad.

Henry was my first boyfriend when I was about fifteen years old. He dumped me because I was addicted to wearing this black boiler suit. I thought I looked good in it. Also, I was flat-chested, which I was well aware of, and I felt that the boiler suit concealed my flat-chestedness. I had gone to the doctor about it at the age of fourteen, and all she said to me was, "Oh, you should have been born a boy." There was no more talk or any counselling, and I would just always feel very conscious of my body until I finally got a boob job when I was thirty years old.

I realised that having breasts made your clothes fit you differently. The nerve endings in my breasts really hurt in certain clothes, so I stopped wearing a bra as it was too painful. Looking back at the *Big Brother* house, I didn't realise how much my breasts bounced about in the tops I wore. I wish I had worn a bra in the *Big Brother* house. I was brought up in a Brethren Church, and we learned that it is a sin to have sex before marriage, and I stuck to that. In my adolescence, I was there to console some of the girls who were in deep distress at school due to a relationship breakup. They found my innocence endearing and embraced me. I didn't know what that heartbreak was. I was so naïve about relationships and never went further than a French kiss, which I had to learn from my primary school friend when we were about fourteen by the trampoline at the YMCA.

Before I met Henry, this eighteen year old wanted to go out with me. My primary school friend tried to show me how to do a French kiss by cupping her hands around her mouth and circling her tongue in and out of her mouth. I tried it when the eighteen year old took me to London Zoo, but it felt like a soggy sponge being shoved in my face. I went to see *On Golden Pond* at the now-gone cinema in Tunbridge Wells with him. I didn't understand the film at all or his sudden pulling of my hand down to his crotch area. That was the end of that relationship. So when I saw Henry as we stacked shelves together at the local Sainsbury's, I must admit it was the first time I felt like I couldn't breathe. I watched him in the aisle and thought he was the most amazing thing I had ever seen. I had no romantic experience and thought it would be a good idea to give Henry one of my broken-off nails, which I cello-taped to a piece of card and placed in an envelope. I remember his look of disgust as he threw it back at me. Even at twenty one years of age, we were still close and went to the Oxford balls together and hung out. I will never understand some things about myself. I don't know why I never let Henry be a real boyfriend. I was a very strong Christian, and then I let someone like Adam come into my life and destroy it at the age of twenty two. The decisions we make are our own undoing.

Ocean (A Poem)
For Henry.

Deep pain is the sudden cold felt when you swim in warm blue foam and go too far- whilst surveying a Monet like surround.

The moment is comforted by the pulsating rhythm of ever increasing now time -a newness.

But if you stay still you sink into the whole dark liquid blue cold tomb that engulfs you in a whole mass.

A dictionary of the past.

The pain is felt consciously but not acknowledged subconsciously.

For hope is the backstroke towards land.

The End.

I informed Tristan that I was in a lesson. I told him I was going into *Big Brother* and already felt unstable. I had the most awful row in Covent Garden with Tristan that evening, before my last day at Sarah Bonnell. You realise some people come into rooms in your life, but they belong in the hoover cupboard. I saw a friendship crumble into hoover dust, like when you break a pearl necklace and all the beads scatter. All of the memories were simply kicked away. I felt so rejected. I can remember him shouting at me, telling me to go home as I had a big day tomorrow. He thought I was having a nervous breakdown and said, " Go home and get some sleep."

I staggered onto the underground, sobbing my guts out after that row in Covent Garden. I didn't sleep at all that last night before my last day at school. I went into the *Big Brother* house with the news in my head that Henry was dead, and I didn't know how to process it.

They do say, "Don't make the same mistake twice." In 1994, I had already given up my flat (which was all in my name) to Adam for the next two and a half years, as I couldn't bear to lose him; I made myself homeless. I had supported him, giving up offers from The Royal Shakespeare Company to work in that video shop in Ashford at the end of my degree. I suffered numerous bouts of jealousy over the years I was with him. Once I came home, and he was jumping all over the landline phone, smashing it to pieces because I had answered it and talked too long to a friend or my mother the night before. Once, I came home to find him ripping up my suits. He was standing on the bed in his underwear, screaming and ripping away. I had no idea what I had done to upset him. But I was worried about him. I don't know why now, years later. He had been my first proper boyfriend despite being away from my faith, and as a Christian, I felt it would be a sin to leave him.

But one night, I entered the flat. He had a file case that had a code on it. For some reason, I knew the number and opened it, and again, for some reason, I knew to look in the fifth file, and there were the photos of the girl he had been having an affair with for two years. My friend Veronica from Australia was staying with us that night, but that didn't stop him from pulling me across the floor by my hair because he was so angry at me for touching his file without permission and for finding and even challenging him with accusations. For whatever reason, deep in my broken heart, I packed all my stuff instead of throwing him out of my flat. I put a lot of my things in the garden shed that had a lockup. Thank God, Paul found me a place at the White Chapel Mission, which was a soup kitchen. In those two and a half years, I paid all of my apartment's bills: lights, heating, everything except the phone bill. I wanted him to finish his PhD by living in my flat. Instead, he moved that girl in that he had been seeing for two years while he had been with me. They got engaged in my flat and left me a scented candle lit in my kitchen when I got the keys back. I would wait for Adam on a Wednesday for two and a half years while he lived in my flat, when I would collect my mail from him in Museum Street at a coffee shop with oversize bright red, blue, and yellow coffee cups. When I got my flat back in early 1997, Emma came around with flowers she had arranged and prayed over the flat. I got a boob job and finally had a pair of breasts at thirty years of age, and I went to Australia. When I went to sell my flat after *Big Brother*, in 2002, I found I had £10,000 extra that had been put on top of my mortgage. I really do not know where that came from. I paid for it. Also, someone had tried, without success, to rip my safe out.

Endless You (A poem)
For Veronica.

I blink at the bright light it trickles in as you put on that music.
    Building waves of emotion rippling and glittering
    Me I am my beauty you recognise and treat me in such a way that I
turn off the function button and all advice and let myself dance.
    You know I will like the tune.
                  The End.

I Met You (A poem)
For Vanessa, my dear friend in Australia.

It was your smile, your keen eagerness
    And gentle amazement in us as a one.
    For it seemed to be as if I had been already inside your chapters.
    We land in the middle of it all awoken in a dream.
                  The End.

Tristan wrote me an upside-down poem of thanks for all my help putting him up at Whitechapel Mission that I could read down under. He had been a trusted friend. Until he sold an outrageous story on me while I was in the *Big Brother* house in 2001, the headline read: "Penny would tap dance naked on the table when I (Tristan) got in from work every night." I don't know how much money he got for it. It was a huge double-page spread of a thing in the tabloids.

I remember standing in the doorway of the staffroom at school with my letter of approval from the governors to go on the show. It read: "Following your request for unpaid leave to participate in the *Big Brother* television programme, I have consulted the Chair of Governors, and your request has been granted. Please note that the leave will begin with the commencement of the *Big Brother* schedule for participants, AND WE WILL EXPECT YOUR RETURN TO

WORK THE DAY AFTER YOU LEAVE THE *BIG BROTHER* SITE. I must however draw to your attention the requirements incumbent on all teaching staff to maintain the school and LEA image under Newham Disciplinary Policy and Procedure Section 2.13, Maintaining the relevant body image. Please find the relevant section attached. I wish you well with this venture, and we look forward to your return at the appropriate date. Signed, Head Teacher."

A copy was sent to the Chair of the Governing Body. Re-reading this letter now, I realise that when I came out of the *Big Brother* house, the school asked me to pay back June's wages, which I did, but I had taken unpaid leave. By expecting me back the very next day after I was evicted, it also shows how no one knew the scale, hype, and success that *Big Brother 2* would become or the creation of reality stars.

I remember so clearly looking at that governor's letter and thinking, *it seems a small wonder within the miracle of my life, yet I can scarcely gaze at this letter. If I gaze too long, it might vanish. To have found my home in this universe. I really had a lovely life full of true friends. Yet to venture into the limitless, or is it entering the limits?*

I did feel like something momentous was going to happen to me. I would be leaving my life off stage, in the shadows, in the wings, and going onto a stage unknown.

Mel was really encouraging; she just told me to use my theatre skills and my talents. She did warn me that if someone is discussing something, listen and see if it is worth reacting to their words. (I wish I had remembered that with the incident with Stuart in the house.)

Mel: "Remember, words will either pull you up or pull you down. They will possibly be quite empty, and these people probably want their moment of fame or something."

Me: "Hopefully there will be conversations going on with more depth to them. I will need to be aware of strife."

Mel: "Yeah, do not cause a clash; you know the moment when the dilemma arises behind the words like it has been hiding there."

Me: "Well, like that time we didn't speak and had to be in the same meetings in the Yellow House. The poor Head of the House was beside herself with the hatred we had for each other. I really had not slept with your boyfriend."

Mel: "Yeah, what a difficult time. I moved into your flat, he came shouting down the road, and I moved out again. Then we had to work together, and we didn't speak for ages."

Me: "That clothes rail and the orchestra of emotions were like a Shakespeare play."

Mel: "Maybe you will get some really quirky, artsy, funny types who are really interesting and well-read and use word juxtaposition without putting the emphasis on the metaphor."

Me: "Ha-ha, Ms Sport's teacher, that just sounds clever. I hope I can be silent with loud words, whisper a rage, and cry a joke. Be reflective, not boring, and be interested and interesting."

I want to add in stories linked to my school at the time, education, and how teachers must have perceived me. It is difficult to write as it still weighs heavily on my heart that, by walking into the *Big Brother* house, I would never be able to teach again like I used to. It's amazing how many stories I am led to believe that my headmistress gave to the newspapers during the two weeks while I was in the *Big Brother* house, completely unaware and unable to defend myself.

I'm told that someone from the school even found some photos in my scrapbooks in my teaching cupboard and sold them to the papers. One of those photos, of me in a schoolgirl outfit, sitting with my form group in 1996, all dressed up, was published in *The Recorder* on 6 June 2001 (a local paper). It was World Book Day, so we dressed up as characters from stories we had read in 1996. The headline read, "Lisa with her clothes on."

Another article in the tabloids read, "Head sack threat to naughty teacher." My headmistress is quoted as saying: "I will sit down with our solicitors and look at the code of conduct in her contract. I gave her all the advice I could before, but obviously, now that she is in the house, I can do no more." It saddens me to read this and realise that no one fought my corner in 2001 at my school of eleven years. Wasn't it obvious that the press was fabricating stories to sell their papers? Could the school not have given me the benefit of the doubt? Could anyone not have seen that it was all exaggerated?

The article continues: "Show producers are terrified about the prospect of charismatic Penny being booted out, knowing it would be a ratings loser."

Another headline in another tabloid reads: "Teacher TV Furore shocking. Teacher Lisa Ellis, whose saucy antics have made her famous to millions, faces a meeting with her shocked and embarrassed boss when she leaves the show."

I never had a meeting. My headmistress never sat down with me to discuss my point of view or how I was mentally. There was a story on the front pages of most of the newspapers for every day I was in the *Big Brother* house. In the "Teacher TV Furore Shocking" article, my headmistress says: "It will not be a disciplinary meeting." The article goes on to say, "my headmistress has taken no calls from parents." One parent said about me, "she's a really good teacher. I don't know why Channel 4 didn't edit it out."

I always wonder what was edited out by Channel 4 of other contestants' antics or language in *Big Brother 2*. Only what you see makes you believe. Twenty four hours edited down to half an hour. I'm sure all of us would be surprised by how we come across. I just paid back my months' wages and politely resigned when I came out of the *Big Brother* house. I couldn't process the emotions I felt, and it impacted my OCD rituals, which became more and more intense over the years, trapping my mind in a coil of fear, shame, and confusion.

I never knew what the other teachers said in 2001, as I never met up with them to talk about all the stories written about me, except for one teacher who said I would definitely get sacked from a photo she saw in *The Daily Star* on 11 June 2001. There I am, standing naked with foam all over me. The headline says: " I still want to teach." On the other side, a subheading reads, "Blowing Bubbles: Thank God I had my breasts done." Quotes from my headmistress in that article read: "No further decision will be made on her future till we have spoken in length."

I never got to talk to her, my union, or my form. I wish I had had the strength to fight for my name and reputation. I talk about this photo of my naked body covered in foam later on in my book. It is very painful to talk about and something I've never talked about before, as it was part of the photos taken for my *OK! Magazine* interview. I reveal the truth behind that photo for the first time later on in my story. If I had purposefully posed for that photo for the tabloids, if I had sold or made a deal with *The Daily Star*, I would have received thousands of pounds that would have set me up for life. I didn't. I did not! I hope my explanation later in my story will make some teachers believe in the truth of the person and teacher I have always been.

Stories sprouted up with photos I had taken in a hotel room just for my *OK! Magazine* interview. Later on, I talk about a story from *The Sunday Express* from 10 June. Again, a photo I had taken for the only interview I did give with *OK! Magazine* (this time I do have my clothes on) seems to read as if I gave that interview as well. It reads: "*Big Brother* Exclusive."

The headline reads: "I'm too much of a woman for the *Big Brother* men." If I had sold that second story myself to *The Sunday Express*, I would have made thousands of pounds. When I was asked to make a decision late at night on 8 June 2001, in my hotel room, I chose *OK! Magazine*'s offer for my story over all the offers from all the major newspapers.

Every newspaper wanted my exclusive. I did not know what to do. *Big Brother* gave me a room in the Charlotte Street Hotel on my eviction night, and it was extremely late because I had my interview with Davina and then had to attend a massive press conference, and I had no idea what had been written about me since I had been in the *Big Brother* house. I was driven to the Charlotte Street Hotel at about midnight. I had one girl with me who was there to "advise" me. I didn't know her and asked her what offer I should take. She said she didn't know what offer I should take, which didn't give me any guidance or insight into what I might not know about what had been said about me or what offer would help me sort the truth from the lies in this window of opportunity I had. So that was no help from her, and I was completely ignorant of what on earth anyone in the world thought of me that night. So, I thought, well, I will take the *OK! Magazine* offer (even though it was loads of money less than the tabloids were offering me), as then it will be a lovely, sophisticated story and I can look quite glamorous and a bit like an actress.

In my naivety, I really thought it would be a nice story in the top magazine, as it was the magazine of the day to be in if you were a very famous actress or a member of the royal family at the time. In 2001, *OK! magazine* featured only the most glamorous, rich, famous, and royalty.

My *OK! Magazine*'s story was on the front page and was about five pages long, with photos and my interview in their next publication. However, in the time before that *OK! Magazine* publication came out on 22 June, my "exclusive" photos, which I had presumed were taken purposefully just for my *OK! Magazine* exclusive, had found their way into all the tabloids, something I had deliberately tried to avoid. I had chosen *OK! Magazine* to have a respectable story about me. I had been told by them when I had my interview with them, as I said earlier on in my story, that I couldn't talk to the press for two weeks, which was my window of opportunity to make money from my "fame." So I was required to remain silent for two weeks.

After that, I didn't sell another story or photo to any of the tabloids. I've never given an interview to a tabloid. The money I could have made!

In 2001, *Heat Magazine* was today's version of Twitter and Instagram. If you were mentioned in *Heat*, then everyone was talking about you, I suppose, like something going viral today. While I was in the house, I was on the most important page of *Heat Magazine*'s June edition. They called that page "Everyone's talking about..." There was a lovely photo of my face smiling as I walked into the house; another photo in the corner shows me with my wet hair all over the place, drying my back with a towel I did not drop; and then, for millions of people to see, my naked body. That photo, 'the towel drop photo,' made me feel suicidal at stages of my life over the next twenty years.

In the article, under the headline "Everyone's talking about Penny," it reads: "Penny seemed the most unlikely to court controversy. After all, who would be interested in a 33-year-old teacher who says she is naïve, has low self-esteem, and is anxious most of the time? But Penny immediately grabbed viewers' attention with her endearing dizziness, shock religious admission (she is a born-again Christian), and general mothering of the others, including almost becoming a permanent fixture in the kitchen. Then the flirting started. The last thing we expected was that the meek teacher would be attracted to Paul, who claims he is 'hung like a donkey' and can 'hump like a rabbit.' Although Paul didn't seem madly into Penny, he is enjoying the attention. But when Penny followed that by flashing her bits twice in one day after dropping her towel, it seems she has gone too far, and her head teacher threatens to sack her. But while Penny's behaviour may grate other housemates, at least it's entertaining. She's provided light relief during those verging-on-tedious moments and is always a talking point the morning after. Gawd bless you. Lady Penny."

Along with my *OK! Magazine* photos turning up as "exclusive" stories in the tabloids that I mention here, it makes me so sad, and my head screams, *Is that fair?* Teachers and friends at church and all over the world would think I had given these interviews and sold these stories and photos to the tabloids. That I wanted to stand naked covered with foam, in *The Daily Star*'s "exclusive" on 11 June 2001. That I wanted the world to know I was too much of a woman for the *Big Brother* men. *The Sunday Express* article on 10 June 2001, was another interview I never gave or received payment for! All these stories used photos that were taken for my *OK! Magazine* interview, the only interview I gave, which came out in the magazine. In *The Sunday Express*, I am supposed to have said about my headmistress, "She is very supportive. If someone has a chance to improve their life, she is all for it." On the front page of

The Mirror on Wednesday 30 May, there was a photo of my headmistress and the headline, "I will sack Penny if she has sex on *Big Brother*." The subtitle reads, "Heads warning to flirty teacher."

Being talked about and written about exacerbated my OCD for the next few years after 2001. I would find myself checking the door hundreds of times. I had diagnosed OCD before I went into *Big Brother*, and I used to check my flat door in Islington so intensely that I snapped my front door key twice, pushing it in and checking that it had locked the door. Then I would have to find a locksmith after working at school to get a new key made to get into my flat again.

When I lived with Peter and Ted when I came out of the *Big Brother* house, Peter noticed my checking and said, "Why don't you just take it with you?" which made me laugh and has helped me over the years when I am mentally rooted to the spot doing my counting in a massive OCD ritual and I say under my breath, "Take it with you" (the door, the tap, the light switch, the gas oven) whatever I am checking that I think a disaster will happen if I don't count my specific numbers a certain amount of times. I imagine myself walking off to another supply job up to 2020, holding a door, a light switch, and a tap that I was checking. His remark helps me ask myself, *Is it safe?* (Whatever I'm checking, it's a Peter.) There was a dreadful OCD attack when I was closing a kitchen cupboard door as the kettle was boiling. I couldn't let go of the kitchen cupboard door till I finished my counting, so the steam from the kettle burned through the skin on my arm nearly to the bone in 2002.

When a massive, horrid, double-page spread appeared in the tabloids all about my church, All Souls in London, in 2001, it ripped out my heart. My lovely Anne Kneller, who was ninety years old, had actually turned on her TV; she never used to watch me on *Big Brother*. She was such a wonderful old Christian lady. She came up to me at church in November 2001 and said, "God saw your heart, Penny." She assured me I was loved. That was an amazing feeling.

My pastor, Richard Bewes, who was always so full of humour, said, "Don't worry Penny, it will all be cast in the sea of forgetfulness."

This is a verse in the Bible that means God will forgive and literally throw away your sins and forget them. In 2001, most news, as I have said, was easily forgotten the next day. That was a forgiving church, full of wise people who were kind and non-judgemental. They really had to handle this media frenzy and did so, unlike my school, in my opinion, with graciousness, quietness, and forgiveness.

My mother was called in Spain while I was in the *Big Brother* house in May 2001, and told by a journalist: "Your granddaughter has died in a car crash" (I didn't have children), to try to get a story about me. How did they find her phone number? There was a story that was going to come out in June if I had stayed in the *Big Brother* house about my sister; something I did not know about her at all until she told me in 2003. How did someone know that? Did they listen to her phone? Was my phone hacked? The things newspapers knew about me and my family in 2001 were staggering. When I went to live with Peter and Ted after my stay at the Charlotte Street Hotel, and I think I mention this fact again, Ted had collected most of the newspapers with front page and double spread stories on me. The pile stood up to my waist—hundreds of stories of interviews I never gave. When I came to sell my flat in 2002, my mother sat on the living room floor of my flat, crying in desperation at the state of my money. She screamed with such worry and said, sobbing, "You have lost everything."

However scary anything becomes in life I would encourage you to just face it head-on. This is the first time I am facing the giants of shame, fear, dread, and despair that I have cowered under for twenty years. If I can do it, so can you. Believe in yourself and live the life you deserve, not the one thrown at you by others.

What irritates me, even more, is that these best friends—whom I don't even know—sold stories about me. All my real best friends could have made so much money selling stories, but they didn't. This one so-called best friend, Charlotte, said, "We told her she has to be careful not to go over the top. She can do some pretty crazy things at times."

I DON'T KNOW A CHARLOTTE, WHO ARE YOU?

Why didn't I confront the school and ask them to believe me that I didn't drop my towel? I should have gone into the head offices of the major newspapers and not left until they put the truth out there. I don't know why I let it all just keep pouring into the papers without reacting.

On Thursday, 12 July 2001, there was another story that I never gave or got paid for in *The Independent*'s Education section. The headline is so weird: "Teachers hate my Brillo Pad haircut." The article says, "An education in the life of former teacher and *Big Brother* contestant Penny Ellis." The article tells my whole life, from my childhood right up to 2001. How did they find out so much very private and incredibly confidential information about me? Even the school that I went to when I lived in Cyprus as a five-year-old, The Black Katz in Limassol; my fantastic

English teacher, Mr Lanaway, who taught me in Tunbridge Wells in 1983; my feelings and relationship with Adam; even the A levels I took. Could I have won against the stories about me? Could I have found out in the years that followed if my phone had been hacked? I don't know because I didn't do anything for so many years. How long do you just let yourself get more and more downtrodden by others' opinions of you? How long do you stay in a place of fear? It is very liberating to tell my story, and I am so grateful someone wants to hear it. I really don't know why I didn't fight to explain the truth. In all honesty, I was just lacking in self-esteem to the point of self-destruction. I've spent the last twenty years apologising in schools and explaining something I never did. It has caused incredible mental health issues for me.

On Friday 6 July 2001, the deputy head of Sarah Bonnell wrote to me, saying, "Hope you're enjoying your newfound fame. I was GLUED TO THE BOX (unusual for me) whilst you were in the house, and I even learned to go on the internet to follow things on the live camera, etc. Considering how useless I am with a computer, that was a real result. There has been an educational spinoff from your adventures."

The rest of the letter asks me to fill in nominations for my form and other bits of schoolwork related to my form and my creative projects. I did it all and sent it back. However, as I write this, I am thinking that not only did the school sell stories to me, but it also did not hear my side of the story by holding a meeting with me and also asked me to do schoolwork despite the fact that I had paid back a month's wages, taken unpaid leave, and was left unemployed.

The letter ends, "See you at the BBQ." I did go to the BBQ in July 2001 and gave a speech in which I said sorry. I felt compelled to apologise. I got a lovely vase as a leaving present, which I still have today. I really had thought I would go back to my job as an English teacher, to my drama group, and to my form. I needed the comfort of the familiar. Your mind cannot envisage the concept of fame when you are in the middle of it. An example is your wedding day when all attention is on you. Imagine you've never seen snowdrops before, and you see them for the first time. This reality TV had just been created. My mind started to thaw like the everlasting winter of Narnia. I had to step out of a newly created reality into the reality I had left behind, but that was out of reach like the horizon, and I was in a celebrity reality that I had only seen in films and had never understood. To think I had not looked at or realised, for years, what was going on the internet about me.

But I lived with so much shame and embarrassment about the stories I knew about. If I had known the extent of media coverage, I wonder if it would have sent me over the edge, as I was extremely vulnerable. I know I have said this earlier, but I just think it is worth repeating. It's like, why increase the pain of it? Maybe I didn't want to know, so I ignored it as we do with bills that are due—we put them in the side cupboard, hide them, and hope they go away. I was so sad to be away from my church, my lovely job, and my sweet friends; it had all ended, and I was ashamed, depressed, and utterly broken. But if you put a monster in a cupboard or a drawer, it grows in the dark. I do think if I had seen all the things about me on the internet over the last twenty years, I would have been mortified.

Friends have pulled me back from the depths of despair. They have shared the joy and wonder of *Big Brother* and have also been there when the fame faded away.

Five reasons to be friends: Peter and Ted.

I have known Peter since the age of twelve. I cut his hair in a lesson outside the music classroom window, and we only got caught as the hair blew into the window we had climbed out of and flew into the teacher's face.

I bumped into him at Charing Cross after losing touch for a while; he was living walking distance from my school.

Broadway DVDs with Ted.

They gave me a home after Big Brother as my flat was taken up by Rika and Mel for over six months in June 2001.

We rode the roller coaster of reality star experiences together at so many events in 2001.

They agreed to see me go into the *Big Brother* house when I went over there for dinner. We chatted and I can remember some of the conversation.

Me: "Maybe the lights in the house won't allow for shadows, and I will see things in the light. We sometimes act in the shadows and not the self; it is like we want ourselves to make a decision."

Peter: "Well, you've made your decision now. You have set this train in motion. The tracks are laid. Ted and I are a bit worried about your state of mind."

Me: "Hey, Ted, I just hope I am worth watching. Like a good play, a big set of characters and a story that demands to be heard."

Ted: "Well I hope it has got something as you do have the best life already. You have life at its best, and I just hope this is a springboard that grows you up beyond your potential."

Me: "Or into my potential. I just need to get balanced and not get into one. To hold onto a sane rhythm and pace and not pick up or be affected by others. I want to be able to keep hold of what is mine. I do let go of the wrong things so many times. Most people might lose a false eyelash at a meet and greet. I seem to blow it big style."

Ted: "We know; we hear the stories. The money for the furniture will cover your month's outgoings".

Me: "I am just so grateful; that is such a relief; then I can have a month without worrying where I am going to get any money from. My finances are in such a mess after leaving Adam in the flat. I have loans on loans. Such a mess of soggy debt."

Peter: "You always have the beauty of the laughter of so many good friends and the truth from their hearts. Remember to feel the love and know that you are cared for and sung to from the heart. The laughter of those who love you as they turn on the TV around 9 p.m."

Me: "Yeah, it will be a butterfly mass flutter of hearts pulsating, a cacophony surrounding me at that time each day."

What wonderful friends they are. And for EVERYONE who watched and loved *Big Brother 2* in 2001, thank you.

Undoing (A poem) For Peter and Ted.

My head has been a plasticine multi coloured fuse box a variety of veins.
All running separate distinct impact.
Colours meaning something but stuck seamless still packet image ribbed of furrowed brow.
Still lurking a set pattern yet and I seem to be OK in separate acts.
Only in my silent days do I peel away
And lay down each separate strand a release of stale air of thoughts see through clear and dark as hidden glue.
It binds and peels plaster off, skin sweat, sticky sweet pain. The undoing frees me to write again.
My breath alone it is a grace, a fingerprint touch as out of despair a despite becomes such a reality.
Like window shutters banging back -freshness enters with such a view of paint dry hope.
The End.

SCENE 4:
The last days before the nation knew my name.

On the last day of school, before I left for work, I laid all my clothes and bits that I was allowed to take on my bed. I was going to pack carefully that night and get a takeaway with Mel for our last evening before I went into *Big Brother*.

Big Brother had a very strict list of what was allowed in. No clocks, no music, no devices, no pens, paper, or pencils. We were allowed one luxury that we could either have for ourselves or share with our housemates. I packed some pretty daft things: a disco ball, juggling balls, and a decorating nail kit. What I should have packed were some presents for my housemates, or at least some wine and maybe some cigarettes to give them. I bought some nice pyjamas from up King's Road when I went to see a play at the Royal Court with Carolyn and Claire, my dear friends from church. I thought I had better look smart in the house.

I still felt sad after my encounter with Tristan the night before. I was folding all my sorrow and sadness into the creases of the clothes I was packing. It felt like there was a frown outline around me; everything felt wrong, crazy, and chaotic. I remember when I left the *Big Brother* house and was told by someone at a party about a morning radio show that would just criticise my dress sense every day that I was in the *Big Brother* house. I don't know why that stuck in my brain.

On my last day at school, I just felt anxious. I thought that stepping into that *Big Brother* house would be a bit like *Blake 7 Land* (a TV show from the 1980s). I can embrace it (maybe) like a comfort blanket where no familiar sounds will be heard—the school bell, my phone. I hoped I would recall the smell of my memories so far in life. I imagined it would be the end of one life and the beginning of another; that I would finally let Adam go and kick all the flabby dead skin off my heel. I really believed the experience would make me let go of the past. It had to be something this dramatic and diverse to pull me away from the ledge of the past.

I had been a three-year-old with building bricks that kept toppling down. It was time I tried to grow up and build something that stayed up. Time to connect to life a bit more normally; I had been sealed off in my own space for too long, full of fear. Most of my friends were the same age as me and were getting married, having children, going on holiday, buying this and that, or going to this great party, and I had just been watching it all and wondering if I would ever have those things. I wanted to step into something real, like a white-water raft, and go over a waterfall. I needed to reconnect with life; I needed to let go of the sadness of losing Adam, of giving him my flat, of the entire bag of wasted years and journey through university, of the years and years like heavy curtains, musty and constricting.

I feared that I would be entering a Tower of Babel, all of us speaking our own language and just being heard, not understood. Those talks that exhaust you and make you feel even more disconnected. Ironically, that is what it was like, in my opinion, at times in the *Big Brother* House. Everyone was talking at times, but not much was said. As the school day ended, Mel found me in my classroom.

Me: "Hey Mel, I am going to be re-potted into this *Big Brother* pot; let's hope I can blossom and grow."

Mel: "I will see you tonight, our last night together before they whisk you away."

Me: "Great! I will get all my lesson plans taped to my desk. All my cupboards are organised; all my notes and plans for my lessons while I am away are in order."

Mel: "See you at the flat later."

So, I walked out of Sarah Bonnell School. It was a crisp, ordinary day.

I was nearly at the train station when I got a phone call from one of the *Big Brother* producers.

Producer: "Hey, Penny, your name has been leaked to the press, so we may not be able to have you as a housemate. If they print your picture, then it is all over, as we are building an atmosphere of suspense."

Me: "I am just leaving Stratford to go home."

Producer: "Look, wait there; we are going to have to take you to a hotel. I believe reporters are at your flat. Can someone else pack your suitcase?"

Me: "I'm glad I laid out most of my clothes. I would have liked time to properly think about what I wanted to take. I had better ring Mel. She will pack it for me."

Producer: "Great, now can you stay there and don't let anyone see you or approach you."

Me: "I feel quite terrified, and I am now hiding in a bush."

This was the beginning of strangeness and extraordinariness invading my ordinary and all that was familiar. This was the time when the clock reached too famous to be ordinary and too ordinary to be famous. All that had been my reality up until then was deleted like a file on a computer. Over the years and years that followed, I would claw back some fresh gasps of air from what had been my normal in the days before May 2001.

The cowboy scene I found myself in, hiding behind a bush, expecting any minute to get attacked by a photographer, was near Stratford station. I was absolutely terrified that I was about to get pounced on by a journalist. I thought, *what if they don't take me into the Big Brother house? I have sold my furniture. The school has a supply teacher to cover for me. I can't live in my flat as Mel and Rika are there. I had a massive farewell party.*

All I could think was how embarrassing it was. I was now ready to attempt to reach the heights that my imagination had already reached. The taxi arrived as the producer said it would.

I was taken to the Thistle Hotel (as it was called then) by Tower Bridge for two days. No TV, no radio. My phone and bag were taken off of me immediately. It was very disorienting, to say the least. After the evening I had the night before and the shock of Henry's death and no sleep, I was panicking. I hoped Mel would pack all the things I had left on my bed. I was running through a list in my head of things I might still need in the bathroom or one of my cupboards. I was trying to calm myself down as my cousin Rika would be arriving tomorrow to move into my bedroom, and I hadn't changed my bed sheets or sorted out my bedroom for her to have. All my things, like my diary, were lying around my room. Oh, it was what my mother always calls pure stress.

A counsellor came into my hotel room.

Counsellor: "So how do you feel?"

Me: (I bounced up and down on the bed.) "Well, I can go from near catatonic (last lesson of the day at school), to relaxed (with the Metro on the tube into central London), to efficient (my coffee at Seattle Coffee House and bagel from Ian Bagel), to neutral (as I wait for a phone call), and to surprise (as something always happens.) There is always somewhere to go in London. I have battled loneliness for so many years now. I hope the house will help me shed this feeling of loss and rejection. I gave so much of myself away for years, and it was like shedding my skin, 'til I had no identity left. I have been self-destructive for a while. I feel like I haven't read my instruction manual. Putting myself through a forty degree wash instead of taking care and handwashing myself."

Counsellor: (lays all these newspapers down on the floor) "This will be you in the next few days. How do you feel about that?"

Me: "I can never be all that people expect or want me to be, and if you continually try to portray an image, you quickly lose your sense of self, which is your only defining characteristic."

The creators of *Big Brother* came into the hotel room with documents I needed to sign. I thought it was nice of them to introduce themselves. I got off the bed to shake their hands. I said, "I was just thinking of all the sounds I won't be able to hear once I am in there." It felt so weird handing over my phone, address book, diary, and keys. We were not allowed any watches, diaries, mobiles, electronic equipment, pens, or paper, as I have said. There would be no clock in the house or any way of knowing what on earth was going on in what would be the outside world.

The creators asked me what I was hoping for by going into the house. I said it would be a wonderful experience, and I was looking forward to having time off school. No more marking for a while. They said they were glad to have found me and said I was quite unique. They also said, based on my recollection of events and what I remember, that they wanted to build a storyline around me, so that's why they asked me to play a mother-type role and nurture others in there. I didn't really understand what they meant and smiled.

Creators said, "Expect the unexpected." Something that was said a lot by *Big Brother* in 2001.

The unexpected and extraordinary can be frightening, yet once accepted, they can be quite stimulating. I mean, look at fairy tales. They include terror and punishment, and they are severe, but the story is about creativity and the release of a burden. I was hoping that some aspects of my life would change forever. I wanted to stop jumping from extremes—from the elation and terror that seemed to be the backdrop of my life. I wanted to swim up, break through the surface, and breathe again. I knew that whether it was a pond or the ocean, fairy-tale surprises would always find me.

I was all alone on the bed and could see Tower Bridge from my window that night. No TV or radio. No music. There was no way of knowing what was going on in the world or in the press about anything. It was an eerie sensation; to be almost inside another new normal yet still unknown to the world that was waiting to create me as a reality star.

The other housemates were also in this hotel, maybe even across the hall from me.

Narinder, 28 years old and married, was an actress who had spent six weeks filming in Bombay for an Asian TV programme.

Ama was 23 years old and a professional table dancer in London.

Helen, 23 years old, taught dance classes in the evenings and was a professional hairdresser by day.

Elizabeth, 27 years old, had travelled a lot.

Stuart was 36 years old, married, and ran a telecommunications firm.

Dean was 37 years old and in a long-term relationship. He also ran his own internet company.

Paul, 25 and single, worked as a computer designer. He lived at home but worked in Germany.

Bubble was 25 years old and had worked in nightclubs.

Brian, who was 23 years old and a cabin crew supervisor, and then me, an English teacher who taught at the school down the road from the *Big Brother* house.

We were the housemates of *Big Brother* 2001.

I could have had some fascinating conversations with each housemate. Each of them had such interesting jobs and life experiences. I spoke German as my mother is German and could have chatted about that with Paul. There was so much to find out about them, but my time in the house would be up in just fifteen days. The ten of us were chosen from two hundred and fifty thousand applications, nine hundred of whom had advanced to the audition stage. All of us, with our fate in the hands of *Big Brother* 2001. I have walked across Brooklyn Bridge, and I love Waterloo Bridge, but I didn't know what was at the other end of this *Big Brother* bridge.

Getting the habit (A poem)
My feelings lying in the hotel room the
night before going into the *Big Brother* house.

On a day when routines are now set in stone for me -and the cocoon has not erupted its butterfly.
On a day as any other on a shore of no shadows – just me.

MEET ME AT THE MIRROR

So, a day I see the tidal wave engulfs you and the friendship breaks like shipwreck wood.

In the drowning they now disturb your water.

Many ripples whisper you are alone now.

In the expanse of the ocean's reality, you do not see the whirlpool becomes the flamenco dress spinning round.

Your tears spill heavy as rocks and a path is mapped out in water never to be found.

Many waves wrap round you; the weight of self-pity can drown you.

End as trust is thrown overboard, and you swim against the current of what you were.

Only a laugh not a tear will help you rise in the morning.

The End.

SCENE 5:
Fragmented Identity.

We were told before entering the house that we couldn't talk about *Big Brother 1* or *Celebrity Big Brother* 2001. I think that might have been to just have the focus on us as the new contestants and our experience. We also had to go for a photo shoot. That is the photo of me in the gold cardigan and bright blue eyeshadow, the one Rylan posted on his Twitter page in 2020. The photo was used time and again over the next twenty years.

We had to stand on a platform that moved around, sort of slowly spinning, so the photographer could get different angles of us. The photos were taken in a big open hanger. It was really quite funny standing on this platform, which was very high up, and seeing all the vast open spaces. I didn't know how to pose, so I just let the cameraman do his thing. I didn't request to see them, and I had no idea or say in which photo was chosen. I didn't know what they needed my photo for. These were the first photos used by the press in all the newspapers to reveal the contestants going into the *Big Brother* house in 2001.

We were allowed one suitcase and a small case. Everyone else packed two bottles of wine, and some people packed beers. They packed sweets and cans of Red Bull. They all packed books to read, as we were allowed to pack two books and two magazines. Some packed cigarettes. Brian had packed the game Twister, Bubble brought a ring in from his daughter, Dean packed a ball and two wooden bats, Elizabeth packed Twister and Cluedo; she also brought some blue cheese, some joss sticks, and marbles, Helen had packed hair colour and lip gloss, and Stuart had packed dice games and trick contact lenses. Everyone also brought in photos of their families. Our suitcases were taken from us and inspected because we were not allowed to bring any electrical equipment with us. They allowed Dean to bring his clippers in as he had a sensitive scalp. We were not allowed any writing material.

Big Brother had taken our phones and placed them in a safe somewhere. We were only allowed one item of each beauty product (moisturiser, mascara, lipstick, shampoo, etc.), and it would have to last us unless we added it to our weekly shopping list. I don't know why I didn't take in any wine. I should have done. I love a glass of wine. In one of my interviews, when the film crew arrived at my flat in Islington, I had lain on my bed and said innocently, "I have Jesus and a bottle of wine."

I was talking about people's different views and how I love having dinner parties and having a drink with friends. I was also trying to talk about my faith, but that sentence, standing on its own out of context, is used in videos of me on YouTube, and I just sound a bit unbalanced. I gave my juggling balls to Bubble when I was evicted. I also packed a scrapbook of photos of my Form 7A from Sarah Bonnell—not really any useful items at all! I wish now that I had packed some bras. Looking at the episodes on YouTube, I can see my breasts were quite exposed in some of the tops I wore in the house. I really hadn't done that intentionally. I really hadn't realised. In my darkest days late in 2002, I put all the clothes I wore in the *Big Brother* house and my eviction dress, as well as dresses I had bought for events I had been invited to, into black sacks. I took about ten black bags to the nearest charity shop in Islington, where I lived in London.

We were allowed two people to see us go into the *Big Brother* house. I think Brian, Paul, and Elizabeth, whom I walked into the house with, had family. I had Peter and Ted. They had to stand behind a little rope that sectioned them off from the steel walkway that led to the entrance to the house. It was very basic, nothing fancy at all.

I was placed behind a high plastic corrugated sheet, similar to a half-cut-out porta-loo and was not permitted to speak. I could see a few of the other housemates' feet on the muddy grass, as we were all standing behind our own plastic sheet dividers, so we couldn't see each other. It was quite eerie, as everyone was very quiet. I was frisked, and I think they used a metal detector as well. There were security guards in a line with vicious-looking Alsatians.

When we were told to walk, I came out onto the steel walkway; there were a few cheers from the few people watching, as there were about ten people in total who saw us go into the house. On the other side of the walkway, there must have been about sixty press photographers clicking away. I had Peter and Ted clapping and smiling encouragement at me.

I walked with Brian, Paul, and Elizabeth. Brian tried to talk to me, and I felt petrified we would be told off, so I hurriedly told him to be quiet as we had our microphones on. I don't remember hearing any noise other than clapping. I didn't look at anyone I was walking with but did smile, even though I was absolutely terrified inside. The photographers caught my face turning back to look at Peter and Ted, smiling. That was the photo used by *Heat* magazine in their June edition when they put me at the front of the magazine in the section "Everyone's Talking About" along with a photo of me naked with my towel.

It didn't feel real walking down that steel pathway to go into the *Big Brother* house. I was in such a chaotic whirl in my head after the events of the last few days. My nerves felt shredded, and part of me wanted to turn around and go home. I felt really uneasy and not at all thrilled. I had such a weird mix of emotions pouring through me all at once. The article that revealed our identities was in the newspaper the next day. Next to my photo with my gold cardigan, it read: "The 33-year-old English teacher from London is a puzzle. She is said to be shy and nervous, yet she can tap dance and juggle." The article headline said: "A lap dancer, a gay air steward, and a bloke who reckons he can hump like a rabbit were among the ten new *Big Brother* housemates who moved into telly's famous house yesterday."

ACT 2:
Behind the Sides of Normal.

SCENE 1:
The *Big Brother* House and my fifteen days.

I shall call Act 2 Behind the Sides of Normal. I think that sums up my time in the house. Another one of my favourite quotes is, "Within us all is the tiniest door so miniscule we lose sight of it."

Did you know things to celebrate in May include: no socks day, dance like a chicken day, and world tuna day? In May 1937, two hundred thousand people celebrated the grand opening of the Golden Gate Bridge by strolling across it. I walked into the *Big Brother* house in May 2001, and the door shut behind us.

I would like to describe the house as it was my home for fifteen days. Thirteen fixed cameras in the house on the wall watched us come in. Remote control cameras were operated in the camera run galley used by the producer, filming us through the one-way mirrors in the runway behind our walls. There were over forty microphones positioned in the house to listen to us. We had a £3,000 microphone we had to wear all the time and could only take it off to go to sleep, and we had to change our batteries twice a day.

The newly modelled house, which had previously been used for *Big Brother 1* in 2000, received a £200,000 makeover, making it larger and smarter, with the designers hoping for a Scandinavian atmosphere. A solar heating panel ran along the exterior wall. Solar panels worth about £100,000 were installed to help with the supply of electricity for cameras that ran twenty four hours a day and lights that were left on all the time. There was a solarium and a spa bath that were all new additions.

The first *Big Brother* house had pastel colours and little furniture.

The first week-long *Celebrity Big Brother* in aid of Comic Relief had used the house only eleven weeks before *Big Brother 2* started. Celebrities included Vanessa Feltz and Jack Dee. The house was redesigned in the weeks after *Celebrity Big Brother* finished. An article mentioned the house being designed with a cabin fever theme, which implied we would go stir crazy. I think I did near the end of my fifteen days; I was becoming neurotic and manic.

I really loved the huge outdoor wooden table as you went through double doors that led out onto a decked patio, and we had most of our evening meals on that wooden table in the dusk of the summer evenings. There were a lot of wood designs in the house. The kitchen had purpose-built units of waxed oak with curved lines. There were no sharp corners. There were bright rugs around a large coffee table in the living room area, where we had a lot of meetings and discussions. We just had a fridge, oven, and sink in the kitchen, which I really liked as it stood in the middle of this big room, so I felt part of other people's interactions whilst I was so busy in the kitchen most of the time.

From the kitchen, you could see the solarium and garden straight ahead of you, and to your right was the open plan living room and door to the boys' bedroom. The wooden beds were all custom built for us. Both bedrooms looked the same, with red, yellow, and orange colours on the bedding and the walls, so either room could be used by both sexes.

The en-suite bathroom in the girl's bedroom could be entered from the hall or the bedroom. It was almost behind me when I stood in the kitchen. There was only one toilet for us all to share, though, which got a bit smelly at times. I had no reservations about cleaning it regularly. The door to the diary room was across from the kitchen on the left side and had the *Big Brother* logo printed on the door. We had a supply room next to the diary room and were given flour, pasta, potatoes, and rice. We were rationed some fish and meat. There was an emergency ration supply if we ran out of food. One article said: "This year the contestants can decide where they sleep, so this could mean mixed sex bedrooms. The garden has decking, a hen house, and a secret den. No doubt there will be a mix of the good, the bad, and the barmy."

Conrad Green, executive producer, said, "I don't normally do a second series of anything, but I thought this could run and run. It's a new drama with no script and ten new people. It's important we keep our nerve and hope the house gets interesting. It is impossible to make these things happen, so it is going to be a fascinating, big adventure. Look at

Celebrity Big Brother. They thought they knew what they were doing, but once the stars got in there, they were surprised by how they responded."

I agree with that, as you do forget the cameras are watching your every move. There were cameras on the walls that whirled around, so you suddenly heard the noise they made and realised they were watching you. I had no idea behind all the massive mirrors were cameras as well; they were literally inches away from us. We were surrounded by mirrors that, from the other side of our walls, looked like windows when you looked into them from that side. So, it was full exposure for us, like being in a goldfish bowl. There were even cameras in the bathrooms and in the shower.

It was so very bright in the house, and I remember feeling glad I had packed my eye mask to wear at night. It was always so light. There was natural light coming through the windows in the bedroom, which didn't have any blinds. Without a clock, I felt uneasy and dislocated from normal. There was some lovely artwork on the walls that came from a local community centre. They had been painted by people going along to the centre who were artists, homeless, drug addicts, or alcoholics. I wish now that we all would have gone to the centre in Hackney when we came out of the house and met the artists. I do hope they got to sell their work.

Over a hundred and fifty producers, editors, directors, production staff, and members of the web team worked on *Big Brother,* with a team of sixty working on each programme. Throughout the night, there were always three producers, two directors, and twenty one other crews on duty. They intended to create surprise.

The voice of *Big Brother* came into the house over a tannoy and was the voice of whichever producer was working that day. They decided to make *Big Brother* "harsher" for our series, and I felt that a lot every time I heard *Big Brother's* voice. Ruth Wrigley called it "upping the ante." However much we pleaded in the diary room, we would always have to wait as the voice of *Big Brother* would say, "We will get back to you." It really frustrated us. Conrad Green said it was "wrong footing the contestants."

There were over nine thousand hours of tape recorded. Then there was the extra coverage on digital Channel 4 and on the web. More than fifty thousand people were actually watching us sleep on our first night in the house at 5 a.m.

If live coverage was not available on E4, it could be seen on the web, which was run by a team of twenty-five people. There were news and gossip, games, and competitions. At least seventeen thousand users could be logged in simultaneously. Web users could find out information on individual contestants and play interactive games. They could go on a video tour of the house and follow any contestant around.

Fans could receive emails and watch "*Big Brother* Confidential." It was a magazine programme just for internet users. There were lots of edits that were not used on TV of the contestant's family and friends and reactions from famous people. This introduced a lot of people to the internet for the first time in their lives. For me, that is mind blowing. Can you imagine that? I will never forget someone running up to me on the street in London, tears of joy streaming down their face, and saying, "I watched your feet all night while you slept."

I am always humbled to have been a part of people's lives, their joys and sorrows, as we were in their living rooms over the summer of 2001. Over twenty-five journalists were monitoring the activities of the housemates over a twenty four hour period, ready to write their stories. As soon as *Big Brother* launched, the press latched onto any behaviour that could be interpreted as risqué, and unbeknownst to me, many stories about me involved sexual chemistry threads that built a huge tapestry that would run and grow and take on its own life all the while I was in the house and still be weaving in 2022. The E4 digital channel gave the audience a chance to monitor the happenings in the house live. They could choose to watch the house live with a ten minute editorial delay or whether to watch it with two or four-hour delays so they could replay it in full several hours later.

It became the start of our compulsive occupation with reality TV, and viewers would tune in at breakfast time just to watch us sleeping. There were eighteen hours of live streaming a day on E4, and you could vote through your remote control. The WAP stood for "wireless application protocol," and it meant mobile phones that could connect to the internet. You didn't have to get a WAP phone, but you could register to receive texts containing *Big Brother* news. You could gift someone a BT voucher for £4.99, and they would get four weeks of text updates from *Big Brother*.

I was in the House during a general election and a Tory party leadership battle, and I was on the front page of every newspaper in the country! The show had taken off, and the nation was gripped. "Penny, the teacher who dropped her towel." It is an honour when you are known for something you can be proud of, like raising money for charity. It's incredible to be known as a global role model for highlighting a cause. However, living with the fame of something you never did is extremely stressful.

I have had times when I really thought I could not carry on living. I don't know what I signed the night before I went into the show. I have not seen that contract since. I have always faced up to my mistakes. But this broke me over the years, as it wasn't what I did, so I could neither defend, apologise, or explain it, as it was a lie that belonged to the media and not to me.

Fame is a responsibility I never imagined I'd have. I never thought I would be famous, but fame, as we have learned over the years, can be done to you. I mean, the media create your fame, but then the world believes that is what you wanted, said, or did. I have described it as trying to hold a boiling bowl of water over your head for twenty four hours a day without spilling a drop. I hope my story will explain the experience, as so much now is social media driven and people do want to be famous. You can never fully get back to the person you were before.

In the *Heat* magazine, which I talk about a few times, there is a column that reads: "It looks like sex could be on the menu in the *Big Brother* house with a set of attractive and mostly single contestants. The new house is cosier. There is a whole section devoted to sex on the website where users can vote how likely they think it is that sex will happen week by week. Every other *Big Brother* around the world has resulted in two contestants having sex. The producers have probably made the contestants very aware of this."

What a dreadful article in my opinion. I was not told about other programmes or activities in the other *Big Brother* shows around the world. This *Heat* magazine edition would be read and reread over the week in people's homes, at work, or on holiday. In 2001, people would focus on one or two stories in the news for a whole week. Imagine spending one week looking at one magazine and being quite satisfied with that one story and all the information in that one *Heat* article.

Newspaper and magazine circulation was massive in 2000: the sixteen daily and Sunday paid-for national newspapers had a combined circulation of twenty one million. The press in those days influenced public opinion. *The Sun* newspaper had a circulation of over three million. *Heat* magazine was up by over a hundred per cent alongside other celebrity news magazines such as *OK!* and *Hello!* It seems everyone was ready and waiting to find out who we were on 25 May 2001.The last decade has seen a huge decline as the growth of mobile technology and social media platforms changed the way readers access the news. As I stepped into the *Big Brother* house, I had no idea I would be forever changed, that my character and reputation would become what millions would read in the tabloids about me.

Catapulted into Insanity (A poem)
My feelings of walking into the *Big Brother* House.

The monotonous dread of a voice of insincerity like a face covered in a jester's smile,

To have to be within a zone of such coldness where dreams are stolen, and words hold double meanings.

I came out of it in an unwound ball of wool and spent however long it takes to regain love for myself, for in love I find my life's breath,

As I breathe in so many dawns rise.

My memories have fallen like dust and formed such shapes so self-contained.

I need to gather enough breath to blow them all away.

Yet again they will land and depending on the day, the mood within the weight of my heart, I will walk through and lay amongst the what might have been. On other days I will chase after my heart that has flown into a million sparks of future surprises and greet a dawn so fresh it causes heartache of beauty in each beat.

The End.

***

Day one in the *Big Brother* House:
25 May 2001, 10.10 a.m.

As I walked up to the entrance, I thought that it would be the last second of being alone in my own space. I was on my way to another shore, still apart but not alone. I wondered what would fall out of my life and land in meaning in this now time. Like the earth has a barrier and the spaceships go through it. I would now have my privacy barrier circled by something called the media. I wondered which parts of me would break through the barrier or which bits would get burnt up!

There was no dramatic entrance of steps to climb down; that came in the later *Big Brother* house. We just walked straight in.

Bubble had gone into the house first on his own, but I was glad to walk in with others. All the interior doors of the house leading to the bedrooms and diary room were locked until we had all entered, so we could all go into them together. Helen and Ama were next in. Stuart, Dean, and Narinder then arrived. Then Brian, me, and Elizabeth were the last ones to come through the door.

I couldn't believe how bright it was; there were so many mirrors and lights. I was surprised by the explosion of noise that hit me as everyone started chatting at once. Also, Brian and Bubble knew each other from one of the auditions, so they embraced with added joy. I felt a pang of jealousy or insecurity as I wished I had met someone I might have gotten along with at one of the auditions. It would have calmed me down if I had seen them again and felt like I knew someone. It is weird turning up somewhere and knowing absolutely no one. That feeling you get when you go to the pub to meet with friends, and no one has shown up yet. You sit there waiting while everyone around you has fun. I felt like that.

Suddenly *Big Brothers'* voice boomed out really loudly: "The front door is now closed; it will not be opened again until the first eviction in two weeks' time."

I found it really unsettling when *Big Brother* would suddenly talk to us or give us instructions over my fifteen days, as it always seemed like a warning or that we were in trouble. *Big Brothers'* voice was always so loud and seemed really strict; it echoed around the open plan space in the house. It's similar to being in a shopping centre and hearing a voice over the tannoy that you didn't expect to hear. It was both ironic and reassuring that I wouldn't have to check or lock the door. I had missed trains while checking the door to my flat. I had shingles twice from the stress of OCD. I mention OCD a few times in my story, and I hope that by doing so, I can help someone else. I could be free of that ritual for two weeks at least. Now there would be nothing to check and nothing to lock in the *Big Brother* house. Some days are worse than others with OCD. Sometimes it breaks out like a chrysalis, and the freedom flutters out like two white petals in a blue sky. For me, I took it a day at a time.

We had entered the open-plan living space, and I didn't think about the door at all again in my time in the house. Instead, my mind was racing with ideas of being accepted and liked, as well as the fact that it was a real-life experiment. In art, a picture can sometimes say something truer than reality. I remember thinking, *was this real or art? The glare will reveal all I am. Was this needless or born out of a need?*

I didn't know if I would be standing on broken glass. Going in felt like I was taking a stand for me to be myself, as loud as rain on a corrugated tin roof. *I am a painting*, I thought, *and you will see all my outlines, and familiar dot-to-dot all joined up. I can only be myself; I will be the painting I have always been.*

I walked down that path, taken away from all I was until I was just a speck on the horizon. I was such an emotional mess and exhausted from everything I had experienced in the run-up to entering the *Big Brother* house. Also, I felt very isolated, as we had been in our hotel rooms away from everything that had been our normal for two days before we entered the house. Based on my recollections of events, and my opinion, I felt I had entered a *Truman Show*, or the "black box" as drama students call it. The challenge of the A level student would begin in this experimental improvised production. My courage failed me almost immediately. No one I met gave me that heart-flipping moment. I had hoped to get that vibe—you know the energy you get when you meet someone, and you just click? I didn't feel any warmth; there was no heater clicking on, blowing a warm, serene heat. The temperature in the house, emotionally, was not consistent in those two weeks; I didn't feel I could relax properly. I didn't know how sincere people were in greeting each other in that first moment. I got panicky, and as I hugged Brian, I blurted out, "I'm a hugger and a groper."

He took it in good jest and said, "Grope away."

When I'm nervous, I spill things out of my mouth and then cringe at what I've said. This was one of those moments. I was suddenly very aware I was in that glass bowl, just like the goldfish we had to take care of in the kitchen. I went over to feed them with Brian and Narinder, who named them Dinky and Darth Vader. Narinder was worried and went to the diary room later that day as Darth Vader was stuffing all the fish pellets and leaving none for Dinky. I did realise over those days in the house that more than one person would feed the goldfish, so they were eating too much. It meant I would try to organise a feeding routine and then would find that no one had fed them, so they were starving. It probably added to some of the contestants' views of me as bossy.

I remember greeting Narinder when I entered the house and admiring her vivacious personality. She would make me laugh over those fifteen days. She seemed very confident and direct and had a lot of opinions. Over the next two weeks, some of her comments about my breasts really made me feel uncomfortable, but we remained close in the house and as friends afterwards. I felt quite old and serious standing there watching everyone. Everyone seemed super excited. Bubble was so confident and cracked jokes about farting down a straw into a pint of beer. He seemed to hit it off with Ama. I said how pretty Helen looked when I greeted her. For the others, I just said hello and wanted so badly to click with someone. I felt like I was at a conference where you are told by the speaker to spend five minutes meeting and greeting each other.

When the interior doors opened after a booming *Big Brother* voice informed us over the tannoy, the contestants ran frantically around to choose a bedroom. Ama got the double bed in what became the girl's bedroom. My bed was in the corner, near the door. I was ok with that, as I had space by that wall to lay out all my stuff. I felt like I had my own safe space. On looking around the girls' bedroom, the boys were a bit annoyed that we had the bedroom with the en-suite, especially Paul. I imagined how trivial our disagreements would be. I said we should toss a coin for that bedroom, and we all suddenly realised we had no money on us; it had also been taken off us when we entered the house. Dean was kind enough to let the girls have the en-suite, as he said, "It would mean more to the girls." We still didn't have an extra toilet in there, which would have been very useful. The Jacuzzi in there could be filled by *Big Brother* with hot water as a treat. That didn't happen while I was in the house, though.

When the first episode of the new series aired, we had already been in the house for thirty-five hours; all those hours were edited into the first *Big Brother* show.

I was glad at first to be free, not rushing around at school or dealing with the demands of my normal everyday life. I found it difficult to have anything in common, though. I could talk about the theatre, art galleries, and my Christian faith, but no one else seemed interested in those things during my fifteen days in the house. I couldn't just sit around; I realised I had to do something as I really didn't know what to say to anyone.

Stuart and Dean said they didn't cook, but we did have a recipe book, which I love to use, so I got myself in the kitchen and just started cooking. Other people did cook that day for lunch (not that we knew what time it was, though, as there were no clocks), and we had pasta with garlic, bacon, and herbs. Paul and Dean had been in the garden trying to construct a sundial, as we only had our own body clocks and daylight to determine when we would eat. It was strange not knowing what time it was.

Ama and Bubble were the only smokers and were in the garden

chatting as others didn't want them smoking in the house, and I don't think they were pleased with that decision. I felt like I might have to be careful around some of the contestants. Some seemed a bit touchy and could be easily offended. I did feel some had already formed their opinion of me and didn't necessarily like me.

Narinder and Brian were the most open, freely chatting about going to the bathroom for the first time, knowing there was a camera in the bathroom. I liked their energy, as they seemed to feed off each other's words.

We had to make bread every day; that was an order from *Big Brother*. That was great for me, as when I lived at home, my dad always made bread three times a week, so that was a wonderful memory and something I loved doing anyway. The fact that the entire house smelled like freshly baked bread gave me confidence. I felt safe in the kitchen, surrounded by smells from the outside world. I think if all your normal is stripped away, the smell of something familiar can give you such pleasure. I loved baking the bread for that reason. I did bake bread the first day and asked Elizabeth to find me some salt. I was never trying to boss anyone around. I only wanted to try to establish some routines and order in the place we would all call home for most of the summer. I had no idea how others were perceiving me. We would make the dough early in the day so it had time to rise, which could take up to two hours. I used my dad's recipe, as I had watched him make bread so many times. It did help to fill us up, as most of the contestants were really hungry every day. There were a lot of us to feed on the £70 weekly allowance.

I did try to instil some order into our first day and called a meeting in the living room after I checked out the supplies in the storeroom. I couldn't believe how little food we had. I was glad that other than the rice, pasta, and flour, we had a few vegetables in the garden. I hoped we could maintain that mini allotment as we had lettuce, potatoes, broccoli, cabbage, and cauliflower all growing.

We established a chair in the living room area, and if anyone sat in that chair, it was their turn to talk, and we all had to listen. I was never trying to be bossy, but I must have been a bit, making Brian say, "Penny's a plant; she is *Big Brother*."

We decided on chicken, mashed potatoes, and peas that evening, and I said, "We have chicken in the freezer, but don't tell the hens."

We ate our first dinner really late that evening. The menial was magnified in the house; things that wouldn't hold our attention or that we would have never given a second thought about suddenly became hugely important. We all had a lot of time and not a lot to do to fill it. My days in the house were filled with conversations about food and, on occasion, the subject of eviction. I liked dinner time as all of us would sit around the table in the living room area or outside, and I felt like part of the group. They would always compliment me on the food I cooked, and it was the only time of my day I felt connected to some of them. I felt safe and happy in the kitchen; it became my comfort zone. By cooking and serving the food, I felt like the real me, the person my family and friends knew I was.

While I was making bread earlier, I could see Bubble trying to use a skipping rope in the garden, which the others found really funny. It was the only entertainment to watch. We had deck chairs in the garden, and the boys were sitting out there as it was sunny, and they had unpacked really quickly. I took my time laying all my things out in my space by the wall. I had brought my manicure set and my Bible.

Ama had realised her cat had peed on a pair of trousers as she unpacked her case. She came into the kitchen to get a bucket to soak them in and looked really annoyed. Everyone was fascinated by her job. I would have liked to talk with her more as her mother is a Christian; I did talk to her briefly about her mother's Christian faith, and even in the group later when we all sat together. They were all talking about issues that might open a can of worms. I said that it isn't popular to talk about my faith, and no one did during my time in the house. Narinder was relieved that I was religious, as she was a Sikh. I wish I had talked with her about religion in the house. I don't know why I said that about my faith. I don't think I wanted to hear their opinion on my beliefs, as I already felt like an outsider.

I loved the hens and rooster despite being amazed by how much they pooed each day. It was extremely smelly, and there was a lot of it. If they had laid eggs, it became one of the highlights of our entire day. "I won't let any foxes get to you," I would say to them most days.

I liked talking to them in the mornings, as I would get up first and do my exercises and have my prayer time. I always got up very early at home and had that same routine of exercising and praying before my long journey from Islington to Stratford to teach at Sarah Bonnell. The hens had such a great hen house, which was on two levels. It had a room where they could roost at night. We were given strict instructions to lock them in at night as foxes roamed the area. I used to double-check that they were safe and secure. I did notice my OCD creeping back in as I checked that their door was locked. I felt really protective towards them. We have always had animals at home, and they are a real part of our family. They would overtake the house, and life would revolve around them, so I have always loved taking care of animals. I didn't really trust anyone else to look after the chickens. I would always go and double-check on them throughout the day. I would talk to them and liked being with them.

Narinder, Brian, Helen, and I went outside to name them on that first day. We decided on naming them after the Spice Girls. I had no idea that after being evicted, I would be personally invited to Emma Bunton's birthday party, where I would meet the Spice Girls and a new friend I had made – Duncan from the boyband Blue.

Over those two weeks, people would come and find me in the kitchen and start talking to me. On the first day, while I was busy in the kitchen getting dinner prepared, Paul decided to tell me a story about a charity run he was supposed to do. He said he was going to do it naked and run up hundreds of stairs in a religious building. He realised that would be inappropriate. I said he could have worn a loincloth. He then confessed that he had made the whole thing up. I found that really funny and flicked him with a tea towel, something we did at home in my family as a silly gesture and a sign of affection when we washed up the dishes. He actually thought I was really annoyed. I think not just the menial tasks but also everyone's reactions were magnified in the house.

We had no radio, TV, or anything else to distract us. So any actions or words said would be overanalysed by those watching or listening, as there was nowhere else to go and nothing else to see. We spent the entire day together. I think most of us experienced a similar feeling later during lockdown, stuck in our houses, trying to find something to fill our day with our families, spending every hour with them. I assured him I found his windup funny. I felt then that I would have to try and be a little less eccentric and tone my way of being down a bit, but with nothing else to do, I did act out at times. For me, I was just being theatrical and wacky, but in that intense environment and in the edited versions shown on TV, it appears I am actually that way or meant to say that.

Big Brother boomed into the house over the tannoy to announce that the door to the outside den was unlocked. It meant huge squeals and screams from some of the contestants as they scrambled to be the first to reach the den. We found a ragdoll and hoisted it out into the garden to bring it into the main house. I was worried and said, "Don't frighten the chickens with it."

It had a sign saying it was the eleventh housemate and would join the house when the first contestant was evicted. Everyone got overexcited, and I thought if I acted like that, they would look at me as if I were weird. I didn't understand why, during those two weeks, everyone thought it was funny when some of the contestants said really rude things, acted out in unusual ways, or were quite extreme. Yet most of the contestants thought I was unstable because of my behaviour. I really didn't understand that at all.

I was determined to have a bit of a holiday away from all my worries and chill out, but a competitive streak hung in the air like burnt tar, along with sensitive egos, during those fifteen days. The problem was that I was hypersensitive. I picked up moods like a sponge. I was easily derailed by other people's moods, and I felt compelled to please everyone. It really was not the best environment for someone like me to be in. Some found my niceness annoying, and others were disgruntled about me being in the kitchen all the time, but what do you do when there is nothing to do?

I was just getting on with it. I didn't realise it was such a huge topic of conversation when I started cooking in the house. For years after, I would be stopped on the street and people would shout with joy, "In the kitchen, out the kitchen." That evening I went to bed exhausted after hearing more squeals and shouts as Bubble put the rag doll in Brian's bed. Everyone was laughing as I fell asleep.

***

Day two in the *Big Brother* House:
Saturday, 26 May 2001

I got up early, about 6 a.m., I think, although I had no idea of the time. I went straight out in my pyjamas to check on the chickens. I would always say hello to them and ask if they were alright every morning. It is funny how we talk to our pets as if we are having a two-way conversation and they really understand what we are saying. We have always done that with our pets in my family.

After that, I would make porridge for breakfast for everyone most days, and I could see from the kitchen area that day that a lot of the boys were starting their day by doing exercises in the garden. It was quite funny to watch Stuart do sit-ups, Paul do press-ups, and Dean lift weights. The weather was lovely that summer, and it felt good when I had a chance to relax in the sunshine, which wasn't very often.

I was back in the kitchen later, preparing the bread dough that Bubble was kindly kneading for me when I suddenly realised that I hadn't put any yeast in the mix. What a disaster, especially as we had to be careful not to waste any ingredients. Bubble Paul and Brian, who had joined us in the kitchen area, started throwing the bread dough in a game of catch, and we all ran around the living room laughing, trying to catch it like a ball. That was one of my best memories, and I really enjoyed the energy. I'm sure I baked it anyway. I would have just called it flatbread!

Our first task was set that day. The booming voice of *Big Brother* sent shivers down my spine. We had to build a fire and ensure it stayed lit for five days. The storeroom was opened for us to collect the equipment for the task. I just thought the whole idea of building a fire was utterly stressful and boring, adding to the tedious hours we spent with nothing to do. Hours of sitting by a fire and keeping it alight tested my nerves and made me quite agitated. We had to light the fire by midday.

Everyone went into the storage room to get the equipment, as we had to assemble it too. It reminded me of an IKEA flat pack, and I watched the boys as they figured out how to put it together. Stuart had taken control of the task and was giving instructions that he had collected from the diary room. He stood by the designated chair, unfolded a piece of paper, and read it out to us, telling us the task was to keep a fire alight. I always thought he had a really swanky home and a classy life because he seemed very self-assured and always looked posh. When we got the wood from the storage room, there was only enough for the task, so we had to be careful not to burn it too quickly to keep it alight. It was to be attended day and night. One hundred and twenty hours over five days.

My reaction was to go and drink coffee! The only benefit of that task was that we were given a clock to time the rotas that everyone had to do. We were allowed to keep the clock afterwards too, which was great to be able to cook the dinners I made without having to guess the time. It is amazing how important such a small thing is when it is taken away from you. It was such a relief to know what time it was.

For each task, *Big Brother* would call someone into the diary room, and they would find a folder in there with instructions in it. Stuart sat with the folder in the designated chair to plan a rota. Everyone was talking at once, just like when we first arrived at the house. It took ages for us all to figure out a rota and whom we would work with. It got really stressful later that day as two people always needed to be outside tending to the fire. Helen went inside, but she was on rota, and thank goodness Dean was outside by chance with Stuart, who was also on rota, so it covered us as two people were outside. Everyone was getting quite tetchy, and I just saw chaos looming as the responsibility was intense.

I was concerned about the chickens being interrupted day and night by people outside tending the fire and that they might get agitated and stop laying eggs. We were allowed to bet a percentage of our shopping budget and picked thirty per cent after a lot of discussion that went on forever. If we won this task, we would get thirty per cent more money added to our shopping budget for the following week. If we won, we would get £91.00; if we lost, we would get just £49.00 to feed everyone. We would only know if we passed or failed on Thursday. We got the fire assembled with all the bits of wood and lit it just in time. Everyone started discussing what rota to take again, and it got heated, unlike the fire, as we suddenly realised it had gone out! It stressed me out thinking about how we had to keep an eye on it every second and wondering how we would keep this fire burning if there were thunderstorms.

I made omelettes for lunch, and I must have come across as a bit bossy again when I told Ama, who was cooking with me, to put the onion on the side for our cheese and onion omelettes. My mother is allergic to onions, and I didn't know if anyone in the house might just not like them in an omelette. I found it difficult to talk to her or Elizabeth and would only talk to them if we were in the kitchen together. I just couldn't think of any topic of conversation that would flow with either them or with Helen or Stuart. I did have a nice chat with Dean, who was always so calm. He said how he was missing home, and I told him I longed to have children. It was a really lovely, heartfelt chat, and I felt it was a really normal, sane conversation.

I just overheard a lot of the others, and the subject seemed to be all about sex, and I didn't want to join in at all. On top of the stress of the fire task, *Big Brother's* booming voice said that we would have to nominate someone to be evicted on Friday. I turned to Brian and said, "I know you will vote for me, but just remember the chickens; they will die." I was really upset to leave them when I was actually evicted. I hoped the others would look after them properly and talk to them like I did.

A lot of chats continued that day around the kitchen area, as I was always in the kitchen and some of the contestants would find me deliberately and talk to me. I was actually quite happy to be left alone to cook. Brian would perch on the table seat around the side of the kitchen area and start talking. I found him hysterical. Even when he was being quite insulting in jest, it sounded funny. Narinder would join him, and sometimes Bubble and Paul would join him as well. They were the main contestants I talked to during my time in the house. Brian started talking about my breasts that day, asking if they were real and how big they were, and I tried to veer the conversation away from something I would never bring up as a topic of conversation. I was bemused that my housemates wanted to talk about my breasts over those fifteen days. I found it embarrassing and too personal. Narinder said they were lovely, and Brian said he would like a feel. I found it difficult to talk about them, not realising it would be the topic of every tabloid paper in the country in the following days.

The others were in the garden as it was a boiling hot sunny day, and the girls were asking the boys what they would do if a naked girl walked into their room. When I was out there taking a break from the kitchen, someone voted for me to snog Brian, and I refused because that is my father's name. With all of this attention on my breasts and sex talk, and with people involving me in their conversations, I was starting to feel vulnerable. I did manage to have one nice conversation with all the girls as we talked about beauty routines, and I shared that I loved my face packs and manicured my own nails and feet.

Narinder was struggling with people getting her name wrong; they were calling her all sorts of variations of her name or forgetting her name entirely. It was her sixth wedding anniversary that day, and as we congratulated her with a toast at dinner time, she said, "Just call me Lola." I realised I had gotten her name wrong too and just did what I always did with my friends – I gave her a big hug and called her a little love. That was something else that was said to me over the years when people recognised me on the street.

It is funny to see that *Big Brother* had a psychologist on the show to analyse our behaviour when it aired in the evenings. Dr Peter Collet called the hugs "upgraded actions." He said when we all entered the house, it was more formal, with Bubble shaking hands with Ama and Helen. By the time Brian, Paul, and I came in, everyone had "upgraded actions." I found that weird, as to me, it is natural to embrace someone and set a tone of positivity. I even gave some people a massage on their shoulders that day. I certainly didn't intend for any of my actions to have a sexual connotation. I didn't realise my hugs in the house would be analysed by people as sexual or intended as wanting sex. My motto is: "Be nice, be kind, and share some genuine love." I was again pretty exhausted and was glad not to be on overnight duty tending the fire. It allowed at least two people to stay up all night talking about their experiences in the house and their thoughts on other housemates. Naively, during those fifteen days, I never thought I would be talked about behind my back by the others.

***

Day three in the *Big Brother House*:
Sunday, 27 May.

I was tending to the fire on an early shift with Paul. We'd been sitting there for a long time and were getting bored. It was during those times that I made banter and chatted away, trying to make the time go faster and have a bit of a laugh. We chatted about me not having a boyfriend and how he might get a lot of interest from girls when he leaves the house. I was just making conversation and was not flirting with or trying to be sexual with Paul.

Narinder and Brian joined us and continued the conversation about relationships. They added that they thought I was going to shag Paul. It was all said as a joke. I was a bit taken aback but went along with it as there was nothing else to do. Brian said that someone has to shag, as it would be good for the ratings. He was so funny in the way he just said things. We were all having a laugh and did not mean what was said. We all got along really well and just carried on chatting in this absurd way as it relieved our boredom.

I remember saying to Paul that I didn't want to shag him. And as we all laughed, I said, "Tell me you're not going to shag me. I will cut it off with a knife." It was all in jest, with nothing else to do or talk about. I jumped on him on his deck chair to make the others laugh in the midst of a silly conversation we were all having. I didn't think at all about how I might come across on TV, as I didn't think about the cameras. It was just silly conversation in the garden like you'd have on a night out saying things for a laugh.

I didn't know that the tabloid papers were starting to write about me. Headlines were starting to come out on the front page of every tabloid in the country:

Penny 6ft Sex on Legs

The article read: "The teacher got frisky yesterday, whipping Paul with a wet tea towel. A *Big Brother* source said, 'Viewers should keep tuned in because things are almost certain to move up a gear.' It even mentions Paul's mother saying, 'He'd go through all the women.'

Then there is that CHARLOTTE, who I really don't know. My so-called best friend, that I've mentioned before, gave a story in another article. She certainly made the rounds talking about me! She says, "Penny has had dozens of one-night stands. She told me she will do whatever it takes to win and thinks it will help her win if she sleeps with one of the men." She also called me "a real man-eater!" She also says I was briefed by the producers and told it was a good idea to liven up the show! What a load of crap, in my opinion. My reputation and life were in the hands of the journalist's ink. WHO IS CHARLOTTE? I DON'T KNOW WHO YOU ARE! The article says: "*Big Brother* was off to a roaring start with 3.3 million viewers and a million hits on the live website cams."

We innocently got busy tending the fire that day. I looked in the instruction folder and realised I had to dress Brian in the specific gloves he had to wear and the goggles before he could chop the wood, which was fun dressing him up. He was so funny and said, with his outfit on, "I'm going in; wish me luck." It got funnier as he smashed down on a piece of wood and broke the axe. All chaos broke loose, as we didn't know if *Big Brother* would replace it or if we would get into trouble. We waited in anticipation for *Big Brother* to get back to us about a new axe head. We were so relieved that they gave us a new one.

Everyone was outside sunbathing and started talking about things they had done that had been embarrassing. One said they had nearly had sex in a lift with their partner; another said their breasts had fallen out while dancing and they hadn't realised; and another said that on a night out dressed as a woman, they had snogged a girl. None of these made headline news, nor did their responses and attitudes towards sex in the many conversations I overheard them having.

Sunday was the day we had to write our shopping list. It was on a chalkboard like I used at school. I took charge, not thinking if that might have come across as overbearing, especially when I said, "I'm the director; I feel like God here." I was trying to make it fun. I got really frustrated trying to figure out what to get and almost shouted at the group in my frustration, "I'm trying to plan a meal a day or we will be buggered."

I was only trying to organise and plan meals for the week. I knew what we already had in the storage room and what people liked to eat.

Maybe I should have kept quiet. I checked about ketchup, tea bags, and sugar. One of the housemates noticed we had no wine on our shopping list, and another said about getting some: "Go for the cheapest shit."

I was frantically flicking through the laminated folder we had been given. There were pages of it with the price next to it. We only had a certain amount of time to finish our shopping list. It was really manic as we only got the booklet for a short period of time, and then we had to hand it back by placing it in the storage room. I wished we could keep the booklet as we had so little time to browse through it, as well as add all the prices up to exactly £70.00. We added the item and the price next to it, and in the last few seconds, we added up our total before we had to return the shopping list to the diary room. The chalk kept snapping, and the board looked really messy. *Big Brother* stressed me out even more by blaring into the living room: "You have fifteen minutes to complete your shopping list."

I said, "This bloody thing is doing my head in." I had to go into the diary room with the blackboard and read it out to *Big Brother*. I realised we hadn't added yeast, but *Big Brother* let us have it as we had calculated our total amount wrong and had some spare change.

I was scared of the diary room and only went in it if they summoned me. I don't know why, but I found it spooky in there. It seemed like an unfinished room. It was small, with panels on the wall that looked like they needed decorating. The chair was black and white and really uncomfortable. There was no colour or anything to make you feel calm in there. The floor was a thin bit of grey carpet, and when you sat down, you just looked at this black box and the black curtain behind it. It was really unfriendly and nothing like the glamorous diary rooms of the following series of *Big Brother*.

I felt like I had been summoned to the head's office at school and was in trouble whenever I went in there. I still wish I had relaxed and gone in there more often and talked to *Big Brother* instead of trying to bottle up all my anxieties. I went in there that day and didn't know what I was supposed to do with the blackboard. *Big Brother* said to hold the blackboard on my lap and read it out. It was a lot to get through, and in the middle of it all, Bubble dashed in as some of the group wanted to change the four bottles of wine for cider as it was only £3.19 for two litres so people could get pissed. It was too late to change it, I think. I maybe should have changed it, but I just wanted to get out of the diary room as fast as possible.

I really did dread going in there. I spent the rest of the day in the kitchen, preparing a beef chilli. Bubble told me that I was doing too much. I was just getting on with it, but I did say to him, "I am being a bit of a servant." It was lovely, though, and as I served it up on our massive wooden table on the decking, they all clapped me. It was another nice memory of a moment of unity and happiness for me. It was fabulous sitting around that huge wooden table in the dusk of the day. It felt like you were on holiday, and I enjoyed eating outside.

I lived in a small flat in London and never sat or ate in the garden area at the back of my flat. It was a really nice experience to sit around and hear the birds and the chickens making sounds and smell the air on a hot summer evening. Dean was funny as he asked if I cooked like that at home. I said I always had dinner parties for lots of people. He was astounded that I cooked for lots of friends regularly. I tried to do the washing up but was told I had done too much. There was nothing else for others to do, but I just wasn't used to sitting around anyway. I went off to bed feeling upset that they wanted me out of the kitchen.

***

Day four in the *Big Brother house*:
Monday 28 May.

I was on a twelve-hour fire-watching shift with Paul, and we talked about our jobs. I chatted with him about my love for poetry. Bubble came to join me do my exercises. I tried to get him to take it seriously, but he just watched me, making comments and laughing. I guess I was stretching in my pyjamas in a strange garden; I probably looked a sight.

It started to rain that morning, and we were frantically trying to keep the fire alight. Stuart, Narinder, and Brian came out to help. Fortunately, it was only a light rain that soon stopped. Stuart decided to make bread once the conversation dried up. It was nice as I helped Helen make brioche bread, and we finally spent some time together and had something to talk about. It didn't bake well, and I was upset for her as I really wanted it to work. It was again the only thing other than the fire to concentrate on and fill our time.

Again, some of the contestants, when we sat in the garden on the deck chairs, talked about my breasts and asked if I had a boob job. It was wearing me out, but I didn't have the confidence to tell them to stop it.

Some wanted to squeeze them, and I got upset and went inside for a bit. Paul made me laugh by calling me "a big old girl." He said, "I do have respect for you." I think some of them just used these topics to again bring a bit of laughter into a very boring situation. I was OK with everyone; I just hoped they were joking about some of the things they said about me.

Brian said: "You could beat Penny up, take all her clothes, her money, and leave her on the side of the road. You would come back the next day, and she would say, 'That's OK.'"

While we were in the garden, *Big Brothers'* voice boomed into the house, which distracted us from any further chatting about me. Paul collected a folder of instructions and a camera from the diary room. We all sat in the living room area, with him in the designated chair. We would do that every time we got given a task. This time it was quite fun, as we had to create our own house calendar.

Paul decided to direct it and informed *Big Brother*, as he had to go back into the diary room with the decisions we had made about the calendar. He told *Big Brother* that the shoot would reflect our personalities and characters. *Big Brother* accepted Paul's decision. Everyone got really excited. Elizabeth went into the den, draped a scarf over her naked breasts, and held up a magazine. Bubble pretended to steal a chicken. Helen did the splits in her bikini, Dean posed with his guitar, and Brian took an outdoor shower; we all laughed as the foam from the shampoo swirled down onto his swim trunks. It looked suggestive, but it was also very funny. I stood in the kitchen holding a plunger by the sink in the red sequin dress I wore for my *OK! Magazine* photo and interview. Everyone made such a great shot. That is another one of my best memories.

We all got along and laughed so much, which made it a very special time. Dinner was outside again in the lovely evening summer air, and Ama had cooked a lovely chilli. Helen was chatting about her brioche and saying people don't take her seriously, and Dean retorted that some laughed only because it was rubbish bread – it wasn't about her being blonde. I understood, while we all sat around eating, how she felt, as I felt slightly picked on and vulnerable.

Paul was in agony as he had fallen on his ankle in the garden after tripping over a football after the photo shoot. *Big Brother* gave him some frozen peas for the swelling, which we were not allowed to keep for food and had to return to *Big Brother*. He got crutches later that evening, when a doctor met him in the diary room. We were all quite thrilled at the prospect of someone else being in the house. I remember it feeling strange, as we just hadn't had any contact whatsoever with the outside world.

Earlier that day as well, something had been thrown over our wall. I thought it might be a message for one of the housemates. As soon as it landed in the garden, *Big Brother's* voice boomed out and ordered us to get into the boys' bedroom as quickly as we could. It was exciting to know someone was in the *Big Brother* house and walking in the garden. There were some conversations around the table that evening again about people wanting to do more, especially in the kitchen. People were saying that some people don't listen, do too much, and take over. They said they haven't had the chance to get into the kitchen. It was fine with me. I only did all the cooking because I thought no one else was interested. In those first few days, I hadn't seen anyone really keen to cook, so I was a bit perturbed by their comments.

I went to the diary room, which was my last resort as I didn't want to cry in front of them or get angry and say something rude about their behaviour or conversations. I waffled on to *Big Brother* about how chaotic all the conversations seem to be, jumping from topic to topic. Some people just wanted to banter, be loud, and have a laugh. I mentioned seeing the girls chatting about alcohol and relationships and not feeling invited to join them. I said I didn't pick up at all on why some of my housemates really didn't like me. I went to bed confused and feeling a bit sad. I left a few of them tending the fire and again talking about sex.

***

Day five in the *Big Brother house*:
Tuesday, 29 May.

I was on fire duty at 6 a.m. with Dean and Brian. I was really weepy and said, "I'm just this kitchen woman." I felt very vulnerable. I felt some were constantly moaning and whispering about what I was doing and the way I said things, and I started to feel paranoid. For me, I always think, *live in the moment. I mean, just get busy living or go away.*

Brian tried to lighten the mood and agreed with me that others should just say they want to be cooking in the kitchen.

Helen was up for doing haircuts, and I asked her to cut my hair. She brought out her scissors and then dropped them between the slates on the decking. Finally, Bubble retrieved them with everyone cheering him on. It was the highlight of the morning. I was glad, as I didn't want to get blamed for anything else. We went inside to finish cutting my hair. I went back to bed after that, exhausted emotionally. This experience was nothing like I expected, with housemates telling me what I shouldn't do.

While Elizabeth and Helen were watching the fire later that day, Helen went inside to get one of her dresses. There had been talk about being evicted and about who might go first and what our eviction outfit would be. By leaving the fire station, the rule that two people must be present at all times was broken. I got out of bed and joined a heated discussion with everyone in the garden, as we were all a bit bewildered as to whether we should continue with this task or call it quits. Helen was understandably devastated, and everyone rallied around to reassure her it was OK, although I could see some of them were pretty angry at her. We all decided to carry on with the task, as we hoped we might still pass it. I don't think any of us fully comprehended that *Big Brother* saw absolutely everything we did.

We all sat around in the garden, and Brian was dancing in front of Narinder and Ama, and they were telling him how to treat a customer if he were a table dancer. There was nothing to do other than sit in the garden, and *Big Brother*'s voice once again boomed through the house and called each of us to the diary room to talk to them.

I was called to the diary room, which still filled me with dread, and I was asked if I was OK. I felt really upset, but should I have said how I felt? I don't know why I didn't. I said, "I'm fine being here. They are all genuine people. I can get bewildered very quickly. I am shocked by some conversations. I just don't talk like that with my friends. I am glad to be contributing."

What I should have said is, "Why is everyone constantly telling me to stop doing kitchen things and commenting on my breasts?"

I said I thought everyone was playful, and I feel like the sensible one. I also said I was quite upset about all the swearing every day and some of the conversations. I hoped talking to *Big Brother* would help me, but it just made me feel like I had talked about people behind their backs, and I felt worse. There was a noise over the wall in the garden while we had dinner outside again that evening, which I hadn't cooked. Some of my students from my school were shouting their love into the garden. I was really uplifted before the voice of *Big Brother* ordered us inside and said we had to shut the door to the garden and wait until we were instructed to go back outside.

When we all were allowed outside again, we got into a group circle and hugged, and I said, "Fancy my kids bringing us together at last." Little did I know that the towel drop story was being printed for distribution in the morning tabloids for the next day. That story became a shackle around my ankle, stopping me from finding sanity, peace, and happiness until 2020. How apt that the girls from my school came to find me that evening and screamed their love to me! I thank them; they are ribbons tied around my heart.

The tabloids for the next day included headlines and front pages of me:

Big Brother is Watching You.

Head Sack to Naughty Teacher.

Headmistress says: It all depends on her and whether she wants to remain in *Big Brother* at all costs."

The article read: "Inside the house, Penny was in more hot water despite being favourite with the bookies. Coral slashed the odds of her being evicted from 10-1 to 3-1 after other contestants were seen complaining about her to each other.

"Imagine what Christian Penny would pull off if she were an atheist. She is arguably the first star of terrestrial televisions lurch into soft porn. She should open a prep school. She can teach Lady Chatterley's Lover and act it out too. An image comes to mind of an S and M version of Hogwarts Express, and she can double up as a religious instruction teacher."

Craig Phillips, who won *Big Brother 1*, said in his column: "I'm not sure when she dropped her towel, but it was probably an accident."

Thank you so much, Craig.

Another article says I dropped my towel on the Monday and *Big Brother* had to put up an apology on screen on the digital service of E4 fifteen minutes after I did it. Why wait fifteen minutes and let it digest as a truth in people's memories, *Big Brother*? My head screams!

My head teacher is in another article, saying how I got a letter weeks before I went into *Big Brother* about the school's "Code of Conduct." I don't remember getting that. There is a quote from a parent from my school in the article saying she can't believe I taught her daughter. There were comments that Paul and I would be the first to have sex on a reality show. It mentions that my school was visited by Prince Charles (now King Charles) in 1998.

To top it all off, on 29 May 2001, Peter Clarke published an article in *The Evening Standard* with the headline:

Babs did it better.

There is a photo of the late Barbara Winsor in a towel showing her breasts, and a photo of me with my towel beside hers, showing mine. He says, "There can be no clearer indication of how bored we are with politics than our utter obsession with reality TV. We have decided to forget about the pressing issues of the day: health, education, transport, and the euro, in favour of examining minute details of the lives of complete strangers. Naturally, the minute detail we are interested in is sex and its close proximity to nudity." He implies the *Big Brother* bosses and *Survivor* are hell-bent on pushing the boundaries in order to boost ratings.

He goes on to say, "Christian Penny has dropped her bath towel perhaps in a moment of religious fervour and exposed her naughty parts to the all-seeing camera. I hope I am not alone in detecting a whiff of desperation in these crude manoeuvres. Shows that are built on the notion of voyeurism are inevitably caught up in the law of diminishing returns constantly being obliged to show more and more to retain the same level of interest. The sad fact is nothing seems to be able to raise the right amount of fascinated outrage as nudity and sex. It has turned us into rather a seedy bunch. Remember Late Barbara Winsor did all this sort of thing in her heyday she was really saucy."

All I was worried about on 29 May 2001 was that the goldfish were OK, as I had taken them to the diary room that evening as one of them looked really unwell. I went to bed completely unaware of what was being said about me on the outside world.

**

**Day six in the *Big Brother* house:
Wednesday, 30 May.**

This was the day of the row with Stuart. This was the day my towel-dropping story appeared in all the papers in England, with news also spreading around the world to my aunt in Canada and my friends in Australia. Another layer was added on top of the stories already published about me – wanting to and possibly having sex in the *Big Brother* house.

Ironically, I had a lovely chat with Stuart as everyone else was still asleep, and we sat tending the fire in the morning. I told him of my dreams to become an actress and about my long-term relationship with Adam. He listened really patiently. Later that day, I became very upset because I had dropped my microphone down the toilet after telling everyone to take very good care of theirs! They were worth £3,000 each!

It was also the day, as reported in Jean Ritchie's book, that Brian accidentally flashed his assets, and Narinder said, "I've never seen a white one." I quote from Jean Ritchie's book, "Brian laughs and spreads his legs to give her another eyeful." It was playful banter, and we were all trying to just create a bit of drama that would make us laugh. It was unbelievably boring at times in the house, and we all said or did things just to make each other laugh. I just wonder why my nakedness was such a dramatic headline and why it became front page news. Others discussed sex and whether they would consider snogging each other. I think all the talks were just banter to while away the time, and no one, including myself, meant anything by it. No one was talking seriously about sex. I had my Christian beliefs, and I was a teacher. I guess that is the answer, in my opinion, to why I was the focus of stories in the press.

Outside in the garden, I realised how easily I could have left the fire unattended. I said to Paul, "Well, Brian and I were mucking about and nearly went inside at one point." I was tending the fire and getting excited about the jelly I had made. The menial tasks are so magnified in the house; we were really bored with nothing to do. My jelly was the highlight and excitement of my morning. I was hoping it had set. I got up and nearly went inside to check, then suddenly realised and said, "Oh, I can't move," as that would have left one person again by the fire and broken the rules. Some of the others were inside, talking about sex with a woman.

I was sitting in the garden, as I had deliberately left the kitchen open to anyone who wanted to take control of the cooking that day. It was a really sunny day, and I chatted away to Paul, which caused comments by some of the other housemates that I was "gagging" for it. I just tried to ignore the comments and thought about getting a tan as the weather was so lovely. Bubble asked me what we were going to have for dinner after telling me the other day that I did too much in the kitchen. I said, "Chicken, chips, and peas."

He said, "Who's cooking?"

I said, "Whoever wants to."

I did have a nice chat with Bubble that day; I found him incredibly full of life. I said I would have liked to have taught him. He said he had read a lot of literature and enjoyed the classics. I could see he had potential, and I had the opportunity to help him sort out his audition speeches for drama school; I wasn't surprised that he got in and also became a playwright. I went to see his plays in Edinburgh and another in London with my friend Paul Bedsprings in the years that followed *Big Brother*.

We didn't have a washing machine in the house, so we had to hand wash our clothes and then use the mangle. It was such hard work, but it was so funny watching Bubble use the old-fashioned mangle to rinse the water out of his clothes, and it filled in time and gave us something to do.

Later that day, we got the calendar from the diary room after *Big Brother* informed us it was there. It was marvellous! I was on week seven. It was just such good quality, and we all looked amazing. We all sat and looked at each page carefully. It was a wonderful positive group discussion, full of laughter and joy, and it reminded me of the atmosphere at my dinner parties in my flat in Islington. We hung it up on one of the walls by the kitchen.

Helen's birthday was also that day. I had wrapped her present with Ama and Bubble in the girl's bedroom. I went back outside on my own, as they seemed to have found a really strong friendship. Paul, still with his ankle bandaged up, was painting his toenails with Dean and having a talk about cross dressing. We all got dressed up, and Stuart frightened us with his cat eye contact lenses. We had pizza and six bottles of champagne on our table outside.

Helen had been called into the diary room and had chosen the party instead of the other offer of Gucci shoes and a Gucci handbag that *Big Brother* had left on the diary room chair for her. We all sprayed our hair with spray colours from the birthday decorations box we were given; it was absolutely lovely. Another surprise was a huge chocolate birthday cake, *Big Brother* informed us that it was in the diary room from Helen's mum. It had a lovely picture of Helen on it, and Ama brought it out with Brian with all the candles lit. We sang Happy Birthday to her as we sat around our table outside. It was a lovely time.

But again, I was asked stuff as I was about to make custard. Did I find Paul good-looking, and did I think he was a bit boring?

I just replied, "I've got friends like him, but they are more interesting."

I don't know why I was asked so many leading questions in the house. It was as if some people wanted me to say something inappropriate. Maybe I was getting paranoid, but some of the questioning could easily have made me say something outrageous just to be silly. I just wouldn't ask people questions like they did. I didn't make the custard in the end because, with all the champagne, I thought it would probably make people throw up!

Around the table, there was once again a lot of sex talk. We all ended up sitting in a circle on the decking, and then there were the questions of who you would sleep with in the house. I was so fed up with all this talk of sex. I found it very rude. I believe that in any concentrated environment, we can all become slightly paranoid and thrown off balance. I had to answer, and I said "Brian" when I was asked who I would sleep with.

I don't know why Stuart hesitated or complicated the question. Everyone was saying to him, "Just pick one person." However, for whatever reason, he chose to answer the simple question with, "I wouldn't sleep with Penny, but I would sleep with the rest of you."

Suddenly, it seemed like, in slow motion, chaos was unfolding. Paul became a subject as Stuart said something about Paul and me; Paul then came to my defence, and I said, "Don't mock my friendship with Paul," and like with any concentrated tensions, possibly in my opinion only, jealousies and dislikes boiled over.

I was already exhausted from all the sex conversations and conversations over those days about my breasts, and I was fed up, so I said, "Fuck you, arsehole."

It just hit a nerve because I was tired of being the subject matter of this sort of conversation about sex. I had been worn down since the comments started on day one. What I meant by those words was to stop making me the main topic of a conversation or asking me a question I hadn't even asked. It was the final straw after days and hours of me being the focus of talks about sex. His face and reaction reminded me of Adam when he got really affronted. I had been in situations with Adam years before when I had tried to defend myself. I was very broken from Adam's abuse and felt very timid now that I had asserted myself with Stuart.

Stuart asked me to repeat myself, and I think I just blurted it out again. Then there was the whole begging him to forgive me thing, which only made matters worse. I was actually frightened to see how angry he was. Narinder was really sweet, telling me I do everything for everyone, and Bubble was hysterically funny, saying that if it helped, he would sleep with me just to make me laugh and break the tension. Brian was really concerned. I did ask Stuart to forgive me, but he just said I had shown myself to be shallow.

I staggered off to the diary room, telling *Big Brother* that I hadn't meant it horribly and that I was trying to pull everyone together and encourage them in the house. I said Stuart had knocked me back a few times with comments, and I thought tonight we were all just mucking about. I said I was so tired of the comments about my friendship with Paul, and Stuart didn't have to say that Paul was "going with me."

It was just so intense and so ridiculous, but in that house, there was an absolutely horrendous tension and atmosphere. I suppose that being cooped up away from emotions, partners, and familiar comforts, everyone was coping with different tensions of their own. A lot of emotions were released that night. I left them all and went to bed; some were drunk in the garden, and others sat around talking about sex again. Helen, on the other hand, was fast asleep and missed the entire row saga.

I felt awful, as the students at my school would have heard me swear. I felt dreadful as now they would all have another topic of conversation in the *Big Brother* house about me, as what else is there to talk about when you have nothing to do? This was the first and only time I suddenly thought about the cameras picking up on my swearing and that going out on TV. It's so easy to forget that cameras are watching. I was suddenly terrified. It was a sudden realisation that this could be shown to the public.

I had no idea I was all over the front pages, and this was just another chapter in the long story of me being all over the papers and the internet. I had no idea before then that the cameras would ever pick up a story on me at all. I used to laugh about the camera on the wall in the girl's bedroom, as it moved every time I did, and the ones in the living space on the walls were always moving around every time I was moving around.

Even though I didn't know then that they were also behind our mirrors and that they layered the walls of the house, I joked about the camera on our wall in the bedroom, but that was made into a story in the papers that had sexual connotations as I had nicknamed the camera "Pervy." There was a huge, massive double spread in the tabloids about that "Pervy Camera," with a huge photo of me naked in the shower. It is amazing how stories are created from one word or one action. I felt an overwhelming emotional burnout from those first few days of trying to adjust to life in this space. I was struggling, weeping, and manic.

It was only day six!

It was so intense and exploded in that concentrated space we were all locked into. Those who were still awake were summoned inside from the garden at 1 a.m. because fireworks were being set off over the wall. It was a day of fireworks – literally and metaphorically.

***

Day seven in the *Big Brother* house:
Thursday, 31 May.

I was outside tending the fire with Paul early. I hadn't slept well at all. I felt sick and uneasy and expressed to Paul my wish that Stuart would get over it.

"I'm willing to take a punch on the chin," I said.

"Something like this was going to happen soon as this is all a big change for everyone and we don't know each other well enough to know how we are going to react," Paul added.

Paul was really kind, and I appreciated his insights. Stuart came out and gave me a hug, which was such a relief to me, but over my shoulder he winked at Paul. Unbeknownst to me, the row and the wink had become media fodder, with stories in tabloid newspapers and even on radio show discussions. I didn't know about the wink and was grateful there was no horrible lingering tension left from the previous night. At the time, I was just relieved that the row was over as a silly outburst of emotions and exhaustion.

At 11 a.m., we found out that we had failed the fire task, but we were allowed to keep the clock, which was a huge relief to me. If I woke up in the middle of the night at home and didn't know what time it was, I always felt very strange.

My anxiety was worse in the house, in such unfamiliar territory. Everyone realised we only had £49.00 to spend on our weekly shopping. We did bond as a group by doing a countdown from ten to one as the fire task officially ended at 11.59 a.m. after one hundred and twenty hours, but *Big Brother* had stopped it early at 11 a.m. *Big Brother* had said that there were a few reasons we failed the task, which caused tension as some wanted to know who else was to blame. There was so much blame flying around and a lot of accusations that it was once again a toxic environment.

Narinder was chatting to me about Paul, and by now I was just amusing myself by making up answers to make her laugh. I said he wasn't in my league. I think in that environment, you just make your own entertainment. We were called into the living room by *Big Brother* and told we would have to make our nominations at 10 p.m. the following evening. We had all presumed we would be nominating on Monday. Tomorrow would be Friday, and then, to add to the stress, we would have to wait until Monday to find out who had been nominated. I hate it when, in life, you have to wait over the weekend to find out something really important. It hangs over you all weekend and is in your mind as to what the outcome will be. Then those nominated would have to wait a whole week until Friday to see which one would go. *What a lot of stress*, I thought. I felt sick to my stomach. We were all really shocked that the nominations were happening so quickly. No one really knew who they wanted to nominate as we were all still getting to know each other. It made me realise how little I knew about some of the contestants. I didn't even think that one person I could nominate could be Stuart, because that row had been forgiven and forgotten by me.

I was called into the Diary room and *Big Brother* wanted to know if I was OK after the row. I said: "I feel slightly paranoid, and it might be in people's memories for a while. But please tell my girls at school not to swear and I'm sorry for swearing. But *Big Brother* it does upset me as I begged for Stuart's forgiveness, and I believe if someone begs you to forgive them, they should forgive you. I am now wary of how I approach certain people as their egos get injured quite quickly. I am disappointed in myself and feel I have let myself down. I feel a bit older than everyone. I just need to be strong and face it."

I came out of the diary room, and Brian hugged me and asked me what we were having for dinner. I said, "SOMEONE needs to put the chicken on." I had enough whirling around in my brain before I suddenly realised that Ama was in the kitchen. I didn't feel like she wanted me to help, so I said to Brian, " I am in the kitchen, out the kitchen." He found it absolutely hysterical, so I just acted out a little scene of me jumping in and out the kitchen whilst describing how to prepare a roast chicken about rubbing it in oil and putting garlic under the skin. Brian played along while others watched me. I enjoyed myself, and I have no idea what anyone else thought of me.

That was another fun moment in the house for me. Over the years people have shouted or run at me on the street chanting, "In the kitchen out the kitchen." I went to bed early, and a lot of the housemates stayed up into the early hours as they did most nights.

***

Day eight in the *Big* Brother house:
Friday, 1 June.

On the *Big Brother* show, a psychologist advised *Big Brother* that we keep the clock to help regulate our sleeping patterns. I was really grateful for the clock, as it helped me organise my mind and got me through the day. My OCD and anxieties were overwhelming me, and I tried to keep calm. I would look at the clock and think of what I would be doing at that time in the outside world. It helped me feel normal to remember something like being off to work, to my church, or to a theatre production. I was feeling really homesick and felt a cloak of depression covering me. A clock, such a small thing we all take for granted in our everyday lives, meant so much in the *Big Brother* house.

Another psychologist that analysed our behaviour regularly had a slot on the *Big Brother* show in the evenings was talking about me and said, "Some have control issues." He mentioned comments made about me, as contestants were still talking about me without me knowing.

They had said things like:

"I don't like her treating me like a child."

"Why is she telling me I'm very good with eggs?"

"She is too physical for me."

"Does she not realise we are in a public environment?"

I was always just myself in the *Big Brother* house and driven by my emotional state, which was a mess, I admit, but I am much stronger and whole today. I was incredibly broken and fragile mentally and emotionally in 2001. It took a lot of years, right into 2020, to be free from mental illness.

Today was nominations day, and we had been told by *Big Brother* that we would be nominating at 10 p.m. It was also the day that Josh would become the eleventh housemate to enter the house. The day was consumed with washing our bedding. Some of the contestants had a rash, and we had to wash our bedding in non-biological powder, which we collected from the storage room. Hand washing the sheets and then squeezing them through the mangle required such monumental efforts. It was such an old, rusty mangle, and the handle could have done with some oil as it was really hard to turn. We hung as much as we could on the washing line, and it collapsed. Bubble managed to fix it.

The excitement of the day was that it started to pour with rain, and we all rushed out to bring the washing in, or we wouldn't have had any bedding to sleep in that night. Also, we were told to go into the boys' bedroom so that *Big Brother* could come in and fix the washing line properly. With nothing else to do except wait to nominate, some housemates collected stones in the garden and placed them in the shape of the initials of their partner before being told by *Big Brother* to stop as there was to be no contact with the outside world.

I found the house quiet that day, which was nice. I felt on edge, as everyone else probably did. Later that day, everyone started talking about nominations. Some of them were looking forward to it, while others were dreading it. I just found it all a bit surreal. I really didn't know who to nominate. I knew I wanted Brian, Paul, Narinder, and Dean to be on this journey in the house with me if I stayed, as they had shown real care and concern towards me, and I had had some good chats with them. I was OK with Stuart now, and I thought it might be best to keep an older contestant in the house to look after the chickens, as some of the others were so childish, and I had found the chickens without any water and was worried about who would look after them consistently.

That left Elizabeth, whom I didn't really know very well and who hadn't talked too much, but whom I thought was a sensible person who could organise things in the house. Bubble was quite funny, and I thought at least he brought some energy to the tedious hours, even if he was a bit brash at times. Then that left me with Ama, who I just couldn't figure out, and Helen, who seemed to just say whatever was in her head a lot of the time, and I had no idea what she was talking about. *Big Brother* boomed into the living room, telling us to stop talking about nominations as it became a subject of conversation. I just went off to bed late in the afternoon. I felt really vulnerable.

We all had to sit in the living room area and wait for our turn to go into the diary room to nominate. To break the tension, we started singing the Beatles song, *Ob-La-Di-Ob-La-Da.*

Ama was first and nominated Paul and me. We all had to give reasons why, and she said I was being patronising towards her.

Brian chose Helen and Elizabeth.

Bubble voted for Paul and me, and he said it was because I put the photos of his daughter up on the bedroom wall for the world to see.

There was no social media where we could post cute pictures of our children back then – how times have changed. I had only put them up with some glow stars I had brought into the house in my suitcase, as I thought it would be a lovely gesture. I always put photos of my family and friends up at home.

Dean nominated Narinder and me. He said that I caused friction.

Elizabeth nominated me and Helen. She said that I wasn't a good contributor or a good influence on the group.

Helen nominated Narinder and Bubble.

Narinder nominated Helen and Bubble.

Paul nominated Ama and Helen.

I nominated Ama and Helen. I said Helen was tactless, and Ama didn't do anything she didn't want to do.

Stuart nominated me, saying I mothered the group and it was suffocating. Ironically, *Big Brother* had initially asked me to play a "motherly role," which I hadn't; I was just myself in the house.

In comparison to how I was portrayed in the tabloid press as a sex maniac, showering naked, and showing off my private parts, the comments of my housemates compared to the journalist's headlines the day of the nominations were much kinder.

I cleaned the kitchen once the nominations ended. Brian followed me to the kitchen and asked if this might be our last week together. I told him that the way people were looking at me, it was definitely my last week. I did feel people were thinking about and watching me in the house. Some really set the tone when they talked to me, making me feel really bad about myself. I had started to feel out of place and more neurotic.

I went off to bed, leaving everyone talking again about nominations. We didn't know it had been broadcast to the nation live. You could cut the atmosphere with a knife that evening when we all sat there waiting our turn to go into the diary room. As I went to bed, I felt extremely vulnerable because I was being judged by others who had not seen the best of me.

Davina said in the live show that evening: "Bookies had Bubble and Penny for the chop. But it is finally up to you, the public. It is your show. Is Penny bottom of the class?" She then gave a phone number for the audience to vote and went on to say, "It is totally your vote, and may *Big Brother* be with you." We had no idea that everyone in the outside world knew who was up for eviction and had the opportunity to vote. Watching that episode on YouTube, I realised I used the *Star*

Wars analogy at the start of this book. I didn't know Davina had said that, and I only watched this episode on YouTube the other day for the first time! I definitely felt like I was in a far-away galaxy while I was in the *Big Brother* house!

The next day, *Heat* magazine came out, and I became the topic of the entire week in the first section of the magazine, 'Everyone's Talking About,' with a photo of my naked body. That was the 2001 equivalent of me going viral today.

***

Day nine in the *Big Brother* house:
Saturday, 2 June.

The day began with everyone being very quiet in the house. Lots of the contestants went to the diary room throughout the morning as they wanted to talk about their feelings and thoughts about who they nominated.

I felt the sudden realisation that two people in the house really didn't like me and had nominated me. It is such an odd feeling as you look around and wonder who it might be. I did feel that some were resentful of me and maybe even jealous. It was a mixed bag of emotions, and part of me wanted to leave right away rather than wait until the following Friday.

In their comments in the diary room, one of the housemates said they could spend weeks in here and that it would be better if I wasn't around. I went back into the kitchen, as I felt at home in that space. I was glad the chickens had given us an egg that day, as we were really low on all our supplies. Elizabeth was in the kitchen, trying to make bread with what we had left. I wanted to do some cooking and felt upset that people had made me feel like I wasn't allowed. To entertain myself, I thought I would try to make whatever recipe the laminated cook book opened on. We had a recipe book we could keep, although I cooked most of the meals from my memory of cooking them for friends. I said to myself, "Let's just flip it open." I looked in the cupboards and realised there was hardly anything left. I don't know if those who had been cooking had rationed portions appropriately. I was just starting to feel desperate about everything. Everyone else was eating porridge and talking about fighting. They were all in the garden.

For the first time, it was actually a relief to hear *Big Brother*'s booming voice. We were given a new task to revise and learn. It was for a real first aid test. We had four days to learn it all. Brian collected the instructions from the diary room. He stood by the designated chair and unfolded a piece of paper to read out what the task was. My heart sank as it was another difficult task. I was hoping for something fun to do.

Brian got excited about the task as he was an air steward and knew all about bandaging, fractures, burns, and shock. He said, "This is me." He took on the task of training us and did bring some fun to it with his dry sense of humour and the way he could just say things without sounding insulting when he was testing us with questions we had revised. We had a limited time to decide if we wanted to gamble some of our shopping budget. We decided on sixty per cent, as everyone felt we could pass this task. We were given one booklet a day and had four of them to get through.

The first one was about resuscitation procedures. Brian tested me on my knowledge as I cooked dinner later that day with anything I could find in the cupboards. He did make me laugh a lot with the way he tested my knowledge. There was so much information to get through. I found it really draining, like I was in an exam. It just made me feel really tense. Helen wanted rice and pasta for her dinner, and I said, "Ok, babes." I always find you can make any dish tasty with pasta, and I just chucked in what I found in the fridge. They all loved my pasta dish, which cheered me up.

After dinner, *Big Brother* set us another task – to talk about life changing events in a discussion. This was at 10:29 p.m. I thought about whether I should talk about the abuse I went through as a child in Cyprus with my neighbour, whom I then saw shot in front of me as we were caught up in the 1974 war, in which I saw some truly dreadful things.

I wondered whether I should discuss abusive relationships, someone's untimely death, or my mental illness and OCD? No, I decided to talk about my breasts, which, ironically, were the topic of the day in the outside world again anyway. I said how I had a boob job done at thirty and finally felt more like a woman. I didn't go on about the doctor telling me I should have been a boy or the mental anguish it had caused me over the years. Everyone clapped. That was the end of my sharing.

I was very moved by some of the others' stories as they spoke from the heart and as we all sat there in the living room area talking openly and about really deep examples of life changing experiences. I felt others had shown a really genuine side of themselves and had really wanted to unburden themselves. It was a wonderful atmosphere of peace, kindness, understanding, and calm that I felt for the first time in the *Big Brother* house. I slept really well that night.

***

Day ten in the *Big* Brother house: Sunday, 3 June.

It was shopping list day. I wasn't there in the living room discussing what should be bought with the £49.00. I was having a shower.

A photo of me, naked, bending forward in the shower and washing my leg, found its way into the tabloid newspapers in a massive two page spread. It also became one of the photos added to the pages of my *OK!* Magazine interview. I was blissfully unaware I was being filmed in the shower and had no idea that a photo of me naked would appear in the tabloids. At the time I was just glad not to be involved in the shopping list this week. Watching the episode on YouTube, I am amazed that the filming for the *Big Brother* show edits between the living room with the rest of the contestants talking about what to put on the list and then back to me in the shower. It cuts back to the group in the living room, then to me again with a bath towel around me, cleaning out the Jacuzzi bath.

That day, I talked to some of them about my Sunday routine over breakfast, and it made my heart ache. I would be having a lovely morning at home, listening to Christian radio. I would tape the omnibus edition of *The Archers* to send to my mum in Spain on a cassette tape. She was missing the show and, like me, was useless with computers, so she relied on my cassette tape recordings. I would go into London and meet a friend for coffee and go to All Souls Church in the evening. I would be praising God and meeting my beautiful, creative friends. I felt a pang of panic in my stomach as I realised how lost I was in there. I also had my friend Mel and my cousin Rika living in my flat, and I had no idea where I would go when I was evicted from the house.

I had some time with Narinder and Brian in the kitchen. We discussed how little food was ordered. I said it would be great when there were only a few of us left and that there would be more than enough eggs from the chickens and other supplies for us to eat like kings. I felt depleted of all energy and enthusiasm. I forced myself to study the next booklet we received and tried to remember what I was reading for the first aid task, but my mind was so foggy with thoughts of home and the life I had left behind.

Early in the evening, *Big Brother* ordered us to stay inside as they put a tub in the garden without our knowledge. The storage room was declared open, and we found several crates of grapes. There were instructions that we had to crush them with our feet. When we got back into the garden, everyone squealed with surprise at seeing the tub, and all of us could get in it with a squeeze. For every three bottles we filled, we would get one bottle of proper wine. We managed to win six bottles of wine as we filled eighteen bottles with the grape juice that we swapped for the wine. I found the whole task hysterical. I absolutely loved it as it was so different, silly, and quite theatrical. We were allowed to keep the grape skins, and Paul and I found plastic containers in the garden, so we squeezed the remainder of the juice into those. As I collected them from around the garden, I said, "I hope a bird hasn't done a poo in them."

I also suggested we make grape skin turnovers for a pudding, but no one agreed. We managed to squeeze five bottles of grape skin juice and drank that in the evening, saving our six proper bottles of wine for another day. As we were drinking it, one person said, "Well, I've only got two verruca!."

Suddenly we all realised we were drinking this juice that our naked feet had been squelching in the tub! I said, "I've got hard callouses, and I think the grapes helped to get rid of them." That didn't go down as a joke at all. It was amusing to see the disgust on some of their faces. We all started singing *Big spender*, and I got carried away in the joy of it, as I love musical theatre, and stood up belting out part of the song. I loved that. It is edited into my best bits, and looking at it, some might get my sense of humour, while others might think I am an absolute lunatic! I don't know what the housemates thought, but I was just so glad to feel happy again. We had all been singing the song and putting our own expression into it; it just so happened that me standing up and singing was edited into one of the clips of my best bits. Anything edited is out of context with the actual energy and moment it was part of.

The contestants were talking about clothes and money that evening. Narinder and Stuart had cards from their partners, as it was both their wedding anniversaries. I tried to join in the conversation and said, "I used to be a man." Someone had approached me when I was getting the tube into town one night in London, dressed up with very high heels on. He had come up to me and said I was a beautiful man. I think some of them thought I was going slightly crazy, which I really was. One of the producers told me when I met them after *Big Brother* ended that I had caused mayhem in their offices as they scrambled around to find out if what I had said was true. Everyone was a bit tipsy that night, and we all stumbled off to bed at different times.

***

Day eleven in the *Big Brother* house:
Monday, 4 June.

The storeroom opened, and we could collect our shopping. One of the housemates was irritated because the sizes of the juice and other items were so small that there wasn't enough to feed everyone. There didn't seem to be very much stuff at all. I kept quiet and didn't offer any opinions.

There was a weird atmosphere, as we all knew that we would find out who had been nominated that day. I did some washing up, and no one was talking. We were all studying for the first aid task, and I couldn't believe how much information we had to learn.

Suddenly, at 2:15 p.m., we heard *Big Brother*'s voice announcing, "The results of the nominations will be given in an hour's time." I was chatting with Dean, and we both were saying how we didn't mind going home. I just felt very disconnected from the whole group. Narinder and Brian were dancing and doing role plays, which were absolutely hilarious to watch. I started cleaning, as that is what I did at home when I was stressed. I moved behind them, trying to clean a massive stain off the table, but it wouldn't come off. I got really frustrated and said, "This table is fucked." I felt like I was having a nervous breakdown. I tried pulling myself together while singing *Whole Again* by Atomic Kitten. I didn't know I would later end up working with Atomic Kitten in Liverpool for a charity event when I came out of the *Big Brother* house.

We were all sat around the table in the living room area when I found out that I was up for eviction. When I heard my name booming into the living room from *Big Brother*, I felt terror and relief all at the same time. It was a strange sensation I had never felt before. I then felt vulnerable, rejected, and pathetic. It did send me over the edge emotionally, as it was just so much to take in. It seems like none of this stuff is at all serious, but in the *Big Brother* house, it was my whole reality. It was all I had to hold onto. I caved in mentally. It is a bit like being a caged animal, and I felt trapped, controlled, and under attack. Paul gave me a hug, as did Narinder and Brian, as soon as my name was called out. I told them I was OK and was a tough old bird. Narinder could tell I was an emotional wreck. We continued our day as I asked Bubble to check for eggs. He went outside with Brian, who said, "I really get on with Penny." They came back in having forgotten to check for eggs, and we all realised how shocked we were and couldn't think straight.

Everyone was going through their own emotional response to the nominations that day. I had to go to the bedroom at 3:15 p.m. and I sobbed my heart out. Bubble came in and tried to cheer me up, and he did make me laugh. He said that I was talented, sensational, and clever. He also assured me I may not go as the public might want to keep me in as the mad woman in the kitchen. He was so funny and said how lucky I was to get on the show and meet him. He reminded me we have to revise for the first aid task, which none of us were in the mood to do at all.

That day, I also got closer to Helen and sat with her on my bed, reading her stars, something I didn't usually do. I told her that her stars said she would earn lots of money and need an accountant to help her, and she would get some freebies. She said she didn't have an accountant, and I said she would need one. The stars also said she needed to look the part, and I said that won't be a problem as she is so pretty. It was a nice moment.

Dean and Elizabeth made the most fabulous homemade pizzas that evening, which were so big and really tasty. I did go into the diary room and tell *Big Brother* that I was dazed by the whole day. I was afraid of my students' reactions, as I said teenagers might mock me. I left the diary room feeling worse. I was falling apart inside. I write a lot of poems and weave them through my stories, as I find I can say what I feel more clearly in a poem.

Spoon face (A poem)
Feelings of Anxiety and OCD.

It is a hidden disease.
　　It holds its own heartbeat.
　　So that the functions are like a video player within a room.
　　Both are real within themselves.

I hold it.

Sometimes.

Caressing it and then throwing it up against the wall.

But it seems to have a root so deep despite being a shadow.

It drowns me into unreality like having an operation while awake (absorbing self) or laughing when you really want to cry.

The moment in the day unfolds onto another and another like a book being read by someone passed on to you, and you are here.

You know too much of the other and the pull is between the dark and the light.

How can we skip and dance when we know the death, the suffering is as real?

Why cuddle into warmth when the reality is so much worse within the reality around you.

To hold onto the beautiful the moments the splash a watercolour like spray across the dawn a pink so real yet it is too beautiful.

I can only be happy when I let go of you.

Let go of the doing of one thing when I mean another.

The saying of one thing when I mean another.

The living of one life when I mean another.

Look with awake eyes that can see despite the dark.

Oh, capture a box of moonlight.

The End.

***

Day twelve in the *Big Brother* house:
Tuesday, 5 June.

I have a vague memory of asking *Big Brother* for a dentist for Brian because I could tell he had a tooth that needed attention that morning. Maybe because I was learning about first aid, I noticed it.

I also remember me and Narinder waiting for Elizabeth, who had made a flan for lunch. We were starving, so we wacked it in the oven early and didn't let it rise in the fridge, which angered Elizabeth. We both felt like naughty schoolgirls, as we just found it funny. Someone had made porridge and burned it that morning. No one could eat it. This led to one of them saying, "If I hadn't seen the bottom of Penny's feet, I might have drunk some of the grape skin juice!" We were all really hungry and ready for lunch. It is amazing how important dinner time became. They were the most important parts of our days, which otherwise stretched ahead of us with nothing to look forward to.

The day was taken up with frantically trying to revise as the last booklet would be taken from us at midday. I was exhausted from learning all of these facts as well as imagining what I would do when I left. I had no home to go back to. *Why did I do that to myself?*

While we studied in the garden in the sunshine, the others chatted about taking revenge on an ex and what they would do. There were suggestions of putting pig semen into an ex-partner's toothpaste and freezing poo and hurling it at someone's window. I didn't join in and let all the chatter wash over me. I was feeling really isolated and spaced out. I was suddenly called to the diary room, and I really didn't feel like talking to a disembodied voice that just filled me with dread. I tried to get out of there as quickly as I could. I told *Big Brother* I felt like I was back at university with all the studying. I said that I liked Dean as he made me feel calm and seemed really grounded. I also added that I had chatted with Stuart and Elizabeth but was worried that Bubble was sleeping too much.

I was pleased I could do the cooking that night with the meagre supplies we had. I filled everyone up with a lot of mashed potatoes. We sat at our table outside in the dusk of the day for dinner, but the atmosphere was fraught and stilted.

Brian and Narinder practised first aid on each other while waiting for dinner by the kitchen, and it was so comical to watch the scenes they enacted as I cooked. It is a serious subject, and I realised I had learned a lot of vital skills in preparation for this task. I was pleased to have learned so much.

Big Brother asked me to come to the diary room again with the first aid booklets at midnight, and I told *Big Brother* I was feeling anxious and weepy about the first aid exam tomorrow and the fact I have been nominated. I said that I was scared to be voted off the show. Then I said, "Most of all, I'm concerned that we pass this first aid task, or there will be no food next week, and that will be a real disaster." I was glad to leave the diary room and go to sleep. It took a while for me to get to sleep as the boys had put stones in our beds as a joke, so the girls were pretty annoyed and all up talking in the bedroom.

Stuart, Dean, and Bubble were still chatting in the living room, and I had no idea they were talking about me being the first to go, based on how I acted and what the viewers would have seen. I just felt like I was having an out of body experience. I felt utterly lost inside.

***

Day thirteen in the *Big Brother* house:
Wednesday, 6 June.

At 7.15 a.m., there were huge bangs and whistles going off all over the house, just like someone was clashing saucepans. We had not been told how we would be tested for the first aid task, but we were about to find out.

Big Brother's voice boomed into the house, saying that a meteor had crashed in the garden and we had two minutes to put on our microphones, dress, and gather in the kitchen. We were all trying to wake up in the midst of this noise and sudden announcement. I was shocked and thought people had broken into the *Big Brother* house. It was terrifying for a few seconds. One of the girls was shouting over all the commotion, "Dress in what?" Someone else shouted back, "Clothes!"

I found that really funny, even though I had no idea what on earth was going on. *Big Brother*'s voice continued above all the clashing noises, saying if we were not all in the kitchen area in less than two minutes, we would fail the task. Most of us dashed to the kitchen, and there were a few split seconds as we desperately waited for a couple of the others. The terror on our faces was something to behold, as we didn't know how much of the two minutes we had already used up. *Big Brother* continued once we were all assembled in the kitchen area. I was just so relieved everyone got to the kitchen in time. We were told to read out the instructions taped to the patio door, which was shut. Dean read it out. The garden was a disaster zone, with four life-size dummies strewn around it. If any of the four died, we would fail the task.

Everyone dashed outside, where the whole garden was covered in broken bits of meteorite and four dummies. I didn't know which casualty to go to first, so I followed Bubble and Dean. Helen called for an ambulance as she saw a red phone box in the garden. If we failed, we would only have £28.00 for our shopping next week.

The four dummies each had a label on them describing the extent and severity of their injuries. Someone was moaning as they were really desperate for the toilet, but we all agreed to stay focused. I followed Bubble and Dean to find a motorcyclist who had back pain. I don't know why, but they suddenly went off together and told me to stay with the motorcyclist and keep talking to him. Of all the stuff I had learned, I was not putting any of it into practice.

Brian and Narinder were in full swing doing mouth-to-mouth and chest compressions on an injured lady. Elizabeth, Ama, and Helen were attempting to treat a burn victim. Paul Stuart and Dean revived a woman who couldn't breathe. All the while, I was standing by this motorcyclist, saying, "Don't worry, mate, you're going to be fine." Paul came up to me to see if I was OK. I said to him, "They told me to stand here; I am really pissed off. I feel like a twit and don't know what to say." Paul went off, and I turned to the motorcyclist and said, "Don't worry, mate, keep breathing; we are doing our best."

The next thing I knew, a siren went off, and *Big Brother* informed us the task was complete. It took only about a half hour after all that preparation over the last four days. I was extremely disappointed because I had anticipated four challenges throughout the day that would have encouraged team building amongst us. I had hoped for a day of lots of challenges and time to get to know and work with some of the contestants who I didn't spend time with. We all went back to bed at 8:16 a.m. as *Big Brother*, as usual, said, "*Big Brother* will get back to you."

About two hours later, I was in the kitchen making porridge for everyone. Brian asked me how I was. I said I was emotionally drained. His response was, "Again." He just made me smile, even though it sounded like he was fed up with my moods.

We all sat in the living room early in the afternoon holding hands, waiting for the result, and were told by *Big Brother* that we had done the correct procedure on the motorcyclist and the woman who couldn't breathe. When administering CPR, sometimes the stomach rather than the chest was compressed, which made us all feel really nervous that we might have failed again. On the last victim, the procedure for the burns was correct but a bit delayed. We all sat there, holding our breath. It was so tense, and we had so much to lose. Suddenly, *Big Brother*, after a pause that seemed to go on forever, said, "In the opinion of the *Big Brother* first aid expert, all four casualties received correct treatment." The elation we felt was tremendous. We were all screaming with joy. Our shopping budget next week would be £112.00. I felt really glad we had passed it, as I wasn't sure if my talking to the motorcyclist was enough. I had expected to undertake some really big challenges.

There was a massive football match on that evening in the outside world that Dean and Bubble were really upset to be missing, so they sat in the garden, Helen took them homemade cookies, and they pretended they were sitting there watching the match without a TV. Stuart made dinner and cooked some brilliant burgers, with Ama telling him how to cook rice.

We were allowed to vote in the general election, and we had to take our postal vote into the diary room. I told *Big Brother* I had voted for Labour, as I haven't voted in ages. Some of the others chose not to disclose who they voted for.

I felt fed up and upset about how short the challenge had been that day and went to bed at 11:45 p.m. Everyone else sang Happy Birthday to Bubble at midnight; I don't think I was missed. When I watched the YouTube episode of the show, I couldn't believe how much I was talked about by the other contestants. I am talked about by some of the boys as they lie in their bedrooms.

"She is not making any sense."

"She feels rejected as her boyfriend left her for a twenty-two-year-old."

"You're in a game of rejection."

"There is only one person going."

Ironically, I had said to Brian earlier in the kitchen, "I must say, last week I really wanted to go, and didn't feel close to anyone. I was thinking, get me back to my life. But now I am emotionally attached to our little family. The chickens and the way we do our days. It is our little ways, and no one else is experiencing anything like this."

It was what I was genuinely feeling. I think if I had not been evicted, it would have given me back my confidence, and I would have gotten control of myself and started to be the best version of myself. I am talked about again by some of the girls that day, who say about me:

"[She] treats me like a child. If she is still here, I will have to deal with it. She hasn't got allies in the house."

"If she stays, I will stay out of her way and only talk to her if I have to. She rubs people up the wrong way."

***

**Day fourteen in the *Big Brother* house:
Thursday, 7 June.**

We all got up at different times and sat in the garden. We had to get a vet in to look at one of the hens, who had a funny rash on their skin that I had noticed. I thought the poor chickens must have been super stressed from all the commotion yesterday.

It was a strange experience waiting inside the house, knowing someone from the outside world was again in the garden. I wondered what it would feel like to leave this house and step back into the real world.

It was Bubbles' twenty-fifth birthday. It was the day before eviction, and Helen kindly tinted my hair. Brian joined us and gave me a body tan, and Paul gave me a manicure. We all had a nice chat together in the girl's bedroom, and it did feel like real friendships were forming. I did find that if I was with certain housemates, the mood would change instantly if someone else joined us who brought a different vibe. In my classrooms, I've discovered that when one disruptive or negative student is absent, the entire mood of the class changes. Bubble was ecstatic as a journalist with a megaphone shouted the results of the England V Greece football match over the wall. *Big Brother* immediately ordered us inside before the journalist could share any more news of the outside world. I found it intriguing to hear another person's voice other than the contestants' and *Big Brother*'s.

We filled our time creating a song, which all the girls sang at Bubble's party later that evening. We all had to join in on the song *Stuck in the Middle With You*. It was nice to finally do something with all the girls participating. It was the only time we all did something nice together. I wish we had had more challenges that brought us together rather than separated us. We all danced and expressed ourselves, and I don't know why that wasn't a part of the day that was edited into the show.

In the afternoon, I lay on my bed and chatted with Narinder. I just couldn't help myself and blurted out what I thought of everyone. Narinder loved it and thought I was hysterical. I was just venting all the rage I felt about being so judged and saw it as so unfair that others could act wacky and extreme and say really outrageous things that were seen as funny, but when I did it, it was almost as if I had offended someone and they were so affronted and justified in judging me when they themselves acted even more childish and, in my opinion, more weird and strange than I had done.

Finally, at 7 p.m., the storeroom opened and we could collect things for a party for Bubble. It was a football themed party. We collected boxes of blue props to decorate the house with a Chelsea theme. We were all really excited, and all my nervous energy started to explode in manic ways as I couldn't cope with all the experiences that I had gone through over the last thirteen days.

There was a game of table football and a 1970s Chelsea shirt for Bubble to wear. Bubble painted his face blue and white, which looked quite scary and extreme to me. Helen and Ama dressed as cheerleaders and chanted Bubbles' name. All of us had fancy dress outfits to wear. The whole energy was theatrical, which I was used to from having performed in loads of amateur dramatics. I put on a blue wig I found, as I love wigs and have worn them for characters that I had played in theatre productions.

By putting on the wig and a blue dress, I created in my mind a character of a teenager at a football match who goes crazy when their team scores. In the context of that, my behaviour on the night was appropriate. People at football matches go absolutely nuts when their team wins. They pull down their trousers, revealing their football flag on their bum. A medley of Chelsea songs was played in the house. All I did was dance and cheer when I scored against Paul as we played table football. I was a typical teenage character, an excited football fan.

It is a clip still on a YouTube video that, in my opinion, has gotten me sacked over sixteen times from school jobs from 2002-2020, as students would find it and management would frown and then just say my contract was up at their school. They never said directly that I had to leave because I had been on *Big Brother*, but it was always a time of exit at their school that coincided with the Beatles hysteria of students realising I was a reality star after seeing footage of me on social media platforms.

It was just silly dancing at a party. We have all done that. You can imagine how many hours of footage there were to edit into a half hour show. Imagine a scene where you arrive halfway through. For example, you might walk into the staff room where you work to get a coffee. One of your colleagues has his arm around one of the women's shoulders and they are looking into each other's eyes. You immediately form an opinion when you see or overhear part of a conversation. Maybe that woman's dog had just been put down, and in that moment, a colleague hugs her. All I am saying is that what we see is certainly not the whole truth.

Throughout my days in *Big Brother*, I expressed myself and just wanted to have a nice time. However, like in the outside world, we all stop to see a row on the street. We are gripped if something we see is extreme. Maybe you might take a moment and write down a few of the things you said or did today, and then edit them together and see how you might come across. I was manic too, as it would be Eviction Night tomorrow.

The storeroom opened again, and we collected a curry takeaway, blue lemonade, and a cake. We all danced into the garden with the long blue tablecloth over our heads, like one of those dragon dancers you find in Singapore. Someone commented, "I couldn't imagine Penny as a teacher."

Someone else said, "She's not handling it."

Paul did say to me later in the evening, "I don't think you are OK."

I replied, "there are people out there like me who are a bit alternative and creative."

He said kindly, "If you go out tomorrow, go out in style; do yourself justice."

I went to bed at 2:15 a.m. My mother always said to me: "If you can't say something nice, then don't say anything at all."

***

Day fifteen in the *Big Brother* house:
Friday, 8 June.

My last day in the *Big Brother* house started with me checking the chickens. I said to them, "Hey babes, how are you doing? Your skin looks better." I was worried about them and knew I would miss taking care of them.

We all decided to clean the house, so it looked nice for Davina when she spoke to us later. I hadn't thought about the cameras at all. I don't know about the others, but I was nervous that day knowing we would be on live TV. I really hadn't imagined while I was in the house that I was actually being filmed. It is a weird feeling as the *Big Brother* house becomes your reality, and you just get on with the day ahead. Everyone else in the house had dramatic moments; I didn't see that my activities in the house would be shown as much as they were on the evening shows compared to others.

I had made breakfast, our usual porridge, and was trying to keep calm but was struggling. I suffered terribly from anxiety, and it was crippling. I had not sought help because I felt ashamed about it. But I would say to anyone out there, please seek help. I lost years of my life trying to cope with things on my own, while all my friends had no idea how much mental pain I was in.

I tried on my eviction dress in the afternoon just to see if it still fit; I had always felt huge. I had eating disorders, and it is only now that I am happy with me and what I look like. So many years are squandered feeling all the negative words in the dictionary about yourself.

Helen was quite excited, and I was feeling terrified to the point where I couldn't move. Brian helped me walk my little case that I came in with. It was like a dress rehearsal, and I spun around, smiled, and waved to an imaginary audience. Elizabeth was lovely as she came in the bedroom and said, "Penny, dignity, grace, smile, and be calm."

I responded, shaking inside, and said, "No manic-ness." I asked Brian if I looked too tarty and added, "There won't be anyone there, but if there is one person, I shall smile."

After entering the *Big Brother* house, clapped by just my dear friends, Peter and Ted, I couldn't imagine in my wildest dreams that there would be anyone outside to see me leave. My anxiety worsened over the day, and I just tried to get a grip. I did a silly dance in front of Narinder and Brian just to ignore all the panic inside myself. It is a clip added to my best bits, and I look like an absolute lunatic. I wish once again I had worn bras in the house, as the top I was wearing that day, as Davina remarked on in the live show that evening, was very skimpy. I am embarrassed about that, as I didn't realise it. I used to wear tops that made me feel comfortable and didn't aggravate the nerve endings in my breasts.

When the others talked about me that day, Brian came to my defence and said my actions were just my way of coping. I was really at a very low point and felt lost. I finally just sat down with the ragdoll in the living room for a couple of hours.

Rejection: (stream of consciousness.)
Explaining my anxiety.

Wrap up your feelings in soft tissue lined with all the stars of heaven for a while, for they will need your attention. For you know you cannot shine in this place. It is their gawping mouths you enter each day, and in the hyena's attention seeking screech, the individuality is defaced by a moustache drawn onto the beauty. These new sounds of this place have only summoned more of your low self-esteem and self-doubt. I am cornered and don't know what to do. This has not brought me ocean deep joy; no one has taken my hand and danced with me in the dew. Oh, to be strong, I tried to reach for the rose but have cut my hand on the thorns. I am aware of how I am limiting my life, and this is a courage I must find to fight the hardest battle, as it is the overcoming in the undoing of everything. I'm now here in this, and to turn over a piece of wood in the garden and see all the insects scurrying so numberless, people who walk around behind secret smiles and agendas in their underside, yet I seem to be the only one freaking out in here. You know "anachronism" is the representation of an event, person, or thing in which it could not have occurred or existed, a person or thing that seems to belong to another time. After being so warm, so natural, and so together, and suddenly becoming so mechanical. This has felt like some underwater event. I felt that they had all nominated me. It was a dull residue, but an acceptance of it, like the coldness of the tiles in the bathroom. I cannot find any sweetness in this. I sit here observing, as if within a battle not of my choosing and unable to decide. The discordant tone echoes like the scraping of plates. I have let things fall out of my mouth like carpets out of the sky, and I realise now this was dead before even the battle began, even though swords have been sharpened repeatedly. Will this be what I am remembered for?

***

I really didn't know what I was feeling; it was a mixture of exhaustion and terror. I was called to the diary room and told *Big Brother* I was just having a prayer time with the ragdoll. I said I was scared and hoped not to say anything wrong in the live interview.

Our dinner (which wasn't grand at all as we had so little rations left) was cooked by Dean and Bubble. They had cooked a sausage pot, and we only had water to drink. Someone suggested Helen and I give a speech. I went second and said, "It has just been a really terrifying experience of my life, being with you all and trying to adapt to that. You have all seen my most neurotic, most manic side, and insecure side. So it would be really lovely to see you in the real world, a normal environment, to see how your lives are moving on, so thanks very much."

We all held hands around the table as we heard Davina's voice say, "This is Davina, please do not swear." I was so thrilled to hear her voice, and suddenly the reality of being on TV struck me. Just by hearing her voice, I suddenly grasped the enormity of being on a TV show and having people watch me on their televisions. It was like a light bulb of realisation and excitement was turned on in my cloudy, confused mind. It was the first time I had felt like that since entering the *Big Brother* house.

There were two shows that evening. This was the first show at 8:30 p.m. and showed the results and then highlights of what we had all been doing that day while I had that time in the house to finish packing. Davina continued by saying, "We got over a million votes more than Labour received in the whole of Scotland." She continued by saying, "The first person leaving the *Big Brother* house is . . ." Then there was the longest pause. I thought it would go on forever, and then suddenly my name was called.

I felt sick and then a wave of relief as I wanted to see friends again who loved and understood me. I needed to get back to my routines, my lovely church, and my fulfilling teaching job. I hadn't expected to win; I was only feeling disappointed because I hadn't shown my whole self.

Brian immediately asked me, "Are you ok?" He crowded around me with Paul and Narinder, who also got up and came over to me immediately. I had an hour and a half to get myself packed so I could take my little case with essentials in it. I would leave my bigger case packed at the end of my bed for *Big Brother* to bring to me in the outside world. I said to Helen, "You better win it."

I gave some bracelets away to Narinder, Brian, and Paul. While I was packing in the bedroom, Paul, Narinder, and Brian came in to help me. They were visibly upset, and that really moved me and made me cry with appreciation. I could see we had a special friendship. I did say to them that I was sorry for my manic behaviour. I did feel very different that evening.

Having had that revelation, albeit a bit too late, when I heard Davina's voice, I suddenly felt in control of myself, strong, and back to normal. It is funny how one thing can snap you out of a weird space in your own head. It was like I had splashed my mind with ice cold water. I think I was now ready to shine in the *Big Brother* house, but of course it was too late and not meant to be. Brian said later to the other housemates who had noticed my transformation and were really surprised, "She seems like a different person."

I was pleased that they all saw the *me* that my friends love so much; unfortunately, it was just as I was leaving. They all formed a guard of honour with their hands linked over their heads as I walked to the front door. I carried my high heels, as earlier Helen had been worried her heels might stick in the steel grating, and I thought I had better do the same just in case. I am glad they kept the tradition of the guard of honour going for every eviction night. The front door was still firmly shut, and music was playing in the house and had been for the last two hours, unbeknownst to us, to drown out the cheering outside. The patio doors were locked, and the garden had been out of bounds since late afternoon.

I had wanted to have my last dinner at the outside table, but we hadn't been allowed outside. We heard Davina's voice saying, "Penny, I am coming to get you." Then she started a countdown, and in those ten seconds, I hugged Dean, then Paul, then Stuart, then Narinder and Brian, and finally Helen. The door slid open loudly and so quickly. There were security men who were really tall standing either side of the door. Everyone wanted a peek outside, but the security guards deliberately stood in the way of anyone trying to peer out. They looked very threatening. I could hear barking as well. We all heard cheering as loud as a thunderstorm. It was an incredible atmosphere, and someone said, "There for you too, Helen."

In what was called the nerve centre, where the interview would take place, were family and friends. Peter was there and had been interviewed by Davina on the earlier show about my behaviour that day. He said to Davina, "She has got it out of her system. She has got the manic bit out."

He was sitting with Paul, whom I had met at Reading University when I did my teaching PGCE, when I was with Adam, and hadn't seen for years. My neighbour from Islington was also there, who I had only ever talked to a few times. I was surprised they were sitting with Peter as if they were my closest friends when I entered the nerve centre that evening.

I did have about twenty of my best friends in the audience as well. The producers said to me at the wrap party that they couldn't believe how many I had. I was sorry for not involving my neighbour from Islington in events I went to once I was out of the house. I wasn't living in my flat, and I felt bad not meeting up with her. Ironically, when I got my job at Cavendish School in 2014, her best friend was my boss! How funny it is that life brings things and people full circle!

During the show, Davina cut to the "incredible travelling diary room chair," and people around the country commented about *Big Brother* while sitting in the chair.

A waitress said, "Keep Penny in; she is fun-loving." Josie, a TV presenter, said: "in the kitchen out the kitchen."

Some other bloke said to keep Helen in and hoped she would wear the bikini she wore for the calendar.

I got 624,786 votes, (fifty-eight per cent of the total), and Helen got 447,337 votes.

I didn't realise I left to the song by ABBA, *Gimme! Gimme! Gimme!* The words in the song reflected, in my opinion, what was being said about me on the outside world.

Dance you Life's' Dance (A poem)
How I felt when I stepped out of the *Big Brother* house and the door slid shut and locked behind me.

Now you have found the tempo- the tune-the beat.

It isn't a methodical beat nor is it a sporadic one but is totally fun and slightly erratic yet full of punch and zest of life and joy.

Be who you really know you are. Claim your drumbeats as you need to be quiet enough to hear it and then courageous enough to take up the dance even if no one around you can hear it, even if the sounds around you are too loud.

It is your quiet one or if you hear it, you will realize it beats in time with your heartbeat as that is what it is all about.

The joy of life is found in this quiet expanse of ever increasing rays of sound that go on and on. So a note held too tight will be crushed, so a note let go of will lose its place and lose its perspective. But a note observed in the centre of your heart is truth is light is sensitivity is where life is found.

Always in the right song and despite yourself you cannot help but shine and be as you are so subtly dancing so quietly jigging so wonderfully gliding at last can life become free.

Can I dance into the light and into life itself to become the zero-balance oneness?

The End.

SCENE 2:
My Interview with Davina McCall on my eviction night.

I stood there for a second, dazed like a rabbit in the headlights, as the door slid shut really fast behind me. I remember thinking about one of my colleagues at work as I stood in the staffroom doorway, saying, "If you don't do it, you will never know," "and I thought, *I don't know!*

I really didn't know what to think. I felt just as confused and bewildered as when I first went into the house. I thought this as I walked really fast down what I remember being a really long walkway. There were high metal fences with barbed wire on the top. It looked very menacing. The lights that were like floodlights were so bright and shining on me so I couldn't see clearly where I was going.

There were security guards lined up either side holding the lead of a scary looking huge Alsatian dog. So many were on either side of me, each on a thick black dog lead, barking viciously, and I remember thinking, *is that necessary?* I tried to walk faster and was dragging my case while trying to smile and swinging my heels with the other hand. I was glad I hadn't worn my heels. At the end of this walkway were more burly security guards with more barking Alsatians on leads, and I went through a huge double metal gate that they shut behind me. I was relieved to get away from them. Everything looked completely different, and I was trying to get my bearings.

I suddenly realised that this was the same walkway I had taken into the house fifteen days earlier that was completely renovated now. In front of me was a huge bridge to cross, and I could see in the distance another long walkway at the end of the bridge. I was exhausted and wondered where on earth I was going. As I got up to the bridge, I suddenly heard the cheers. It was such a loud sound, and it seemed to hit me physically as it just poured all over me. I had to stop to catch my breath. I was so shocked.

I started walking again and saw crowds of people ahead of me that looked like millions of people. There were posters bouncing in the air saying, "the Penny has dropped." I remember thinking, *this can't be for me*. Peter came up on the bridge to get me. I remember crying out to him, "Do they hate me?" because I was still upset with myself for swearing at Stuart.

Peter said, "The press know you. You're a household name and your job is safe." None of it sunk in, and I had no idea what he was talking about. It was just wonderful to see his gorgeous smile.

He led me onto the second walkway, which was lined with hundreds of people on either side. People were calling my name and clapping and cheering. There were banners waving in the air and flowers being thrown at me. A little stuffed dormouse toy was shoved into my hands, which I still have today.

I realised that two men were standing very close to me and Peter, and it took a while for me to realise they were bodyguards as the crowd tried to touch me and reach over the barriers to grab me. It was like a scene from a movie. I realised I felt the thrill of what I had expected the experience to be like. I wanted so much to be liked. This outpouring of love and crazy hysteria had just exposed the deepest inner fear and longing that still hung in my soul as I was overwhelmed by the love and affection I felt from the crowd. There is always a little 'four-year-old lost in the supermarket feeling,' and you try to fill it with more acceptances. I had hoped to feel that affection in the *Big Brother* house. I can only compare what I had hoped the *Big Brother* house would be like to when your work sends you all off for a group building exercise and you come back more bonded, more focused, and with a better understanding of each other. I felt that from the crowd that had made the effort on their Friday night to come and see me evicted. I will always be grateful and thankful for that amazing support.

Fame brings up the question: Can you face who you are perceived as in the light of what you have become because you can never undo it? Davina, who was very heavily pregnant, appeared on the walkway. It must have been about 10:25 p.m., and the live show was about to start in five minutes. I remember she looked radiant, but I also thought, *what if she goes into labour with all this going on?*

She took my shoes off, which I thought was nice but unnecessary. A security man had my small suitcase. I watched him take it into the nerve centre as I was walking towards it, with Davina and Peter.

Just before the entrance, there was an explosion of light, clicks, flashes, and shouts: "Look this way." There were hundreds of press and cameramen on both sides of the barriers wanting me to stop and take my photo. I had to turn around a few times to make sure both sides got their photo. Davina took my hand and tried to move me forward towards the nerve centre, as I suppose we had limited time. I just ran off towards the crowd to shake people's hands and hug them, as I wanted them to know how much it meant to me that they had bothered to come out to see me.

Davina, who was still holding my shoes, said to the camera, "She has nothing on her feet." In the nerve centre, I was so pleased to see my friends all in tiered seating, just like at a theatre. I sat down in the chair opposite hers and stared and waved at my friends. Davina said, "What a mixture of feelings you must be feeling right now. What is it like being the first one out?"

All I could really think about was so many hands reaching out in the crowd, so many faces, and the loudest cheers and screams. All these people had made the effort to come out and support me, possibly, or to be there because it was *Big Brother* eviction night. They came all that way to stand outside and see me in the flesh. It was quite humbling.

I entered the nerve centre and was led to a chair opposite Davina, who had sat down. I just sat there for a second or two to take it all in. I looked back around at my friends. There were one or two faces that I thought, *you're not my friend.* That is how it goes, though—some come out of the woodwork because you're famous. Some were there that I hadn't seen for ages, like the girl whose wedding I was a bridesmaid at in New York. Also, Ian bagel from Covent Garden reminded me of that sudden divide of time before and after. The last time he saw me, I said I might be going on *Big Brother*, and he looked at me in disbelief. Now he was cheering, and he became a friend for a while. He is such a good person.

I felt like I was between times—before, when absolutely no one knew who I was, and now, everyone I didn't know knew me—the time when I was living and breathing as an ordinary human being, and no one discussed my every move. It was the time before I stepped into the mirror, revealing everything I did, from sleeping to being. I looked around and saw I was being looked back at, yet I was now inside the mirror of who I was and who I am now. I took a deep breath and was so relieved to see Peter was there in the centre of all these friends smiling at me as I finally answered Davina's first question: "I think I've blown it." Everyone laughed and thought I was joking.

I felt confused, lost, and really pathetic. Davina was very upbeat and seemed almost delighted to see me. I thought, *oh good, she likes me; that's OK.*

My sister met her in 2020, when Davina's dog ran up to her, and without looking up, my sister said, "Does it bite?"

Davina replied "No."

My sister looked up and said, "Oh, you know my sister Penny."

Davina said, " I have only ever known one Penny; give her my love."

I thought that was quite nice. I said to justify my answer to her first question that I felt the press must hate me, which is why I am out first. Davina assured me I wasn't hated. She didn't expand any further on what I could be worried about with the press in that question.

She asked me if the house was what I expected. I said that I was bewildered by it and didn't form a natural bond with my housemates. I said I had some nice individual moments. I guessed quite well when she asked her third question—who I thought had nominated me. I was right for everyone who I thought had nominated me except Dean, and I added that I was surprised he had nominated me as he was always so nice to me in the house.

Davina assured me it wasn't a negative that he nominated me, as he thought I would be better off out of the *Big Brother* house. I said I never got to the core of anyone in there. She said that I had become more insecure and less confident over the days, and I had come up against brick walls and misunderstandings. She asked me for one-word answers for my response to the names.

For Ama, I said, "Elusive."

For Bubble, "Direct."

For Dean, "Hidden."

For Elizabeth, "Quiet."

For Stuart, I said, "Poser," and the studio erupted in laughter.

Inside I was thinking how bizarre it was that my time in the *Big Brother* house was this interesting and thought it would just be this chat with Davina that would be my five minutes of fame, as it were, and it would be over. I just did not take the questions seriously, as I saw it all as just a nice chat. A bit like when you chat with friends about a night out and the daft things you did, but it was all just a laugh in moments of banter, boredom, topics of discussion that were a bit superficial and silly, and a row. I had no idea how all my moments had been shaped by the media of 2001. I wonder now if, if I had known, I would have confronted Davina in that crucial first interview, cleared my name, and challenged the lies. In my opinion, I did not know I was fighting for my life and reputation.

Davina asked me why I didn't nominate Stuart. I said I felt it was my fault for getting so emotional. I said at home I have parties and we all get drunk as lords, but we never have that sort of atmosphere or conversations about subjects of sex or sleeping with someone.

Davina moved on and said Stuart got no nominations. I was quite surprised by that. Davina then talked about how I had cooked in the house and showed my best bits. I just laughed and was quite embarrassed by some of the clips, especially the way they were edited together and, in my opinion, taken out of context. In the clips, one minute I am talking about Jesus, and the next it looks like I have jumped on Paul on the deckchair in the *Big Brother* garden. I was so embarrassed. I just clapped and laughed along with everyone in the studio. I didn't say to Davina how embarrassed I felt by how those clips were edited together.

But you don't start saying some of those clips are out of context on live TV, do you? I was sitting there overwhelmed as all my friends were there, and I was talking to a famous presenter, Davina McCall. I am star struck myself. Please believe me when I say, I had no idea I had been on the front page of every newspaper for two weeks.

I had no idea what Davina was talking about. She then said that I had a lot of press coverage and "we saw you drop your towel and show your nether regions," but she said immediately after her comment about my towel drop. "What about this?" and she held up a tabloid front page newspaper she has folded in half. The headline read, "Penny, I want to go all the way." It was advertised as an exclusive interview. People will think that is another interview I gave for money, which I never did.

I forgot immediately that she had somehow mentioned a "towel drop" and had no reason to question her talking about a towel, as I didn't understand what she meant anyway. I was now defending the fact that I wouldn't have sex on TV, and in my brain, I couldn't actually believe she was being serious. I don't know why she folded the paper and just showed me half of it. I couldn't believe I was actually on the front page of a newspaper.

I wonder now if my towel drop photo was also on that front page when she folded it in half in 2001. If I had seen that photo at my eviction interview, I would have defended myself. I would have grabbed the paper and stared at me holding a towel completely naked and probably screamed the studio down.

In my head, I am convinced that all the questions she has asked me are just to make the eviction night show interesting. Once I said categorically that I really would not have had sex on live TV in answer to her question, she hurried me outside to see my school girls, whom I embraced. I was so happy to see them. I had put my shoes back on by then and towered above her.

As she led me out again towards the crowds, I said, "Are they real, or did you have to pay for them to cheer?"

Davina laughed and said, "No."

I couldn't believe how many people were cheering again. I met as many people in the crowd as I could. I didn't get a chance to see my friends again that evening, which was disappointing. I could have had a meaningful chat with them and gotten their advice. When I saw the episode back on YouTube, I saw the camera cut to the house, and they were still locked inside, not able to go in the garden. Dean says of the cheering, "It is a tape; no crowd can keep cheering like that," but the crowd, bless them, were still cheering.

In *The Sunday People* newspaper on June 10, 2001, it read: "Yesterday Penny spent hours with a trained psychiatrist paid for by *Big Brother* as she tries to get over her two-week ordeal." On 9 June, I was at my *OK!* magazine interview. I did not have hours of help or aftercare, and certainly not on the 9th of June, as the paper suggests. At last, a nice friend who isn't named is in this article, said, "This is supposed to be a TV show; Penny didn't realise they were trying to shoot a piece of porn and she was to be its star." In this article, it also says, "She insists it is *Big Brother* that let her down, and she has done nothing to harm her pupils."

In another article in a different tabloid newspaper that same weekend, it described my eviction interview and what I was asked: "Penny described her *Big Brother* experience as amazing, incredible, and bewildering. When asked about the infamous towel drop, she said in her interview with Davina, "I don't remember it. Did I do the dance of the seven veils? If I had done it deliberately, I would have done the whole dance."" I never was asked to explain or given a chance to defend myself in my eviction interview about the towel drop, and I never said those quotes. I never gave those interviews, and I never got paid for all those interviews I was supposed to have done. I was now in another realm. Out of my ordinary. Out of the reality star's home, the *Big Brother* house. Now I was facing the vast landscape. How was I supposed to navigate myself across all this new terrain? I had no help. No manager. No one who knew what to do with this new reality star I had become.

I was then led into another room, where there must have been over fifty journalists and cameras. It was a massive press conference at about 11.30 p.m. I was exhausted. I stood there like a rabbit in the headlights. I was led up to a platform and sat down in front of a huge microphone. I must have had people from *Big Brother* next to me, but I don't know who they were. I have no idea what the questions meant that suddenly exploded from the floor. I didn't understand at all why they kept asking about a towel dropping incident.

I waffled on about the *Big Brother* house, and I just quoted Miranda from *The Tempest* by Shakespeare: "Oh brave new world that has such people in it." They all just stared at me rather strangely. I thought it was a good quote as it is the first time Miranda sees other humans for the first time in her life. It was like arriving on a new planet, and I didn't understand their language that evening.

It was too overwhelming to be in front of all these people after fifteen days of such isolation in the *Big Brother* house and going through the evening's events, which were all so completely new and terrifying for an ordinary person. I had no friends or family by my side to explain the questions to me or guide me in what I should say. I was surrounded by strangers. For me, I had entered a new time zone, a new galaxy. I was absolutely overwhelmed, as nothing about all of this was normal to me.

In 2001, the TV sat in your living room, and you watched the news, films, life stories, and documentaries. Then you switched it off. It wasn't a reality you stepped into and accepted as a normal part of your life, like we do today with the social media platforms we interact with. I had no idea how to answer their questions, as I had absolutely no idea that I should be defending myself and fighting for my job and my whole life as I had known it.

Whatever they wrote from what I said in that press conference would be the stories on the front page of all the newspapers that my friend Marie would see on her way through the airport on her way back from her honeymoon on 10 June 2001. That my girls from school would see, that my church would see, that my family would see. In my opinion, people would assume that I had given those interviews and said those things the way the journalists would have written them up. My friends, school, and church would think I got paid for all those stories. My whole life, character, and reputation were formed by the ink of the journalists into how the world then viewed me from that day onward, in my opinion and from my recollection.

I was still ashamed of the row with Stuart and felt very embarrassed about it at the press conference. I found the press conference bizarre. I still had no idea there was any coverage on a story of my so called "towel dropping" or the effect of that story on my job and mental health over the next twenty years. I didn't study the tabloid stories about me or look at anything on the internet for years about me in *Big Brother*, as I keep saying in my story. I wonder now if that saved me from doing something desperate to myself.

I didn't realise the extent of coverage on me until 2016, when a friend helped me request from Google that they take down about six hundred sites. By then, I had been in the depths of despair, facing rejection and chaos for years. In June 2001, a journalist parked up and slept in his car outside my sister's home for two weeks to get stories on me. He would put notes through her door for any story about me. I thought that by ignoring it all and hiding away, it would all go away. I thought that by moving home in 2002 and leaving London, no one would bother me. I have realised that you cannot ignore giants in your life. You have to face what you've buried deep inside yourself. Once you face the giant, other extremes in your life will flee. I found in 2020 that I was strong enough to face the giant of 'Penny from *Big Brother* who dropped her towel.' When I did, extremes like depression, OCD mood swings, anxiety, and fear fled.

I found that through my faith in God, as I surrendered my life to him, he gave me my real identity back. I gave him my confusion and shame, and he swapped them for a life put right through his death and resurrection. His blood paid the price of my sins. I hope I can share my story with people. We are all allowed a second chance to live, free from whatever has held us back for years.

After my eviction interview, I honestly thought it would be left there, like a good night out, and everyone would have a laugh. I laughed with Davina at having a row I didn't mean and flirting, which I didn't mean, and I didn't really know how it might have been edited or how I might have come across, but I just thought to myself that it was nothing and that I had just been myself, just being a bit daft, and it was all quite harmless. Loads of us go out for a night out and have a bit of a laugh. We might do a funky chicken dance, be a bit silly chatting to someone we don't know or do something to make our friends laugh. That is part of a night out for most people; it is part of having a good time and a bit of a laugh. That saying, "What happens in Vegas stays in Vegas," But it has meant for me, as "Penny who dropped her towel," that I lost some friends, my church, my job, my home, my life as I knew it, my dignity, my sanity, and my reputation.

Imagine coming back from a two-week holiday and finding that life as you knew it was over. That is not funny. This story is to make you smile and to encourage you that whatever we face, we can get through it. I am so glad that people got a lot of happiness from my TV appearance, and that in those fifteen days, a lot of people had a good time. I love that and love them, as life must be about caring and being there for others. I got to share your lives. I got to be in your living room and share precious moments of what you were doing in the days I was in the house.

I received thousands of emails with so much love in them that I have kept them all. You tell me about a significant moment you went through from 25 May – 8 June 2001, and I was there with you; it is very touching and humbling. It was an honour to share a time in your life. Endemol got so many emails for me that they put thousands on a zip disc. To preserve space, as there were so many, they wrapped them in a post-box file. The letter with my zip file read: "You may be insulted by a few, but I advise you not to take it personally as these emails are clearly from people reacting to your 'character' in the *Big Brother* gameshow." The emails I read were of people who saw I was being raw, genuine, kind, and caring, the realest me. Thank you again for your precious emails. I treasure them. Despite stories about me in the tabloids in 2001 that have already digested into people's opinions and beliefs about me; they have been chewed, regurgitated, spat out, or swallowed like a tasty treat I know I was very loved by the public when I did venture out. There was so much love, and I thank you, whoever you are, for your lovely love.

SCENE 3:
The Fallout.

I suddenly thought, once I started writing this book, about what the girls from my school, Sarah Bonnell (some from my form and others in my English classes), had actually experienced during that time in 2001. I had never asked them, so I contacted them. It was quite emotional to hear their responses. I heard myself say separately to each of them that I was sorry I left them.

Despite it being twenty years later, they all said it meant so much to hear me tell them I was sorry for leaving them. Their emotional reaction bowled me over. I had never thought about the impact it had on them or what it took away from them. I love them with my whole heart and feel they are the children I could never have. They are a dream come true for me, my beautiful girls.

Lizzie (age 15 in 2001):
I was her form tutor from 1997, and she stayed with me on different occasions, including Easter one year. So incredibly sweet and beautiful, she really filled such a hole in my heart when I met her. We went to a Christian camp where Claire was her tent leader. Everything she does, she achieves with such grace: horse-riding, playing the violin, and speaking numerous languages. We also went to theatres and other events over the years. It was wonderful to go to her wedding just a few years ago. She now lives in Norway.

These are her words based on what she remembers, her recollection of events, and her opinion:

"It was such early days for social media, and we didn't really have the tools to understand it all. The whole form was so sad to lose you. We felt we had lost our safe space and felt like we were grieving. We missed

your energy and felt disappointed. Some of the form didn't watch it, as everyone's parents had different rules for TV viewing.

The school didn't say anything it was just hushed up. I wish we had had a voice and could have talked with the leadership team about how we all felt. There were no bitchy comments from any of the form or other students. We all knew who you were as a form teacher as well as a person, and we did not recognise the way you were represented on TV. We didn't believe the newspapers either, as that just wasn't you.

It was the first time I realised the magazines actually didn't tell the whole truth. I found that to be a big awakening, as before that I thought they just wrote the truth. I realised that again when I saw you when you were out of the house. You told me about a magazine interview that was coming out. You told me what they had asked and what you said to them. When the article came out, I was so shocked because it was completely different; nothing you said was in the article, and it was nothing like what you expected. At that age, I believed life was fair, but it awoke me to the fact that it isn't. I felt unsettled and had a feeling that it was all a bit sinister."

Zainab (age 18 in 2001):

I was her English teacher. Over the years, we always called each other on a Friday. We visited each other in Hastings and London and always told each other exactly what we thought. I have known Zainab since 1995. She is strong and has so much wisdom for her age, as well as being incredibly striking and glamorous.

These are her words, based on her recollections of events and her opinion:

"I remember getting a card from you telling me you were going on Big Brother. I was shocked. I remember going back to the school from college as there was a film crew in your form room filming. Lizzie was there too. They filmed some of your teaching and the interaction with your students. I don't think they ever used that footage, which is a shame. I found it difficult to watch when the show was on because I knew the real you. I really wanted them to show the person I knew you to be. You have always been a person who loves her students and friends truthfully. I do remember watching the episode where the girls were trying to call to you over the wall of the Big Brother house and encourage you, telling you how much they loved you.

Big Brother made you all go back into the living room and shut the door to the garden. A car came to pick me up and take me to the studio on your eviction night. I cried when you were voted out, but I was relieved as that experience was now over. People latched onto you because of the fame, and I have seen you have some brilliant and also horrendous experiences over the years. I am glad that now you just have the people who really know you and love you as your friends."

Heena (I have known her since 1994; she was in my year 11 GCSE English class in 2001):

We call each other on WhatsApp now as she lives in Singapore. She travels extensively and is so perceptive and knowledgeable. Her views and opinions are full of wisdom and kindness. She is a sophisticated, beautiful soul.

These are her words, based on her recollection of events and her opinion:

"We got a permanent supply; I think she was from New Zealand. She didn't really inspire me. I missed you so much. I just remember not having anyone to go to in the school to voice my concerns or even ask for help with regards to my GCSE English.

I felt very positive despite the stories in the papers, as it made me take the reins and be fearless. I really found my personality and have blossomed, and I am proud to be a 'kickass' woman. I know we lost touch for a while, and it made me sad, but I was always proud and happy. You had actually gone and done something momentous.

I am a writer, and I am so pleased that you are re-owning your own narrative. It is life affirming. I am so glad we are always here for each other. I have embraced writing, traveling, and creative projects, as well as living abroad Let us see everything as an opportunity."

Ironically, it is these girls that have inspired me. They have been there just at the right moment. They make me believe that all is well. I don't know what words could describe the love I have for them and the love I have felt from them.

Kuljeet (in my form in 2001; I have known her since 1997):

She was such a beautiful member of the form, helping and encouraging others. She made up the scrapbooks of our form activities. I value all her Christmas cards and other cards she has sent me over the years, which are full of messages of love. She has a heart full of love and radiates such gentleness. A beautiful girl, sensitive, kind, and loving.

These are her words, based on her recollection of events and her opinion:

"I remember walking into the classroom and even by the lockers outside the form room, the buzzing conversation, 'Have your parents written a complaint?' 'Did you see what happened?'

It was just after being told that you would not be returning to the school. Then there was another conversation where we were told we would have yet another stand in form tutor. Not much else was said to us. The memory that sparks in my mind is the confused chatter of opinions around the class.

'It's not fair.' 'She shouldn't have done it.' 'It was an accident; she didn't do it on purpose.' 'She can't teach in a girls' school now.' 'She did it on purpose.' 'How can you say that she isn't even here to tell her side of the story?' 'She's been an amazing form tutor; you just can't make her go.'

I remember feeling an overwhelming weight of sadness as we digested the information that you weren't our form tutor any more. That is something everyone in the class couldn't deny, regardless of opinions or judgements. I wonder now how much of those conversations were influenced by parental conversations. Personally, my father asked me if he should send a letter of concern once it all blew up on TV. I told him not to. It wasn't necessary, and I don't remember having any more conversations at home.

I remember sitting in an assembly; I am not sure if it was a whole school one. We were warned about speaking to any reporters who may approach us and ask us about the situation or Ms. Ellis. We were warned that our words might be twisted, although they would seem friendly and may tell us they are being helpful. Our form moved to the science block. She was fine, but I don't remember her name. I can sort of remember what she looked like, but our form was never the same again. We had no form class celebrations. The form became segregated. We had lost our anchor. We all had growing pains. I felt a sense of loss and sadness. I am just grateful that we have a relationship now, and we are growing stronger together."

Emma (I've known Emma since 1992, when I started at Sarah Bonnell School):
I was glad she could talk to me about anything that concerned her.

When she left in year 11, we would meet up each week and go for a coffee. I can still remember standing on the school steps and seeing her come down the road to meet me. We have such a beautiful friendship, and I feel privileged to have her in my life.

These are her opinions and what she remembers about the events:

"My English teacher was a whirlwind, eccentric, and fun—model like with crazy hair and so different from any other teacher I'd ever had. She was so passionate about her subject that the class, which used to exist alongside the usual dullness of an all-girls school in East London, suddenly became enjoyable. She believed in those who were used to being ignored, and I, like the others, began to love literature, and I credit her with the love I now have of plays, theatre, and reading in general.

Lisa (her first name) was around ten years older than me, and she became a brilliant friend. She would offer advice on anything and knew the ways of the world, so she was never shocked at anything I ever asked or said. It was lovely to have someone in my life who truly cared and with whom I could be myself. She too had insecurities and OCD, just as I did as a teenager, and if she wasn't a freak, neither was I.

It was an adventure whenever we went out; we never knew what was going to happen. We got into places, and I remember feeling a million miles away from East London while drinking cocktails in the fifth floor bar in Harvey Nichols. She introduced me to a different kind of life, and I loved it. I had just started my first job at an investment bank when Lisa went into Big Brother. I wasn't one of the kids who waited outside the Big Brother house and called out a few times. But I was amazed and excited at the concept that these people would be watched twenty-four hours a day, and I couldn't believe my friend was going to be a TV star. Big Brother was huge, and everyone was watching it, including me when I came home from work. Nothing had ever been done like Big Brother before, and it was incredible. Lisa appeared in newspapers and OK! magazine, and I thought she was living the dream. It was only a couple of years later that I found out how it had all spiralled out of control, and I was sad that I couldn't have helped her through what was one of the most difficult times for her. I had no idea."

***

While I was in the *Big Brother* house, friends of my aunt, who worked at

Harvard University, were discussing me. Friends in Australia overheard others talking about me; Veronica was serving coffee at her coffee bar in Melbourne, and customers were discussing me. Everyone saw these stories around the world. They saw them in June 2001, and again and again they cropped up right up to February 2020, where I lost yet another teaching job and where people judged me and ridiculed me.

I just wanted to share this part, even though it is a bit negative, but I am explaining it as it was and has been for me. I am not trying to vent any bitterness or moan; I am describing honestly what happened and how I felt. I just felt embarrassed. I really didn't realise I probably could have walked into the offices of one of the papers and given a real-life story and all my views, cleared the air, and said my piece, but I didn't realise I was that important at all, even just for what people call "the window of opportunity."

I vaguely remember *Big Brother* asking me to go back into the *Big Brother* house in 2004. I even had a letter from my mother, who was in Spain; in her letter, she wrote out a website that my aunt at Harvard University had said I should update. I had not even created a website, and my own aunt believed it belonged to me. I have no idea what that might have contained over the years. I never even looked at anything and had no idea that there were so many hundreds of sites and news feeds on me, all created without my knowledge, and some of them I found out about in 2016. I wonder how long others fed off my fame while I walked in ignorance. How stupid was I? That moment briefly when I was 'super famous.' How funny is that? How naïve was I?

On 8 June, after the interview with Davina and the press conference, I sat on the bed at the Charlotte Street hotel and was just relieved to get my handbag back. I wish I had called friends or family for advice. I remember looking at the girl who was there to advise me and thinking that she looked so young. I wish Peter had been there, as I was frazzled. It was so late, and it had been such an emotional day and evening as well as a really stressful fifteen days.

My handbag was flattened like an ironed t-shirt and looked ever so small. It just looked like it didn't belong to me and had lost that zing, that spark, that had made me buy it in the first place. It is weird what we focus on in times of great stress. I didn't know what advising meant in this media world. I had already chatted with all the press. *What else is there to say?* I thought. These offers from the newspapers and magazines were "life changing," as an editor who I bumped into at a music event reiterated to me months later while I was looking at Dannielle Westbrook sitting on the grass and thinking, *Oh, I know who that is.* I remember looking up at him and thinking, *Really?*

But I missed so many opportunities, wasted money, lost money, gave away money, and used it to pay off my debts that I had accumulated before *Big Brother*. By the time I went home in 2002, I was broke. A lot of 'new friends' come around you 'when you are in the spotlight.' They stay while your purse is full of money. I am so deeply grateful for the ones I met during that time who only ever gave me their real friendship, love, and support. I love you and am so honoured to have you as my friends to this day. Gary, Ant, Ben, Paul Bedsprings, and Dean.

The Charlotte Street hotel became my home for about five days. I went downstairs in my dressing gown and pyjamas for breakfast once, I think, and I can vaguely remember having my own table. Everyone said farewell to me when I left, with all the staff lining up to shake my hand! Such a beautiful, humbling memory. What a wonderful hotel.

I accepted the offer from *OK!* Magazine and recall leaving the Charlotte Street hotel on 9 June, getting into my chauffeur-driven black Mercedes car to go to the interview in a lovely hotel room at The Waldorf Meridian hotel in Aldwych. I felt like a superstar as I left the hotel, clicking across the hotel lobby in high heels. This account is based on my opinion and my memory of events. Because I chose *Ok!* magazine for my exclusive interview, it meant, as I said earlier, I couldn't talk to any other press or go to some events. What upset me was that I couldn't go to Ascot's Ladies Day, even though they invited me. I was gutted, as I have always wondered what that would be like.

Also, I had to decline some red-carpet premieres and TV interviews. I had been invited to absolutely everything in those first few days after leaving the *Big Brother* house. I wonder what people I would have met and what opportunities I missed by not being able to go.

I took my own clothes for the shoot. I had been hoping they might provide some lovely designer dresses. I was a bit disappointed as I really thought they might dress me all up in clothes, bags, and jewellery with accessories to match, which I would never have been able to afford to buy. There I am on the front cover of *Ok!* magazine in my £3.99 top that I bought at a market stall in Islington and a pair of £1.99 knickers! There I am on the front of this amazingly glamorous, shiny magazine, whose front cover had under its title, "First for Celebrity News. Issue 269. 22nd June 2001." So I'm wondering why my interview didn't appear in an earlier edition of the magazine, and maybe then I could have attended some of the events. It says, "*Big Brother* Penny reveals all in her world exclusive first interview." I couldn't believe they had used that photo for the front cover of the magazine.

Inside the magazine, there are some lovely photos of me posing in a red sequin dress I bought in the sale at Karen Millen. I had worn that same dress in the *Big Brother* house when we did our calendar shoot. There are also photos of me in some of my other clothes that I had taken into the *Big Brother* house, including a red sequin skirt and a couple of tops that I had again bought at market stalls.

Reading back on some of the things I must have said makes my eyes roll. On 9 June, I still had no idea about any stories written about me. I had no idea how famous I was. I had no idea I could have negotiated a huge amount of money for my story. I had no idea that I could have taken control of the situation. It was that moment, that day, that week, when I had the opportunity to say and do things that reflected the best of me. I was so ignorant of the opportunity that was open to me in those first two weeks.

The introduction starts with: "Following a string of high-profile incidents—dropping her towel and exposing herself to the hidden cameras . . ."

Then I say to various questions:

"*I'd seen the hype the first series had received so you know what is going to happen.*"

"*I'm known as a ditzy weirdo, and thankfully I had my breasts done.*"

"*I don't think the school will sack me as they believe in me.*"

"*I think you can allow destructive cycles in your life. I went out with someone who was manipulative, controlling, and judged everything I did.*"

"*I would have given part of the money, if I had won, to an orphanage me and all my family have supported for years in India.*"

"*I don't know what the future holds but I would like to maybe do some voice over work.*"

I started to feel uncomfortable when they said they would take a photo of me on the bed. I was wearing bikini top and knickers, and I squashed and angled myself around, so I tried to hide the back of me. I felt odd, but what do you say? From my recollection, it was then that they said I needed to get in the bath. I said I wouldn't do that, and they said if I didn't, they wouldn't pay me. I was absolutely petrified, as I really needed some money to pay my bills for the next month.

I thought, *what do I do?* I closed the bathroom door with this girl, who was helping the photographer. They said I had to be naked. By this point, I felt really scared. I had nobody there to speak for me, nobody to stand up for me. I waited for the bath to fill up and put my hand in to make the bath foam bubble up to the top of the bath. I sat in the bath and added more bath bubbles, keeping my body low. Then they said I had to stand up, and the photographer was clicking away while one of them was trying to brush the bubble foam off my breasts, so I suppose they would get a nipple shot. I swiped their hand, and I think I said, "fuck off" under my breath. I felt sick. I have never told anyone about this before.

This is the photo I was talking about earlier in my book that appeared in *The Daily Star* on 11 June. This is the photo a teacher at Sarah Bonnell was looking at that Monday morning, probably after picking up the paper on her way to school. She commented to colleagues in the staffroom that because of that photo, "I will definitely get sacked."

The Daily Star, 11 June 2001, would be looked at as it lay in the staff room of Sarah Bonnell. Teachers I had worked with for eleven years would have their coffee break and stare at my breasts covered in foam and read the words: "I still want to teach."

They would go back to their classroom, maybe wondering how much money I must have made and if it was worth it to degrade myself in such a photo. I want to shout out to them, "It is a degrading photo done under such pressure," and scream that I never got paid for it by *The Daily Star.*

Also in my *OK!* Magazine interview, which came out on 22 June, are smaller photos of me washing completely naked in the shower in the *Big Brother* house. There are smaller photos of me in the bubble bath, sipping champagne. I didn't get paid for my interview for *OK!* Magazine for ages. I had to beg an outside agency to help me get my money, as I was desperate! They finally paid me.

My mother always used to say to me, "A lot of people made a lot of money from you." I think I agree. That was painful to write about— why there is a photo of me naked, covered in foam in a tabloid paper. I am glad I can tell you now.

I tried not to think about *Big Brother*, but it hasn't left me as I have been regularly recognised for the last twenty years. I never bring it up at any job or at home.

I only put Penny Ellis' name on my first book, *A River Through My Desert*, the day it was going to print in 2020. My husband Mark said that I should use my *Big Brother* name, Penny. We had never talked about *Big Brother* in the eleven years we had known each other. He had found it mildly amusing that some people called me Penny and others called me Lisa.

It has always been like that since I was about seventeen. Penelope is my middle name, and my friends just adopted whichever one they felt suited me. My school had only known me as Lisa, so all the quoting of "sacking Penny" by my (very busy with the media) headmistress was a bit weird to read.

My lovely, kind church, All Souls Langham Place, knew me as Penny. It still makes me cringe at how they dealt with the media and the stories they got caught up in because of me. I am so sorry.

Anyway, as much as Mark had seen me come home time and time again crying at how the staff and students had treated me at teaching jobs, and how many times he saw me sacked, he really had no idea of the enormity of the show. We were just busy with life.

Then, one day, I thought, *why am I hiding and quaking and constantly in fear of judgement?* I was at the point of just being sick of it. My book, *A River Through My Desert*, is about finding our way out of our terrors, and I wrote it when I came out of *Big Brother* as I found my faith in Jesus Christ again. I don't think I would otherwise be here.

My parents, my sister, my faith, and my true friends all pulled me back from the darkest of pits. *So why not put my name to it and be brave?* I was walking to a supply job, ironically my last ever teaching job, in March 2020, when I emailed Austin Macaulay, my publishers, and asked them to put my name as Penny Ellis. They said it was just in time as it was about to be printed. Mark had not seen or known about *Big Brother*, but following this, in 2020, he saw the stuff still on the internet. He read through the whole lot before I got home from work. There are some very suggestive stories still floating around. That evening we had such a dreadful time as I found myself again in a situation when I got home where I had to explain that I didn't drop my towel, this time to my darling husband of ten years.

That was probably a necessary conversation, but it made me realise how much *Big Brother* is still affecting my entire life, both personally and professionally. I just let out the loudest screams for ages. Mark looked at me. I let go of all that pain, embarrassment, and judgement. To have to explain yourself for twenty years is exhausting.

To finally have peace and acceptance, you must face this giant, knowing you're stronger than it. Whatever we are afraid to face, bring it out into the light and let it show its true colours. This is another reason I am writing this book now: to tell the truth of my journey and show you that I turned the "light" on and have found a life worth living. There is hope and a future, and from any situation, there are always gold nuggets that, because of that experience, enable us to be strong and to reach out and add beauty and colour to a world that needs love.

My casting photo for *Big Brother 2*.

We were set a task by *Big Brother* to create a calender. I chose to be in kitchen for my photograph (above), taken by my fellow contestant Paul.

Eviction night 8 June 2001. I was overwhelmed by the amount of people who turned up to greet me. It was amazing!

THE Mirror 32

Wednesday May 30 2001

I'll sack Penny if she has sex on Big Brother

HEAD'S WARNING TO FLIRTY SCHOOL TEACHER: PAGE 7

Head's sack threat to naughty teacher

By **TOM NEWTON DUNN** and **LORRAINE FISHER**

BIG Brother flirt Penny Ellis is facing the sack from her teaching job – AND eviction from the TV house.

Her school future was in the balance last night after she was seen naked on screen and also gave fellow housemate Paul a deep and lingering kiss.

Penny, 33, has even jokingly promised to have sex on camera.

Cauthar Tooley, head of the girls-only Sarah Bonnell School in Stratford, East London, where Penny teaches drama, said last night: "I will sit down with our solicitor and look at the code of conduct provisions in her contract.

"That gives me discretion to sack her if she brings the school into disrepute. It all depends on her and whether she wants to remain on Big Brother at all costs.

"I gave her all the advice I could beforehand but obviously now that she is inside the house I can't do any more. If she had sex with a housemate that would be totally unacceptable."

Channel 4's cable channel E4 had to broadcast an apology to viewers after Penny's towel slipped off when she was drying

The official BIG BROTHER paper

leader Nigel de Gruchy gave her a black mark.

He said last night: "I don't know if this woman is one of our members, but if she is I would say it was inadvisable for her to do something like that if she is interested in keeping her job."

Inside the house Penny was in more hot water despite being a favourite with viewers.

Bookies Coral slashed the odds against her being an eviction nominee on Friday from 10-1 to 3-1 after other contestants were seen complaining about her.

Show producers are terrified about the prospect of charismatic Penny being booted out, knowing it would be a ratings loser.

But Penny, from North London, has become a lonely figure after dissolving in tears because of a bad-tempered house meeting on Monday evening.

She has been accused of tak-

ing "too motherly". Yesterday she steered clear of her housemates. While the other nine contestants relaxed in the garden during the afternoon, she retreated to the girls' bedroom.

Penny cleaned and clipped her nails then went to sleep.

She told musician Dean and airline steward Brian the stormy meeting had been very upsetting.

Penny said: "When I went to bed last night I was a bit weepy.

"I've been trying to help but I have just become this kitchen woman."

She was close to tears again later after Brian squeezed her breast and Narinder speculated that she had implants.

Narinder, who had asked the boys if they could tell the difference when they hugged Penny, protested: "I said you had lovely tits."

Warehouseman Bubble called out: "Penny, can I feel your boobs please." Brian then pinched them. Penny composed herself and shared a hug with her three tormentors.

Her best friend Charlotte Price last night said she feared for Penny's future. "We told her she had to be careful not to go over the top," she said. "She can do some pretty crazy things at times."

Headline maker: I was on the front page of all the tabloid newspapers for a few weeks.

PENNY: I WANT TO GO ALL THE WAY

■ by RUTH HUGHES

PRIM and proper teacher Penny, 33, has turned into a man-eater days after going into the Big Brother house.

Former Catholic school-girl Penny, 33, has already snogged hunky housemate Paul Clarke, 25.

But she's told pals she's willing to have sex on telly to scoop the £70,000 prize.

Millions saw the sexy smacker screened live on the website yesterday just 48 hours after she moved in.

Penny, whose real name is Lisa Ellis, pounced on Paul.

Turn to Page 7

BIG BOSS IS WATCHING YOU PENNY

SNOGGING: Paul gets a kiss

BARING: Penny's towel falls off   GROPING: Brian's boob squeeze

● Lisa Ellis

'Teacher's shocking'

By SUSAN SMITH

TEACHER Lisa Ellis, whose saucy antics on TV's Big Brother have made her famous to millions, faces a meeting with her shocked and embarrassed boss when she leaves the show.

Cauthar Tooley, head teacher of Sarah Bonnell Girls' School in Stratford, said no decision about Lisa's future will be made until she has been 'evicted' from the show's house.

Pictures of Lisa, 33, who is using the name Penny on the show, were plastered all over the national Press after she bared all for the cameras by dropping her towel when coming out of a shower.

She is also reported to have said she would sleep with one of her fellow contestants to scoop the £70,000 prize.

Conduct

Ms Tooley said seeing the coverage of Lisa in the national media was "quite shocking" and felt "very disappointed and embarrassed for her".

She added it was up to her to make sure teachers kept to the school's code of conduct. "We wouldn't want they feel proud to go."

But she went on to say Lisa who has been at the school for nine years and is a "very relaxed" relationship with the pupils.

She participates fully in school life, often organising many extra-curricular activities, she said.

Even after Lisa leaves the programme, Ms Tooley is aware she will probably have to wait in line behind the nation's media to talk to her.

She said: "I have spoken to an officer from the education department and it's clear that we would not be able to make any decision until she is out of the house.

"We will then have a meeting and discuss the situation with her. There's a whole procedure that would need to be followed and having a meeting with her is the first part of that." But she insisted it would not be a disciplinary meeting.

● A censored view of Lisa's nude antics

Ms Tooley said she had not taken any calls from parents regarding Lisa.

Last week, a group of Sarah Bonnell pupils were heard on the show outside the house in Stratford calling for her.

But other pupils have been less impressed. Danni Bertie, 13, said: "It's not a very good example. I reckon she'll get the sack and I think that's good."

Her father, Brian, said "I think it's disgusting. It's terrible and a bad example to the children."

But Hannah Christian, 16, said "I think it's OK because she's a really good teacher.

"It's not something that most teachers would do, but it's her life. When she dropped her towel, Channel 4 should've edited it.

"I think she should be allowed to come back to school."

Lisa is one of two contestants who have been nominated for 'eviction' from the show on Friday. Viewers will vote to decide which one goes.

Cauthar Tooley

I became close friends with *Big Brother 2* winner Brian Dowling.

With Jeremy Phillips, *Big Brother* producer, at my birthday party.

Paul, Narinder and myself at the *Big Brother* wrap party.

With fellow contestants and producers at the final live show.

The *Big Brother 2* cast at our book launch.
From left to right, back row: Stuart Hoskins, Josh Rafter, Bubble (Paul Ferguson),
me, Elizabeth Woodcock, Amma Antwi-Agyei, and Dean O'Loughlin.
Front row: Narinder Kaur, Paul Clarke, Brian Dowling, and Helen Adams.

Bubble, Josh and I took part in Macmillans annual 'Big Hush'
to raise money to support people affected by cancer.

Here I am abseiling 159 ft down the side of
Beaufort House, London to raise money for
Dr. Barnardos charity.

I cut the ribbon for the opening of the
Dixons store in Oxford Street, London.

I was fortunate enough to be invited to
the premiere of the film *A Knight's Tale*.

It was a huge honour to meet the late,
great, Sir Norman Wisdom.

I met Duncan, from the boyband Blue, when I appeared on the *Big Breakfast* show.

Watching Steps peform at Mardi Gras on 28 June 2001
after Graham Norton and I had introduced them on stage.

I really enjoyed starring in two pantomines, in
2001 and 2004, and received great reviews.

I was also featured in *Closer* magaine in 2002.

SCENE 4:
Being Famous.

While staying at the Charlotte Street Hotel for those few days, I had in my contract various radio shows that I had to go to and give an interview to. I remember meeting the late 'Jono and the morning crew' at Heart Radio. I had such a laugh and still have the big mug he gave me, which I use for my coffee in the morning. I think they must have been mugs they gave out as prizes on the show. I have a postcard of him, and he has signed it: "Hi Penny, you're my girl."

I was whisked to so many radio stations and had no time to think at all. I was walking into places and meeting people I had only ever heard on the radio or seen on TV, and suddenly I was their best friend, and it was, as Ted used to say, "all about me." I didn't have time to think about how I was being portrayed, and I should have made a plan for what to say. I trusted everyone. I was so ignorant for years. Call me naïve. Call me stupid. I have to laugh at myself now. I had no idea that I was just adding fuel to the fire under all the stories about me already out there.

I couldn't go outside on my own as I was swamped by paparazzi and fans. It was intense and humbling. People shouted on the street, "In the kitchen, out the kitchen." People shouted, "I watched your feet while you slept." People would want autographs; I have signed all sorts, including till receipts, restaurant napkins, and an umbrella!

The emails I reread are so valuable, and I want to thank everyone. Ironically, most of the emails have the same tone and message. Some were also from doctors and other professions, and they all said what a shame I didn't have a soulmate in there, how the others didn't really get me. I remember thinking that was how I felt. I do still think that Josh and I would have brought out the best in each other in a genuine way if he had already been in the house. I just thought that in comparison to the brutality and shrieking madness in my opinion of the newspapers' tone and insinuations in the stories written about me, these emails were at last the truth and a breath of fresh air. I could almost hear these people talking as I reread their emails. I can feel genuine love, kindness, warmth, and understanding. I am so glad I made these lovely people laugh and be joyful. The emails come from a wide range of people of various ages and backgrounds. Despite being told some might show a dark side and that "those people use anonymity on the internet," I found no weird, cruel, or nasty ones. I have only seen journalists, in my opinion, do that to my life without any shame or anonymity.

I had Fireman Bill as my bodyguard, and he was great. A swanky car, sometimes a limousine, would pick me up, and he would lead me through the paparazzi sometimes over twenty of them, all shouting and trying to take photos. It was just like a film where the actress is hounded by the press and is led into the car. It is such a surreal experience, and it happened hundreds of times over that year. Once the paparazzi crowded around the car, it was being pushed and rocked as they were leaning in to take photos, and thousands of flashing bulbs were all I could see as I cowered in the back seat.

I wish now that I had sold stories, as the press wrote their stories anyway, and I would find myself in another double spread of a tabloid with a story I never gave or got any money for. I remember spending a day at Bill's fire station, meeting all the team. He took the job of looking after me very seriously, and I felt safe with him. He was really nice and kind. I wish I had asked for his help as the year went on. I can see now why famous people pay a lot for a manager, someone who sorts out the press, someone in charge of legal things, and someone in charge of their money and contracts. Gosh, I really needed a team of people to help me. I had to do it all on my own in a world I didn't know.

It was all so glittering and dazzling as I stepped into yet another out of world experience from 9 June 2001, to about October 2002. It was terrifying trying to do it on my own. I kept trying to pick the person I was back up, but like a shadow, the person I was kept running away from me in all the engagements that came from TV, radio, theatre, and celebrity friends.

Then there were the letters that people had sent to *Big Brother* or to Sarah Bonnell, my school. There was one from Mihuiel, with whom I had done my A-level drama in Newham in 1997. It was an awesome course linked to the National Theatre. This teacher, Karl, was super talented and well known. I was so sad to find out he had died. He was so young and so gifted. He had rung me when the results came in and wanted to tell me himself that I had gotten an A*. He had taught me so much, and I had developed more as an actress in the two years with him than in my three years at London University for my BA Hons. He had posted the results but wanted to hear my reaction on the phone because he knew I wouldn't believe it and he was so proud of me.

Under the guidance of Adam's mom, I had applied and been accepted at Reading University to do my PGCE in Drama and Contextual Studies in 1990. Again, a renowned theatre director ran the course and had offered me the lead role in *Mack the Knife*. I had gone back to the flat in Reading with my news, exuberant at having been given a great opportunity, but Adam had the biggest fit imaginable, so I said I could not do it. After that, my time on the course was soured, but it was better than working at the video shop in Ashford, which got raided one night when I cashed up and closed. I had put the money in a designated place in the wall, and I always wonder if that massive roll of money is still there.

When I worked at Sarah Bonnell in 1992, I remember Adam ripping up my new blue suit while standing on the bed. I just quietly sewed it up and wore it the next day to Parents' evening. I don't know the exact day or time I started to let people do and say what they liked to me.

Finding my faith again has enabled me to stand up and be the person I was always meant to be. The letter from Miheuil was lovely and a real reminder of happy days and good laughs at our A level drama course. I don't remember answering him. What is frightening about being catapulted into fame is that you really stop doing things; there are massive gaps in my memory where I don't know what I was doing.

Also, massive times of extreme loneliness and confusion as you pick up new friends and go to the most bizarre things and stop doing all the normal things you used to do. The trouble is, you're not famous enough at all to sustain that, and you're too famous (yes, really) to go back to the normal.

Could I have gone back into my classroom and picked up teaching again? Even if nothing had been written about me, I always wonder what or how the reaction would have been. In my letter from the school allowing me to go on the show, it makes me laugh to see, and I quote, "we expect your return to work the day after you leave the *Big Brother* site." No one knew how it all expands and takes on its own life form.

I did not expect anything except a bit of a break from teaching and a spotlight on *Big Breakfast* for my theatre company. In fifteen days, what could have been a new experience followed by a quiet return to normalcy became a massive, out-of-control, terrifying monster of a journey. You must take your seat on that ride to realise what you go through mentally and emotionally. Vice gripped on to that *Big Brother* rollercoaster, unable to unbuckle, just going round and round and round.

People would stop me in the street and say, "It was incredible to see you in person," as if Penny from *Big Brother* had just stepped out of the TV! In those days, that was the magic of a reality star. Like many of the emails I have read, I am so humbled that people could relate to me when they met me on the street. What an honour it is to be an inspiration to others, to say to them, "Look, this is me, warts and all. Let's all get busy living."

A letter I did respond to was from Paul Howell. I called him Paul–fan for ages because of his letter. But I was having a conversation on the phone with my mum one night, waiting for him at Bexhill station, and my mum asked me who I was meeting, and I said, "Oh, Paul Bedsprings." There was a huge silence as Paul was suddenly standing next to me.

He said, "What did you call me?"

I got that hot, soaked wash of fear come over me, and I said, "I'm so sorry; I just always have nicknames for people, and I mean it in love."

He absolutely loved it. What a sweet man! He thought it was quite apt, as he did defy and challenge traditional notions of gender, especially with respect to his cross dressing. He calls it gender bending.

In June 2001, I received a letter from him addressed to Sarah Bonnell (so it would land in my pigeon hole). He wrote to me just after the eviction on 8 June 2001. He was determined to keep me in the house, so along with the work experience girl at his work, they made around two hundred calls to vote to keep me in. When I was evicted, he was devastated and decided to write to me. I do remember writing back. Of all the emails and letters, I have such a vivid memory of reading his letter. Paul thought I was "alternative and courageous, and in that house, a square peg in a round hole."

Paul wrote again in 2002, after finding out that I had moved to Hastings, a ten-minute train ride from where he lived in Bexhill. I wrote to him again in 2003, and we finally met up on 20 October 2004 about eight weeks before I was off to Wales to be Katie Cucumber in a pantomime.

There is a gap; there are always gaps in all our lives, I think. There are things we can't even explain to ourselves, which makes them quite frightening. I went through and came out the other side of a very violent and dangerous relationship at that time.

It was 2007, and after coming over for dinner, I showed Paul the only dress I had kept from my time in *Big Brother*. Of course, he tried it on. It was the red sequin one I wore for the *Big Brother* calendar shoot in the house and the one I wore in my *OK!* Magazine interview. His love for "gender bending" as he called it, and adoration of Dusty Springfield shone out. He looked fabulous, and I gave him a pair of sequin shoes to try with it. I took the long mirror from the bedroom, and he posed at the top of the windy stairs. Then, taking a wrong turn, I saw him fall and roll down the curved stairs in my house, narrowly missing Holly, my cocker spaniel. I think she was more upset that some of her favourite toys were being substituted as boobs in the dress! Paul ripped off a nail and broke a vase, but we went out clubbing in Hastings, where we met a French chap who had just had a civil partnership ceremony and wanted us to come over and say a few words.

It was 2009 when Paul and I connected again in Edinburgh during the festival. Although in 2009, Paul was going on and on about a friend of his named Colin who was in fact straight, so any suggestions I offered were all going to end in dismay, and I just lost it. Everything I was saying wouldn't change his mind. It is one of those rows you could only have with a brother or sister. Those raw-to-the-bone frustrated home truths. Mid-row, I dropped my vitamins under the table in the restaurant, and we scrambled about under there to find them when we heard a voice saying, "Hello, darlings." On peeping up from under the table there was the late Lionel Blair! My friendship with Paul has grown and blossomed since then, watered with Gin and shared bottles of red wine in Wetherspoons.

Endless Search (A poem)
For Paul Bedsprings, thank you for everything.

It is over there. The desire for a calm resolution, that whatever is will be.
The bond of communication in the unity of friendship is all that I need to climb out of this.
To reclaim and remember from such a place to now this.
From such a person to now this.
From such a being in life to this used up existence.
I need oxygen and to dive back into laughter.
The End.

I will be weaving a lot more stories in about my friends because they are just so fantastic. The best thing to have come out of *Big Brother* are the relationships I found. I met the truest friends at events and in bars, like the wonderful Gary and Paul, who wrote to me and grew into the best of friends and are amazing and lovely all these years later.

Ben is such a special friend, and he added these words: "I first met Penny in a bar in Soho. It was just after her series of *Big Brother* had finished, and a few of the cast were out and about in Soho. They came into the pub I was in, which my best friend Gary was the manager of at the time. It was that period when the whole of the country knew who they were, and I think they were just glad to be able to get out of the public madness and into relative privacy for a few minutes. Penny and I hit it off straight away and had a blast of a time. Little did I know then that we would become friends for life after just one drink."

I am grateful to the friends who came alongside me and have been such a support over the last twenty years, and the fact that I spent time in 2002 living with my wonderful parents and sister; I didn't appreciate their wisdom and kindness before *Big Brother*. It also meant I met my beautiful husband in 2010. The love of those around you is what is truly important. I am blessed, as I am now crowded with kindness.

With no guidance, I met some incredible and also very dubious people during that time, 2001–2002. I had such a laugh on the *Big Breakfast* TV show because I met Blue and became friends with Duncan for a couple of years. Also, Johnny Vegas was there, and we were trying to find the toilets together. They had built a stage for me, and I closed the show singing *My Way* on that stage with so many famous people watching me and clapping. I went on the *Big Breakfast* TV show again to see former *Big Brother* contestants Stuart, and that was also where I met Josh for the first time. I wish I had asked Stuart and Josh for advice and how they were coping. I'm sure we must have all had our challenges and confusions about what to do. I didn't get management, which would have been someone sorting out my contracts and getting me the right money. I did a lot of engagements for free, as I didn't know how to negotiate any money. I know some of my housemates from 2001 did get management. I really could have done with some sound advice.

Outside the *Big Breakfast* studio, there were fans waiting for me: Steve and Peter, who had created these beautiful posters for me and a card I still have. It must have taken them ages. *Big Breakfast* said they had never seen anything like it before, with fans waiting outside the studio. It was sweet. I took a photo of us together on my camera. In those days, I had a Kodak camera, and I am glad to have lots of personal photos of my own.

I kept thinking that this was what I had hoped for my girls at school, as I had thought I had rung *Big Breakfast* to get them on to read their poems all those weeks ago. *Now look at me, but what am I going to do?* I didn't know what I was going to do about a job or money.

In those first few weeks, I had been a guest presenter for a week on the *Big Breakfast* TV show; I had done an agony aunt slot, "Penny for Your Thought," with Channel 4; and I presented a "Little Sister" competition for Virgin Radio. I have no idea if I asked for any payments; I really think I did most of the events I hosted or took part in for free. I was really so naïve. Every day was busy, but I wasn't going anywhere. I just hoped that something would work out. But, as I've finally learned in life, if you fail to plan, you plan to fail.

The Outside Agency appeared to be there to look after me as a talent agency, but I received no guidance from them, from what I can recall and in my own opinion. I remember walking in and finding a fax from Ricky Gervais about my appearance in the pilot episode of his new show, *The Office*. I have no idea to this day if I called or not.

I had met him on *Big Brother's Little Brother* in June 2001, when I had been evicted. I really did not know how to manage anything in this whole new experience and felt too embarrassed to ask anyone. Life does blur in this paperweight of fame as it tips upside down and back around. I still wonder *what if. The Office* could have given me a break to become an actress—the dream I had given up after university when I met Adam. I had no one in the industry to guide me. I was away from my home and my school, and I just thought I would deal with these first few weeks and then see what I could regain and restore. I didn't realise that would take all these years up to 2020.

I was invited by Dermot O'Leary to be a presenter for *Big Brother's Little Brother* in August 2001, and I thought that would be fun to do as I had not seen the first episode of the show, which had been dedicated to me while I had been in the *Big Brother* house. I did finally watch it in 2022 and was upset by the way I was presented. Dermot put on a suit for me when I joined him as a presenter in 2001, as he said I was "a lady." The tabloids were still full of stories about me: "No, Atomic Kitten hasn't changed their line up but is promoting a special anti-cancer T-shirt with *Big Brother* Penny."

Another story read, "Oh no, the *Big Brother* loiterers are back. Penny is already working the celebrity circuit. She has been a presenter of C4's *Big Breakfast* every day this week. She will join Lesley Joseph, Jane Agutter, and Lisa Riley to give out charity awards at the Intercontinental Hotel next week. Last year's *Big Brother* contestants littered showbiz parties until they got so naff, they were banned from them."

It is hard to explain how difficult it was. No one knew what to do with reality stars in 2001, so you were in limbo between trying to get back to normal and trying to cope with superstardom, which you and most people you met in 2001 found odd. I had to live in that state; it was almost like an out of body experience.

Kindness and support came in the form of Peter and Ted inviting me to live with them. It was Ted who suggested I live with them. They had no idea I had nowhere to go after the Charlotte Street Hotel as Mel and Rika were still in my flat and would be there for the next six months. Knowing them both for so long, and Peter since I was in school, was a huge help. They had graciously agreed to be my family and friends to see me go into the *Big Brother* house and had been called up to the *Big Brother* studio in Bow to be guests on *Big Brother's Little Brother* in May 2001.

The very first *Big Brother's Little Brother* was about to air. If you can imagine, this is again another example of the very beginnings of these sorts of backstage extra bits that all reality TV shows have now. The juicy gossip and the never-before-seen footage. It is so much a part of our lives now, but all the traits of these shows started with *Big Brother*.

Dermot O'Leary began the show by saying there would be behind-the-scenes footage, up-to-date news, breaking news, and people would be ringing in to give their point of view about the BB housemates and "the talking point" of the show, which was me, Penny Ellis! It is still on YouTube. He then jested about me "getting it on in the garden" and asks about Paul and me.

The footage shown, as always, in my opinion, was edited, and even looking at it now, it seems there is absolutely nothing to convey that it was sexual in any way between Paul and me. Peter, who had been invited onto the show, was absolutely brilliant and politely defended me by saying, "When everyone understands her, they will love her. She has always been touchy feely."

He then asked Dermot a question: "Penny had a romp with Brian and hugged him lots; why is that not news?" Dermot didn't answer. The show then gives away a plaster handprint of my hand, with Dermot saying the talking point today is. "Is Penny a pain in the neck or a perfect partner?" The producers and Dermot describe me as being very weepy and having spent most of the day upset in bed. The other news they have from the house is that Narinder had her first poo, and Elizabeth asked Dean if she should eat an apple she put in the bin. They have a cut-out of Stuart's face on a stick and comment on how he has thin lips for kissing.

When calls come in, Peter comes to my defence and says, "Well, who else is going to clean out the chicken poo or do the cooking?" Peter goes on to say that he has been quite worried and unsettled about various stories that have been in the papers and on the front pages. Both Peter and Ted were worried and upset and aired their views about the relentless stories.

There was a part in *Big Brother's Little Brother* for the Stat Monkey with his facts. It is eerie that all three facts about me were correct. Absolutely every personal detail of my life was peeled like an orange in various stories and to varying degrees and was mixed with outrageous suggestions and outright lies that have brought my very character, dignity, freedom of speech, and rights as a free person into disrepute, which is not only shocking but also, in my opinion, completely cruel. Mr Statman talked about my O-level home economics and about my first kiss with the boy at the YMCA who I saw *On Golden Pond* with, and yes, I did fart really loudly in my church when I was about eleven years old. It was a Brethren church, a quiet place of worship. I had taken my doll, Naomi, who I had gotten for Christmas, along. She is about three feet tall. It's funny what you can remember. How did they know these things about me?

The calls into the show varied between people absolutely loving me and absolutely thinking I was domineering. Peter sat through the show and really fought my corner. He ended the show by saying, "You are misunderstanding the direction she is coming from." Ironically, there is a clip of an interview before going in the house that was done at one of those secret location auditions, where I am saying that I really don't like people with too much ego and that people like that upset me.

True friends like Peter and Ted voiced their concerns, but the towel drop seemed too big to be defeated. Not one of my true friends sold a story on me. But as I said already, stories were written anyway. No one talked to me to help clear my name and help me regain my life and my identity. I felt too ashamed to ask anyone and certainly didn't know who I should ask anyway.

In one article was a lovely photo of Faye from Steps and her quote,

"My favourite is Bubble, but I quite like Penny; she is barking mad." I went to live with Peter and Ted, and Peter said to Gary (Clap Clap) in Rupert Street Bar, "She turned our world upside down."

It was fate that I met Gary on a night I was out with Brian Dowling. I call him Gary (Clap Clap), as he is absolutely fabulous with a sparkling personality and has such beautiful joy. He makes you feel happy and excited all at once; he is one of those people who sing on ordinary days. From day one of being out of the *Big Brother* house, there was recognition from absolutely every single person and massive hysteria. Gary said, "*Big Brother* 2 (2001) was the most watched out of all the *Big Brother*s. Over thirteen million saw the eviction night."

Having lived as a reality star, a whole new concept inside people's TV sets, I now had to find out how to live outside of it. You can't just step back into how life was, as absolutely everyone is talking about you. This fame is a gloss; it does sparkle, and I am moving into the part of the book where I tell you about the events and people I got to know and be involved with. Really adventurous and beautiful opportunities and famously talented people crossed my path for nearly two years. Like glossy nail varnish, it was intoxicating, lavish, sophisticated, and glamorous. But I didn't know how to find a way to belong to this life of fame. Like nail vanish, the chips soon start to show. I didn't have any management to help me make the most of contacts, possible jobs, or even how to manage the media.

I had some amazing moments that year, and I was able to share them with my best friends, especially Peter and Ted. I remember Peter taking me on the tube for the first time a few months later. It felt so odd, like I was coming back from outer space. The most ordinary actions are completely out of reach and are unattainable when you have a level of fame, like going on the tube, going shopping, or going to the supermarket. Everything you do—your bad hair day, who you're sitting next to for coffee, what you're wearing—is all lived in the spotlight, written about, and talked about.

I did walk on the moon of fame and came back down to earth with a bump. My walk on the moon started the day I came out of the *Big Brother* house; I was misplaced from my home, my school, and every part of my life that I had taken for granted just fifteen days before.

Those first few days were back-to-back with radio interviews. I didn't see anyone I knew or talk to anyone on my phone. I was again surrounded by people I didn't know. I felt really lost. I was completely isolated from everything that had been my normal. If I had gone home to my flat, sat down with my friend, and talked it all through, I might have given myself a better chance to focus and sort myself out. I didn't do anything, just got caught up in the current and let it take me wherever it wanted. I didn't know what to do and had no plan.

On 13 June, I was invited to the glittery launch of *Eclipse,* a circus musical that opened at Blackpool's Globe Theatre, at Blackpool Pleasure Beach. It had a stunning array of acts performing, including ballet, trapeze acts, and an aerialist who flew at alarming speed through the air dressed in just a highly decorated thong. Donna agreed to come with me. She and Steve lived and worked up the road from my flat and ran a dry cleaners'. They are beautiful people. It was a little overwhelming for both of us, so I was glad she was there to enjoy it as well. Steve rang her lot to see she was OK. They have one of the most wonderful relationships I have ever witnessed. I have lost touch with them over the years, but they were a huge support and so encouraging and kind to me, especially when they redecorated my living room when I had to sell my flat because Mel had gone but left the living room painted blue. They were there for me at the end of my meltdown in the autumn of 2002, and I hear about them from Paul, who is still close to them (the one who helped me get my teaching certificate back).

Anyway, Donna and I went together and had VIP treatment—champagne and a five-course meal—sat with the stars of the show, had a chauffeur driven car, and danced the night away at the after-show and buffet at The Paradise Room. Our accommodation was beautiful. We had breakfast and compliments in our rooms. There was also a VIP champagne reception before the show. When we stepped out of our chauffeur driven car, we walked up the red carpet, met by hundreds of photographers.

I was invited to so many events like this and was pleased to attend. However, I didn't ask for any money, and it never crossed my mind that they should pay me. I now realise that celebrities do get paid for their appearance at an event as it is publicity for that event. I didn't realise that in 2001 and must have missed out on thousands of pounds as everybody was inviting me to the most prestigious events that year.

For a few months, I was one of the people in the celebrity circle who was considered hot property. Like with all fame, you may start as an A celebrity, but without planning or management, I was walking a road to the Z celebrity list. I had no clue how to manage me as this new reality star. I was the featured celebrity at this event. I took the train up with Donna from London. In 2001, there was a column in most magazines that would say who they had seen that week. Most weeks, they would have news of me being spotted doing something or with someone. That particular week I had been "spotted getting a train to Preston and sitting in economy class."

The number of random stories and snippets on me in magazines in 2001 is unbelievable. In one magazine, I was even in the crossword! On everyone's chair at the Blackpool event was a copy of *OK!* Magazine, the edition coming out with my *Big Brother* exclusive interview in it. It was weird to see my name and face on every chair. There were hundreds of copies of the magazine all over the room, and it was funny as some people just sat down on the magazine. I guess it was comfy, like an extra cushion!

I remember being embarrassed and overwhelmed when I saw myself on the front cover wearing knickers and a tiny vest top. Everyone was really nice to us. I had no idea who a lot of them were, but there were stars from the stage and also from the soaps on TV. I had a photo with Louis Emerick that appeared in another edition of *OK!* Magazine. In an article written by a local paper, it reads, "Penny drops in." It goes on to say, "Evicted Penny was relieved to find somewhere that finally welcomed her with open arms. She has been turned away from her church, and her teaching job is on the line. Her behaviour at the event was nothing like as outrageous as her short stay on *Big Brother*, where she said she was willing to have live sex on TV to win the top prize. She also admitted to dating a string of men over the age of sixty."

Do these journalists not realise the impact of the things they write on that person's mental health?

The next day, Blackpool Pleasure Beach was deliberately closed for us all to go on the rides. I had a head of PR from the event as my tour guide. Steps, the band, were there too on the rides, from what I can remember. I don't remember talking to them. But it was enormous fun and very amazing to have the whole park to ourselves. There was a new ride that took you through four sensations. All I remember is the ice one, in which I nearly froze, followed by fire, from which I emerged slightly singed. I wonder if that was the first time that ride had been used.

On 20 June, I abseiled down Beaufort House (in the City of London) for Barnardo's. I was really pleased to be doing something for charity. The photos appeared over two pages in *Heat* magazine with the headline, "What on earth is Penny up to now?" It was a good idea, but you had to willingly jump off the building for the abseil to work. Throw yourself back horizontally. I nearly fainted. I was about eight hundred feet in the air!

The cameramen wanted a photo of me and kept shouting at me to hold my position as they dangled themselves off the roof with their hefty cameras, desperate to get the photo they could sell to a magazine. I was hanging vertically off this huge building, waiting for them to get a photo they liked, for about five minutes, and had to let go with one hand to wave for them. Finally, I started to walk down the building. I just kept focusing on the slabs, which looked like huge tiles, and counted them down one by one.

It was the Great City Abseil and loads of celebrities got involved. There was Paul Danan from *Hollyoaks*, and it was the first time that I would meet Craig, the *Big Brother* winner of 2000. One hundred and eighty people paid to scale down the building, raising £50,000. In the *Heat* article, it reads: "Penny, who is desperate for stardom threw herself off a building on London's Aldgate and abseiled down it for charity. As Penny herself would say, 'bless.'"

It would have been nice to get some advice as to how to handle this experience, but I didn't get to talk to Craig. Over the years, it would have probably helped a lot of contestants if someone (another contestant) had spoken to them about what to really expect, having walked in these unique shoes before. Maybe my book will help those who have no one to talk to and have come out of a reality show. I had no one in the industry to help me know what to really do, so my whole life fell apart. If my story helps someone not do what I did, then that would make me very happy.

The following day, 21 June, was extremely busy. I received a marketing brief outlining my day. I was to open Dixon's new Marble Arch Store; it was their redesigned flagship store. They had organised huge press coverage, and BT Cellnet was sponsoring the event. BT Cellnet was the sponsor for *Big Brother*, so they wanted a *Big Brother* theme. The flies were in the advert when *Big Brother* aired each night. I was accompanied by the fruit fly. We were on the top deck of an open top London bus being driven down Oxford Street, which had been closed for half an hour as the bus drove down. People were cheering and clapping, and I was standing up on the top deck with the fruit fly, waving.

There was a huge crowd when we got to the store, and again, so many tabloids. The surge of people moving towards you with cameras or autograph books is something really hard to describe. The moment I stepped off the bus, there were about a hundred people or more pushing towards me. I enjoyed meeting the staff, asked them for a dust cloth, and started cleaning the glass cabinet inside the new store. I wasn't allowed to give press interviews, as *OK!* magazine had told BT Cellnet too, but I was asked if I would sign autographs and talk to people about my time in the *Big Brother* house.

I was also to sign any voucher packs bought in the store and send a text to a customer's friend of their choice when they purchased a phone. I was asked to cut the ribbon of the new Dixons store in Oxford Street and declare it open. I then had a photo shoot with the flies that were on the BT Cellnet advert that sponsored the *Big Brother* show. I hadn't watched a single episode back, so was quite bemused by Peter recognizing them. I just thought they looked quite cute. I really had no idea who they were. I got a BT cell net T-shirt and a phone, which must have been the top-of-the-line phone in 2001, but I only used it for calls like my old one. I had two phones for ages, which was a bit ridiculous as I didn't even use my phone much.

That evening I put on a lovely long gold dress and was collected by Mercedes and taken to the Charity Awards at the Intercontinental Hotel. The car would drive me back at any time I wanted that evening and would wait for me. It was like living like a film star. I was a celebrity guest and presenter, and I was to say a few lines when the award for the disability category was given out. There was a beautiful five course meal. My co-presenter, Craig, the *Big Brother* 2000 winner, and I were to go on stage together. I was to read out the nominations, and Craig would open the gold envelope and call out the winner. The sponsor of that category, who was Barclays Bank, would hand the winner a trophy, and then we all had to have a formal photo taken in the ballroom. However, for whatever reason, Craig didn't want to give the award away with me. I still had a great night, as I met the late Barry Cryer and had such a laugh with him. It was the second time I had met Craig, and the first time I was to meet and chat with Vanessa Feltz. When I arrived, I was escorted to the Byron Room for VIP guests, where there were several TV and press representatives circulating with an interest in me and offers that I couldn't accept due to my agreement with *OK!* Magazine.

I was really moved to read an article in the Courier (a local newspaper in Tunbridge Wells) that morning over breakfast. Tunbridge Wells was where I had grown up during my teenage years. In the article, Damian, my best friend at the time, said, "She was always a lively girl; we were only talking about her the other day; I wasn't surprised to see her on TV." I will always remember when I locked Damian in a cupboard by accident when we played tricks on our German teacher when we were thirteen years old. He hid in the cupboard, but I hadn't realised the door had locked when I shut it on him. He had, I think, the biggest panic attack, and the cupboard fell over, and I think he broke his nose. We remained close friends until I enrolled in Tunbridge Wells Girls Grammar School for my A levels.

Liz Sharp, a teacher, was very perceptive, as she said in the same article: "She was a lovely girl from an exceptional group of pupils. I am quite disturbed by what is being said."

My hopes to present a beautiful, sophisticated image of myself to the world during this brief window of fame were, in my opinion, well and truly tarnished.

I had another 'down memory lane' experience when I was invited to Soho Theatre to see *School Play* on 28 June. The play was part of the Soho writer's attachment programme. There was a post-performance discussion with the playwright after the show. Ironically, she would be talking about how the writer's programme gave her the tools and confidence to shape some crazy ideas into a story without feeling too shy about it. There was a VIP seat in the second row reserved for me. The seat next to me was spare, and I didn't think anything of it. Then the play commenced, it was a one-hander, and the actress had been one of my best friends when I was at Royal Holloway and Bedford New College London University in the 1990s. I had not seen her for at least ten years. I stared in surprise and then recalled how once on a night out in a pub she had left her whole wage packet behind by accident and lost the lot. We joked once that when we had hardly any money, the only thing we could treat ourselves to would be a new pair of knickers each month. That was our spending treat. The next thing I know, she is mid flow reciting a massive monologue that takes her off stage into the audience, and at the most dramatic bit, she sits in the seat next to me, a spotlight shining on her, and she faces the member of the audience (me) with the most dramatic climactic build-up of her scene. For what seemed like an eternity, our faces locked. I frantically willed her on not to forget her lines. She was as surprised as I was to see it was me. Thank goodness she carried on like the professional actress she was. I bought her a drink afterwards.

On 30 June 2001, it was Mardi Gras, and I was invited to host it with

Graham Norton and Lorraine Kelly. This was the week Ken Livingstone announced that London would allow gay partnerships. That was the day Peter took me on the tube for the first time, I think. I was absolutely terrified, as I had received so much attention from people on the street. I was stopped every few seconds by someone wanting to talk to me, hug me, or sign an autograph. We found quite an empty carriage, and I wore my sunglasses and wrapped a scarf around my head.

We met up with Tim, a theatre producer I became best friends with until I left London in 2002. I went to so many theatre productions with him over those two years and met the most famous theatre actors and directors. The tube got absolutely rammed as we neared the stop near Finsbury Park. It was such a weird experience, in disguise and in the middle of all these wonderful people who were in such a party spirit. We had to find the entrance for the artists who were performing. The whole backstage area was huge, and it was fun to see everyone backstage just sitting around or in groups chatting. Wherever you looked, there was a famous band. I couldn't believe how many famous people were there. I wish I had talked more with them, as everyone knew who I was and wanted to talk to me. Atomic Kitten, Hear Say, Mel B, Sugar Babes, Vanessa Mae, Lisa Stansfield, The Human League.

I found a quiet area backstage to sit down, but that didn't stop the massive surge of famous people coming towards me. One of the magazines did an article that read, and I quote, "Lucky Penny is still star of the show." It went on to say, "Surprisingly, the biggest stir of the day was caused by the arrival of Penny Ellis, the somewhat fraught and unstable teacher from *Big Brother*. Ignoring politicians and celebrities, it was Penny the crowd and photographers descended on as she walked into the VIP enclosure. Even those who ought to be beyond succumbing to the lure of instant 'fame fucking' rushed forward. First to want their picture taken with the initial person to be chucked out of the house was Jeremy Joseph of G.A.Y. and camp comic Graham Norton."

There is a photo of us at the top of the article. I couldn't believe the language this journalist used. The article continued: "Mr. Norton reassured us afterwards that Penny didn't appear to be quite as insane as she had appeared on TV and meeting her was a memorable experience." The article ends with "Oh dear, she did go bonkers on TV."

I was ushered up onto the main stage to introduce Steps for their performance. I must say a big sorry to them for what happened next. I could not have predicted it. I expected to simply say, "Here are Steps," as I walked onto the stage in front of eighty-five thousand people, but the crowd went crazy. I mean, they cheered, chanted "Penny," and clapped, and then, from my recollection of events, started a massive Mexican type of movement and chant of "in the kitchen, out the kitchen." This went on and on, I think, for about twenty minutes. Steps were waiting on the stage's side. No one could get it under control. I looked at Graham Norton. He looked at me. Oh, it was phenomenal. I was so embarrassed. I tried to get the crowd to stop cheering me by waving my pink boa, which I had worn for the day, like I was waving them goodbye. That just got the crowd all excited again. In the end, I just exited quickly, and Steps got on stage.

Looking back, I can see how new this reality star concept was. No one was prepared for it, and especially for talented and hard-working artists who had learned their skills, had talent, and had worked hard for real fame, I think it was difficult for them to accept. Nowadays, it all blends together; reality stars have respect and followers just like famous actors and musicians; all are friends on the same level.

But in 2001, in my opinion and experience, it was, "Who do you think you are?" We were outsiders and seen as slightly desperate and ridiculous. I have experienced what it was like to be on the cusp of a new frontier as one of the first of a new type of star – the reality star, to venture into the celebrity world. It was unknown and completely unrecognised in 2001. It was not normal or even a part of normal at the time. Can you imagine my state of mind in 2001?

Some very influential people did come alongside me from the theatre, music, and art worlds; once some of them met me, they genuinely liked me, and we became good friends for a while.

I will start with the musicians I met and knew for more than a year, while I was at all sorts of events and still living in London. Duncan from Blue was one of them and was very kind. Their first debut single, *All Rise*, reached number four in May 2001, and by August they had a number one with *Too Close*. We went to a theatre production at Soho Theatre and had to walk on opposite sides of the road so the paparazzi couldn't get a picture of us together.

I also met Atomic Kitten, who sang *Whole Again* and their new single *Eternal Flame* at Mardi Gras. I would work with them in Liverpool in December. I met them both again at Party in the Park, which was held by *Capital Radio* on 8 June. It was a very exciting time for both bands, as their careers took off in 2001. It was special to be a very small part of watching that happen. I also met Emma Bunton, who was at the start of her solo career and performed at Party in the Park.

I was invited to various music events at the private clubs through meeting people at different events, so I would naturally bump into the same people. There was a club called Pop, and I remember sitting with Liza Minelli and Westlife. I got along very well with Liza Minelli, but Westlife didn't talk to me, and it was quite a small VIP area. All these talented people with amazing careers made me feel uncomfortable, like I didn't belong. I vaguely remember going to Soho House and Eyelash. There were footballers from the FA Cup final who caused a stir. I would briefly talk and say hello to people I recognised, like Liberty X and the dancers who were rehearsing for Kylie Minogue.

I did an event with Brian, Narinder, and Ama at G.A.Y., hosted by Jeremy Joseph. That night, the crowd went absolutely crazy and hysterical. The intense fame that I was experiencing all day, every day, not just at events but in every waking hour of my day, was incredible.

I enjoyed having a chat with so many of the up-and-coming bands of 2001. I didn't try to be friends with anyone, but I was myself and acted as normal, and if it was an interesting chat then it was worth it. Everyone really liked me. People would come up to me; I found it a bit strange that they knew who I was. I watched Boy George in *Taboo*, and then we all traipsed off to Roadhouse and had a chat for a while as he was the DJ. That was the only time I got a bit flustered and star struck, as me and my mum loved Boy George in the 80s. I was like a giggly schoolgirl, so excited to meet him. I think he just looked at me and might have thought, "Yes, she is as mad as the papers say she is." I couldn't believe even Boy George knew who I was.

I became friends with Jools Holland and his band for over a year. They were wonderful gentlemen, and we went out to quite a few things. I have a photo of me and Dave from the band with Narinder and her husband, whom she said she would never let me meet when we were in the house because I would eat him alive. Of course, she was joking. Peter and Ted were there too, having a meal together.

I did meet up with Narinder and Brian quite a lot, and I wish I had asked them for advice. I don't know why I didn't. I have a lovely memory of watching Jools Holland and his band at the Royal Albert Hall. After the show, I waited at the edge of the stage and thought, *should I just go home?* With that, Jools Holland reached out his hand and hoisted me up on stage, said hello, and introduced me to the band. It was a magical moment and a fantastic evening getting to know them all. I was glad of their friendship during that year. I want to thank him and the band. It is ironic as that was where I had my graduation ceremony from London University. I got given my degree on that stage by Princess Anne; it's funny how things go full circle sometimes.

I got a job presenting a Saturday morning show on Liberty Radio, which would include a section of me talking about various famous people I had met during the week. It was about a five-minute walk from Sarah Bonnell School. I hoped that this would ground me and allow me to pursue a new career as a radio host. I had been on Capital, Heart, and Virgin Radio for chats and enjoyed being behind the scenes in a radio studio. I would be invited to all sorts of music events in London, especially talent shows held at the Roadhouse or other London venues. I became a good friend of a guy that worked closely with Steps, and he had contacts, so I would go to music events with him. I really enjoyed actively searching out bands and having them play live on my radio show, giving them a chance to be heard. I worked hard at making that show fun and insightful.

I invited people I had met who were building a career in music or theatre for an interview. There was always a snippet of a super famous person I had met that week. We had a true or false game and a Remote Rage section where we asked viewers what annoyed them. It was very interactive, with a lot of phone-ins. When it ended in February 2002, I asked for the tapes of all my shows. I had to ask several times before being told they were lost. Again, I really did not know what to do, so I just walked away. My friend Dale had recorded some of my shows and made up a demo CD for me, but I never went around the radio stations asking for a job or asked any of the famous people I met for any advice.

I went back to Tunbridge Wells and did an interview for BBC Kent as they were launching BBC Kent Online, a new website. Seeing that I had grown up in Kent, they asked if I would help. They sent me a lovely letter thanking me and telling me to see the page on BBC.co.uk/ Kent. I didn't look at it as I didn't own a computer.

I was glad to do more charity work, and on 2 July, I agreed to launch the healthy eating programme Take five a Day for Tesco at Cabot Square, Canary Wharf, organised by the Imperial Cancer Research Fund. Again, I just enjoyed meeting people and having a bit of a laugh with the staff. I have no idea why I decided to hold two massive honeydew melons up by my chest. I honestly didn't think about the implications, and most people will either do something unusual for charity or take the mick out of themselves. I think they all saw it as fun, and it was all over the front page, but just in the local Canary Wharf papers. The headline reads: "Oh Brother, Penny gets fruity." It goes on to say: "Juggling a pair of melons, the 33-year-old teacher played it safe and kept her clothes on this time as she kicked off the month-long national campaign aimed at encouraging people to eat more fruit and vegetables. 'I always found her quite annoying,' said one Tesco shopper, 'but she seemed like quite good fun when she turned up here.'"

They sent me a lovely letter afterwards. It read: "Dear Penny. We would like to thank you for kicking off the joint Imperial Cancer Fund and Tesco Take Five a Day campaign. Not only were you a pleasure to work with, but your professionalism and vivacious personality has provided some great photos. As you can see, *The Daily Star* loved you! On behalf of Tesco, we would like to thank you for your support in helping educate Tesco customers to eat healthier. This is a lifesaving cause. We wish you all the best in looking for an agent and future work."

I did another launch that week, for The Sanctuary in Covent Garden. I launched Sanctuary for Your Wellbeing with Jayne Midlemiss, who went on to be the winner of *Love Island* in 2005. I had an event almost every day and was just going along with whatever anyone asked. It wasn't a well-planned strategy but rather a massive whirlwind. I went to Pinewood Studios that week to be a guest on a life panel, and I also went to Capital Radio's Party in the Park. Craig David was there, as were Destiny's Child, Emma Bunton, Gerri Halliwell, Jamiroquai, Nelly Furtado, Ronan Keating, Ricky Martin, and Tom Jones. That's where I saw Danielle Westbrook sitting on the grass while one magazine editor told me, "The money you are making must be life changing." I wasn't making any money.

On 11 July, BT Cellnet invited me on a private yacht down the Thames and to tea at the Ritz. That was wonderful because it was something I had always wanted to do but had never been able to afford. I also had a Mercedes chauffeur me up to The Royal Shakespeare Company in Stratford to watch a theatre play.

The next day, I was back at Soho Theatre judging the Play Stars showcase for the under-11 playwrights. It was great to be back in the theatre, and it was such a superb outpouring of talent. The plays that had been written were really exceptional. One was called "David

Beckham's Birthday Party." Others included "Inside a tomato" and "Only so much you can take." I got such a lovely letter of thanks from the producer's assistant at Soho Theatre thanking me for presenting the awards and saying the children were so very excited to meet me. He invited me to another show of an American artist who was flying over and performing at Soho Theatre, with the idea of working with me to do a benefit show for the Terrence Higgins Trust. He gave me loads of contact numbers and had spoken with the American producer about the idea. I don't know why I didn't follow up on that. Writing about things now, I will probably keep saying this.

I had about four massive boxes of contact phone numbers from all sorts of people who probably wanted to help me or work with me. I never rang them. I just bounced from one event to the next.

The following day, 13 July, I appeared on *The Weakest Link*. I was chauffeured to Shepherd's Bush Pinewood Studios in a black Mercedes. The show was going to be called a Reality Television Special: The Weakest Link. I met a few contestants, as there were only a handful of us in those days from *Big Brother* 1 and 2. I was terrified of having to speak to Anne Robinson while standing on this small platform like a lectern. I got so confused by the first question, which was something like, "What two things do you wear to bed?" And I mumbled something. It was really embarrassing as the actual answer was pyjamas. I just felt so stupid, and I was out of the game first, just like in the *Big Brother* house! *The Weakest Link* green room had the nicest drinks and food; it's funny what you remember. We all sat in there, chatting away and getting to know each other. I honestly cannot remember who on earth was on that show with me, except that I remember Nick Bateman winning it.

I remember having lunch with the late Norman Wisdom, which was phenomenal. What a fabulous star. He knew me and was so happy to meet me. It is so strange that people who are so iconic actually know you when you meet them. I couldn't really get my head around that. Today, it is easy to know who you are in the context of your social media persona, but in 2001, I struggled a lot with the world I had landed in after fifteen days of being in *Big Brother*. I didn't have the vocabulary or mindset to deal with what was happening to me and around me. I had no one to manage me and was offered so much work just by meeting famous people at different events who seemed to really like me.

A really incredible and huge experience in July included my

Royal Shakespeare Company interview in Stratford on 22 July. It was a massive sell-out, bigger than An Audience with Alan Ayckbourn, whose plays I studied at London University. I couldn't believe the crowds. I had lunch at the theatre and then gave an interview to Radio WM. I had to meet with the newspapers and have photos and interviews published in *The Sunday Mercury*, *Birmingham Evening Mail*, and *The Stratford Journal*.

They had to move my interview to a larger venue in one of the other theatres because so many people wanted to hear what I said. All I could see was a sea of faces; there wasn't even standing room left. Nina Nanar interviewed me for nearly two hours, and it was extended as people wanted to stay and hear more. I answered questions and sat there just thinking, *blimey, I'm finally at the Royal Shakespeare Company*, a dream taken from me in the 1990s by Adam. I got driven up there by another well-known theatre director whose name I have completely forgotten but who was a friend for about a year. He gave me a *Big Brother* cup for my birthday in 2001, which I still have. On the way back, Tristan called. I couldn't believe it, as he had sold that story to the tabloids: "Penny tap danced naked when I came home from work." I just answered the phone and told him to fuck off. The following day, I returned to *Big Breakfast*.

Big Brother 2 ended on 27 July 2001. It was an incredible evening. We all sat watching the final outside the *Big Brother* house, along with the hundreds of people who had made the effort to come and share the moment. It was a bigger stage area, and everything was bigger than what I remember from my eviction. There was a circular stage now, and the contestants came down the steps onto that circular stage.

I had a massive walk across loads of steel flooring and a bridge before I even met Peter or Davina, which took me over five minutes. It was much slicker and more impactful now, as well as more immediate, which is ideal for television. Brian stood in the centre of that stage as he came out of the *Big Brother* house as the winner, and I was so happy for him. I have personal photos I took of him with his arms in the air, cheering his victory. It was an incredible evening. I don't remember talking to the other housemates. We all had a drink in a room when the show was over, but it wasn't an amazing reunion for me.

The Wrap Party was on 30 July at Red Cube in Leicester Square. I still have the ticket; it has the *Big Brother* Eye as the background and is numbered 248. The card reads: "Day 67 Task: 30th July 2001. Part 1: 8 p.m. 500 people are nominated for eviction from *Big Brother*.

Part 2: 8:01 Red Cube, Leicester Square, *Big Brother* sets the group a task. They must enjoy themselves for six hours making use of the equipment provided—drinks, food, a DJ, and a dancefloor. Expert Opinion: 'It is likely that a large part of the weekly shopping budget will be lost on taxis home.' Part 3: 2 a.m.; the group pass the task and are rewarded with immediate eviction from *Big Brother*."

It was a wonderful evening. I do remember trying to leave with Brian and some of the others. There were so many tabloid press outside, and we all sat on the stairs of the nightclub, wondering how we were going to get past them. It was like listening to a hornets' nest outside, with the buzz of hundreds of cameramen and journalists waiting for us outside. We sat there for ages before we braced ourselves and went through the Red Cube doors to masses of flashing bulbs and shouts and cheers. It was a "take a deep breath" moment. The constant hysteria in the press and among the excited people we met on the street was overwhelming. When it happened in schools between 2003 and 2020, it was bittersweet, as by then I had lost everything and was at the mercy of those that wanted to judge, ridicule, and bully me.

I did not see any of them again until 9 August, for the launch of *The Official Big Brother 2 Book* by Jean Ritchie. There was a massive photo in *The Sun* the following day; I'm at the back, standing in a pink leather jacket, in between Bubble and Elizabeth. Brian is sitting on the red sofa in front with Helen, and Paul is on the other side with Narinder on his knee. Again, no one shared their experiences, who they might have had contacts with, or how they were coping. I wish so much we had helped each other through those months. The title underneath read: "Reunited – stars of the show." We look like one big happy family holding our own copy of the book. I managed to get my copy signed by most of the housemates. We had to go to the Chanel 4 headquarters. I had received a letter from Endemol. It read: "Dear Penny, I am writing to you regarding the book promotions. A car will pick you up to go to Channel 4's headquarters, Horseferry Road, in London. The launch will be from 3:30–8 p.m., So, put 1:30–9:30 in your diary to allow for travelling time. I will ring you to confirm an exact pick-up time. We will start with a private book signing for competition winners and, at 5:30, a press conference. From 6:15, there will be drinks with key personnel from Channel 4, Endemol, Channel 4 Books, and some competition winners." I wish I had asked for help and asked for advice. I wish I had taken advantage of every opportunity I had to get help with my life, which was unravelling mentally and financially.

There was just such massive hysteria again, and it was quite terrifying when I had to fly to Ireland with Brian on 21 August to do the book signing in Dublin in all the major stores, just the two of us. All the other contestants were paired up to do their book signings together. I am not sure who the others paired up with or where the other book signings happened. The letter had included that information, along with dates and times when the car would collect me and take me to the airport to fly to Dublin. The stores were absolutely swamped, and there was a sea of people flooding the streets. All around us were the police and loads of bodyguards; we could hardly move because everyone was grabbing at us and screaming so loudly. There were cameras and TV vans, and all the media had come out. Other than Mardi Gras, this had to be the second most phenomenal outpouring of love; an experience that really was like the Beatle Hysteria I have seen in the black-and-white footage of the Beatles when they got off the plane.

I appeared on the TV show Kilroy before travelling to Dublin. I was also out at different music events with some of the members of the Jools Holland Band. We watched Marc Almond at a club. I was trying to help some of the bands I had interviewed on my Liberty radio show by getting them a slot to play at certain venues. There was a BT Cellnet party full of celebrities, and I went to a private film viewing and met actors like Rufus Sewell. It was just something every single day.

I had been invited to Emma Bunton's birthday party on 14 August. Getty Images has a photo of me that possibly went into the tabloids and possibly *Cosmopolitan*. I am dressed in a black and white top and skirt, with bunches in my hair. I think it was fancy dress, as I look like a schoolgirl. I had a black sequin tie on, but I lost that along the way. I probably chucked it in the black bags I took to the charity shop in Islington in the autumn of 2002. I was followed by cameramen and hounded by them whenever I went anywhere or came out of an event—a swarm of clicks, flashes, and shouting. It was so intense, and I didn't know how to handle it. I could have talked to them and become friends with a few of them. I watched a programme about the late Jade Goody, and she had befriended a cameraman, who then, from what I can understand, gave her the right press coverage. I had no clue how to manage the media of the day, use it to my advantage, or get them on my side. I walked in, and I saw Emma Bunton in a huge red velvet hat sitting with all the Spice Girls, and she screamed excitedly, "Penny!" She is a lovely, sweet lady.

Blue were there, so I caught up with Duncan again. Michael came along too, who had taken me under his wing. He was the editor of *Closer* magazine. As I've previously said, we frequented the Shadow Lounge together, a private club, and it was there that I met the famous and prestigious people in the entertainment industry. I was friends with him until 2003. I'll always remember Vanessa Feltz, me, and Michael having a lovely meal out at the Bluebird restaurant on Kings Road in Chelsea. I also remember walking in the dusk of the day, and it was still and peaceful and quiet, just bird sounds and our voices chatting about all sorts. That was one of the only times where there were no cameramen, and it felt like I was doing something normal: just meeting up with two friends.

Ironically, I got my pantomime contract through on 9 August, but really, it was my life that was becoming one big spectacle. I got the panto because I met Lee, who worked at Mount View Theatre School, at a theatre event. He got me an audition, and the next thing I knew, I was to be in *Jack and the Beanstalk* in Liverpool in December. We were very good friends for a long time. I got my eyebrows tattooed for charity, and I had my belly button pierced for charity with him. Those are memories I can remember having with him, as well as going to lots of theatre events. I remember going along to Mount View Theatre School and filling envelopes just before I left London.

At that point, I was a complete mess. I was invited to several of the third-year musical showcases held at the Criterion Theatre in 2001. Seeing such amazing talent and young people at the start of a beautiful career in theatre made me feel happy for them, but also really sad, as I knew I was unravelling and making a mess of my life, but I didn't know how to stop it. That feeling was terrifying; I felt it for years. It is like when you pull at a thread and then the whole piece of material falls apart. You can't stop it once that thread is pulled.

I remember being a judge for Collins Performing Arts Limited. It was their summer school talent competition grand finale at Thame Side Theatre in Grays. I got an invite and it read: "You are invited to a VIP pre show buffet in Thame Side two on the third floor from 6:45. Please find your complimentary pass." It was a letter from the head of the school; that meant a lot to me. I was embraced and loved just like I was a movie star amongst all these talented thespians. I do love theatre people, and they brought out my sparkle. That was a lovely experience. I went to meet Rochelle Wiseman, a special guest who was on the adjudication panel with Billy Smith, Lee Ryan's personnel manager. I was listed second, and under my name it said: "professional actress, as seen on *Big Brother 2*." Lee got me into a pantomime again in 2004. After that, in 2005, I believe the friendship simply vanished as I entered a terrible abusive relationship, and no one heard from me for more than a year. Some people are meant to be in your lives for a season, or we lose them due to making the wrong choices. Ironically, I had auditioned for Mount View Theatre School when I was with Adam and didn't get in in 1990.

Life was chaotic in the 1990s, and I was experiencing the same level of chaos again in 2001. I would go through the same chaos and horrible stresses right up to 2020. I don't know why it takes so long to break cycles of self-destructiveness. I think by 2020 I was at last ready to surrender the whole of me to God and trust that he could change me, which he did. That surrender was the hardest thing I had ever done.

On 23 August, I was invited to the premiere of *A Knight's Tale* in Leicester Square. Walking down the red carpet, I was absolutely swamped by the paparazzi again. All these famous people were walking past me, looking at the attention I was getting. The press just kept me posing for ages, snapping away. Loads of super famous people walked past, and yet the press couldn't get enough of me. It was so bizarre. I had to sign autographs on the way in, and it was lovely to chat with people. Some had waited for so long to see me. I couldn't believe they would wait for me.

It was at the after-film drinks at Century I had a moment walking up to the roof terrace, and the late and missed Heath Ledger was standing there on his own. I looked at him, and he looked at me for a while. I said, "Great film," and then I went back down the stairs and sat drinking amazing cocktails with Mark Addy from *The Full Monty,* and we chatted for most of the night; he was a right laugh. I can't remember who else was there, but we were in a club that belonged to Robbie Williams. You do get used to seeing people and forget just how famous they are. If anyone spoke to me, I'd just have a jolly good natter and usually make them laugh. I talked to Hollywood stars, famous musicians, and actors; it was a really lovely time. I kept running into the same people at exclusive clubs like Shadow Lounge. There was another club called Eyelash, and they hosted celebrity parties like Ronnie Wood's fiftieth bash at Cabaret. They would help unsigned bands, which was great for me to meet bands I could get on my Liberty Radio show. I sat with Lulu one night and a host of other famous singers.

My mother said to me when she flew over from Spain in 2001, "The trouble is, Lisa, you came swanning down to Hastings with two phones and full of busy things. You just thought it would never end. Don't regret it, as who gets to have that experience? The only thing I would regret if I were you is not sorting out your money."

She is always so wise and right. What an experience I had! It was like being on a high-speed train, and I didn't know how to work the controls or the brakes.

The month of August ended with a thank you letter from Paul Osbourne, producer on *Big Brother 2*. It reads: "Dear Penny, A big thank you for making *Big Brother 2* such a huge success. It has been a pleasure to watch you and your housemates both during production and in your "new lives" afterwards. I hope that on the whole, you have found *Big Brother* to be a positive experience and that it will bring you opportunities, adventure, and new freedom to explore whatever comes your way. Remember, you can always call me whatever comes up, and that Brett (the counsellor) is available to you should you wish to have a quiet chat with someone who is well versed in the *Big Brother* experience. I hope you continue to work as hard as you have over the past few months to carve out a career for yourself, and I also hope you find someone to support you in that endeavour. Best of luck with Panto this Christmas; I'm sure you will bring the house down (once again). Keep in touch. Paul." He writes underneath in his own handwriting: "Keep going, honey. xx"

There was a laminated card attached with four numbers on it: three for producers and a press hotline number, in case we ever needed to call. I remember getting a letter in January about attending a counselling session. I don't know if I went. It seems to have been 30 January. The letter was again from Paul. I never did call him and say I was not coping. Jeremy, one of the creators of *Big Brother*, rang me personally when I was in pantomime in Liverpool in December 2001 and asked if I was OK. I was shocked to hear from him. I politely said I was OK. In truth, I wasn't, but I was too embarrassed to say that to him. I think he really wanted to help me by calling me directly.

I did see a TV documentary about *Big Brother* in 2020. It was insightful as the photographer who befriended the late Jade Goody said that they would agree to "stage" certain photos. That was something I didn't know you could do and could have really helped me. Paul Osbourne was on the show, and he said that what makes *Big Brother* fun is "tension." An agent called *Big Brother* "the game you have just walked into." Another said the contestants were "perfect fodder for the tabloids." Someone who had been on the show said, "We were thrown to the lions."

On the internet, I discovered an article dated 18 August 2022; it was an interview with Dean from *Big Brother 2*. He said how surprised we all were by how the reality TV genre grew up around us, how our lives and personalities became commodified for entertainment value. It also talks about a company called "Set Welfare," which provided the actual producers with "fitness for inclusion" assessments to help the producers decide who was mentally prepared for the experience and whether that person should go on a reality show.

Dean says, "There is no way anyone sat down with Penny and thought it was a good idea for her to go in front of the nation and bare her soul." I must agree—it was probably never considered a good idea for me, at least.

On 4 September, I flew to Ireland on a private jet, walked down a red carpet flanked by VIPs, and got into a limousine to judge the prestigious Miss Ireland Grand Final. It was absolutely awesome. It was a three-day event and really hard work, but brilliant. I arrived at Shannon airport, came off the plane, and walked across a red carpet to be greeted by dignitaries. They had a limousine, chauffeur driven to my hotel, The South Court hotel and International Conference Centre, waiting for me. I met the Mayor of Limerick at the civic reception, as well as all the Miss Ireland contestants. The competition was for Miss Ireland and Miss Universe.

There was an assembly of guests for a pre-show reception with Boru vodka, and the Miss Ireland Dancers opened the show. The contestants wore knitwear by Caroline Mitchell; beach wear was by Lifestyle Leisurewear; and the evening gown parade was from a designer of their choice. It ended with the crowning of Miss Ireland and a dinner. In the evenings, there were black tie events. On the night of the competition, after the winner was announced, there was the Coronation Ball. I met fashion designers, event organisers, news reporters, and dancers. I even made good friends with the host, Lorcan Murray, and his family, and was invited to his family home for a lovely dinner. They wrote to me when I returned to London, sending me frog cards because they knew I liked frogs, which I did at the time. These were really genuine letters inviting me to come and stay with them; they said they had never met anyone as nice as me. It was a beautiful time, as they were all such good people, and I felt at home and happy with them. I really wish I had kept in touch. I seemed to be hopping from one thing to the next, and I had no idea how to stop myself—just hopping around like a frog!

The *Sun* article that followed read: "Thirty line up for crown. The judges included *Big Brother* star Penny Ellis and former Miss World Diana Hayden. The girls were competing for a place at the glittering Miss World pageant in Sun City, South Africa, and prizes worth £30,000."

I also agreed to be on a panel with Ruth Wrigley for a programme on 29 September called *Making Big Brother Bigger.* She was controller of entertainment at Endemol at the time. I liked the idea as it would mean I could be on the British Film Institute stage. I loved the BFI, and before I was on *Big Brother*, I would go and watch films there. I honestly do not remember what was said, and I wonder now if that was a missed opportunity to get some help regarding all the "towel dropping stories." The letter read: "How do you make a successful TV programme even more successful? Ruth Wrigley, Controller of Entertainment at Endemol Entertainments UK, accepted this challenge. Against the backdrop of a highly competitive TV market, Ruth will talk through how the show was developed, the problems encountered, and how successful or not she was." There was an introduction from a writer and lecturer from the University of Westminster, presentations and VHS video extracts by Ruth, discussions with Josh, Dean, and me, and a Questions and Answers section. After my Liberty Radio show, I was chauffeured to the British Film Institute.

Returning to the influential people I met as well as Michael, the editor of *Closer*, one night at Shadow Lounge, he and I sat and chatted in the VIP area with so many famous people, including the late Cilla Black and the late Dale Winton. No one cared who anyone was, and it was a laid-back fun club where people could be themselves without being on display, networking, or trying to be seen. It became our regular club. I thought Michael was super glamorous, and when he invited me to stay over at his amazing penthouse, I got to sleep in the bed he had bought from Madonna! It was a super stunning bed. I got along so well with him and his partner until our friendship just fizzled out around 2004.

I had a wonderful friend called Tim who was a theatre producer.

We would meet regularly in Soho for a catch up. He was very sweet and very successful. He took me along to all the top shows. We went to see *Peggy Sue Got Married* when it opened in London in August 2001. I went to the after-show party where I got to meet Ruthie Henshall and John Gordon Sinclair, who I had seen in the 1981 film *Gregory's Girl* and had a bit of a schoolgirl crush on in 1981.

I chatted with Christopher Biggins and Su Pollard and said hi to Stefanie Powers, who I used to watch in *Hart to Hart* with my mum and dad. I also saw Cameron Mackintosh and would see him at other theatre shows I went to. I even sat next to him at one of those theatre shows; we must have been in VIP seats as there was Sir Paul McCartney next to him in the same row. I never considered approaching them for advice or an audition at any of these shows. I never asked any of these people for a job. Now that I am finally writing this book, I realise that maybe there were opportunities that I kept missing, if only I had asked.

Tim and I went to see *The Witches of Eastwick* and quite a few opening nights of new shows like *Kiss Me, Kate,* and *Whistle Down the Wind.* We remained firm friends until 2003. It was difficult to maintain contact with such friends after I left London. I wasn't around to go to all the glamorous clubs and parties. I still have a postcard Tim sent me saying, "I miss you." He will always be a treasured friend. It was funny in 2022 when Paul Bedsprings found Tim on Twitter and I added him as a friend. I wonder if he remembers me.

I also became friends with a fantastic musical conductor who worked on the biggest shows. He invited me to the National Theatre, where I sat backstage and saw *South Pacific,* directed by Trevor Nunn, from that vantage point. It was such a surreal experience, as I was sitting behind him as he faced the stage, conducting this massive orchestra. The sounds and experience of watching a production from that area of the stage were so unique. He came along to my birthday bash in Soho in October 2001 at Friendly's, where my birthday was held. I didn't see him again after I left London, but I did see his show when I was in pantomime in Liverpool.

One memorable moment at one of these shows was when the stage manager came up to Dame Maureen Lipman and me and asked us to sign our names in the stage manager's office. It was 30 October 2001, and I was watching *Kiss Me, Kate*. I had gone to see it with Nicky Haslam and Tim. Maureen and I literally skipped off together to sign our names in the stage manager's office. The wall was adorned with large star names from musical theatre stars. We found a gap and scribbled our signatures and had a giggle, then went back to the after-show party. She was so gracious and didn't look at me like, "What are you being asked for?" Such a lovely, talented lady.

I was also dear friends with Nicky Haslam for a time. He is an interior designer and socialite. Before launching her own chain, Cath Kidston worked for him. He wrote a regular column in *The Evening Standard*. I met him at some glamorous event; he was so very sophisticated and took out a super snazzy blank card and signed his name and phone number on it. I had dinner with him, Joan Collins, and the late Cilla Black at The Ivy. He also took me to an art exhibition. We walked in, and Eurythmics, Bob Geldof, Bill Wyman, and Noel Gallagher all looked at me; from my recollection of the event, it seemed that they were all thinking, *what are you doing with her?* Nicky simply stated, "She's with me," and then we all stood there chatting. I do love listening to people and the stories they share. He listed me as one of his friends in the farewell column he wrote for *Metro London*. It read, "Who could fail to be entertained by Nicky's constantly changing coterie of new best friends: the late Dale Winton, Paris Hilton, Penny from *Big Brother*, Chelsea Clinton, and Monica Lewinsky?" I had some lovely evenings with him and took him to see *Kiss Me, Kate*. He is a wonderful person.

I went to see Danny Dyer in his role at the National Theatre's production of *No Man's Land*. He had met me at a different event and asked me to come and see it. I went backstage after to congratulate him. He just looked at me. I think he had forgotten that he had asked me to come along. I was so embarrassed and scuttled off quietly. That was quite funny.

October was my birthday, and this year it was huge. I'd met Gary (Clap Clap) at Rupert Street Bar and Marie, who owned Friendly's, which is under Ann Summers just around the corner from Rupert Street Bar. The Birthday of Penny was essentially organised by these two bars, and with Gary in charge, all the stops were pulled out. He threw himself into it with such passion and style. It felt like my very own Oscars. I got to know Ben, Gary's friend, and still treasure the little statue he gave me for my birthday. He is one of my best friends to this day, and I value him as well as Gary and Ant, who is Gary's partner. I went to their wedding in Islington a few years ago, and it was wonderful to see their joy and to be back in Islington, where I had lived. Gary's style, flair, and organisational skills meant my birthday was the party of the century. He even designed jelly shots for the occasion.

Valerie's, the patisserie in Old Compton Street, made me a birthday cake. It felt like the whole of Soho was celebrating my birthday. I have always loved Old Compton Street and would walk through Soho most days when I would finish at Sarah Bonnell School. It felt like home. My birthday party was glamorous and stylish, and anyone who was anyone was on the guest list. I had producers from *Big Brother,* actors, dancers, theatre people, TV presenters, and people from the music industry. Brian and Narinder were there too, as were my girls from Sarah Bonnell and Mel. The flow of people was amazing, as some would have been on stage in the West End and rushed there once their theatre show ended that evening. All my friends, new and old, mingled and danced until the following day, about 4 a.m. Everyone was made to feel extra happy; it was a beautiful birthday. Peter went around with a massive plastic pineapple and raised money for the Terence Higgins Trust, who had come along to celebrate with us, and I still have the sparkly lava lamp they gave me as a birthday present. I would meet them at Selfridges for another event before going to Liverpool for Pantomime. I was also invited to their traditional 'Ridiculously Early Friends for Life Christmas cocktail party' that they hosted in November. Photos of my birthday were taken and appeared in *Heat* magazine. I had bowls of penny sweets, and Friendly's made a special Penny cocktail.

It was in October that I was approached numerous times by journalists who offered me quite a lot of money if they could get what they called "one tit and two bum shots" of me staggering out of a club or car, revealing one or the other. I said no. Stories were still being written about me, and I really could have still made a lot of money selling my story. I went on *The Ruby Wax Show,* and I remember feeling really uncomfortable with the questions. The late Clive James, who was sitting next to me, suddenly started saying how wonderful I was. I felt so relieved to be defended by him. It felt like a ray of hope. In that same studio was J. John, who gave me his number. He is a renowned Christian. I wish I had called him. I was just so far away from my faith and the life that I had known.

By November, I really did not know what I was going to do. I attended the National Society for the Prevention of Cruelty to Children Crystal Ball at the Waldorf Hotel and danced the night away with Melinda Messenger. Also, I met up with Josh there, and we became friends. It started with a champagne reception in the beautiful art deco palm court, accompanied by Madam JoJo's infamous crystal queens. I was seated at 8 p.m. for a spectacular dinner and auction. The carriages were at 1 p.m. There was music and dancing and a casino. I was slowly realising that I had no direction. I was in danger of wandering aimlessly from event to event, as is known in the industry: "Oh, she goes to everything, even the opening of an envelope."

In December and January, the pantomime season was in full flow. I had to go to a costume fitting and a photo shoot. I received my script and began practising my lines; I felt like a proper actress. I was second billing to Sue Jenkins of *Brookside* in *Jack and the Beanstalk* at the Neptune Theatre. She was portraying the evil witch Queen Blunderbore, and I played Fairy Starlight. In the theatre programme, it reads: "Known simply as Penny to her fans, she gained notoriety this summer by being the first contestant voted out of the *Big Brother 2* and went on to feature in all the daily newspapers and occasionally still does!"

I was part of a fantastic cast. David Paul was an aspiring pop star, flying off to Germany after the pantomime ended to cut a single. Jaime Greer, the Dame, was outstanding. All the cast had a huge repertoire of professional jobs in the theatre world. I was amongst really talented people and had such a wonderful time. We all got so close as we did three shows a day. On our days off, we would go to the cinema. The nights would be spent with other actors from shows in town, and we would talk late into the night. Duncan, from Blue, called to wish me luck while he was abroad on tour. I had bouquets and cards streaming through the backstage area and dressing rooms; they didn't have enough vases to hold all the flowers that kept turning up.

It was such a surprise to get a massive welcome from the City of Liverpool. They even got their gold carriage out just for me, and I sat in it with the rest of the cast trailing behind. Crowds lined the street, and I felt like royalty; I was even given keys to the city by the mayor. The gold carriage went through the centre of Liverpool, which was brimming with crowds waving and cheering. I felt bad for the rest of the cast, as it was a long walk for them, but what a happy bunch of people! I adored Liverpool. It was only about a week into the pantomime before I got handed a pay increase by the panto's director, in the brown wage packets we used to get. We were so surprised by the jump in ticket sales, and they tried to get me to write a *Big Brother* scene into the pantomime. I did try, and they spent ages directing the scene, but it was an awful flop as I just found it uncomfortable to act out. It seemed like everyone wanted to see me! I had a wonderful welcome from the city of Liverpool, totally unforgettable, but while I was there, Lucie Morris and Nadia Cohen were writing in *The Daily Mail* on 22 December that I "dropped my towel on purpose" in yet another article for the papers.

Looking back, I just didn't realise how many people really liked me and wanted to see me. I would meet with the audience at the stage door and sign autographs; I was always so surprised by people's love and reactions. In a world without social media in 2001, I just didn't have a clue about the enormity of my popularity or the opportunities that were there for me at all. I really suffered from low self-esteem and could have embraced that moment and made an impact. Maybe I could have even forged a career in theatre, which was my first love. I did get my equity card, and I did get into Spotlight, the professional casting book for actors, in 2001. I kept my equity card until 2003. I just didn't have the confidence to carve out a career on my own. In this new *Big Brother* scene added to the pantomime, I was supposed to sit on stage as if in the diary room and answer questions from a voice that was supposed to be *Big Brother*. I remember there being total silence in the auditorium when we performed it. It wasn't my moment to shine. I felt so embarrassed. Anyway, my *Big Brother* scene was then cut from the show, but I still had my pay increase.

Everyone turned up on opening night. *Big Brother 1* winner Craig; Bubble and Brian; Gary (clap clap); and Peter and Ted. Gary and I had lunch; it must have been a day off as I remember us spending a lot of time together in Liverpool, and as always, it was a laugh a minute. Our friendship was really strong, like we had known each other for years. I was so glad they all made the effort. The cast were also really good people. I made friends with them, and it was hard for us all to say goodbye after five weeks. We really bonded. They were all going off to jobs in TV, and I still had no idea what to do.

I got along very well with Sue Jenkins. We sat together, chatting and having cups of tea. The whole cast was one big laugh, and we all got along brilliantly well. On the final night, as I came up over the bridge on the stage to take my bow, I literally fell flat on my bum and skidded to the front of the stage. I just sat there, dazed, and received a standing ovation. The cast said it would mean I would be back to tread those boards; it was supposed to be lucky. I believe I was the first *Big Brother* contestant to do Panto, and since then, a slew of other *Big Brother* contestants have followed suit.

Liverpool was magical and so full of atmosphere. We would meet other actors from the various shows, especially *Whistle Down the Wind,* and all go out most evenings after the show to a fabulous bar where we would sing karaoke surrounded by millions of fairy lights, which the bar was famous for. The trouble was, I was staying a train ride away in a room they had rented for me. The boys that lived there were very nice; they had their own bar built into the front room. It would have been better to be just around the corner from the theatre, though, as I had to pay for taxis late at night to get back to my room. I wasn't sorting out my money at all, and I wasn't looking after myself.

The Echo featured Bubble, Suzanne Collins from *Brookside,* Craig, the *Big Brother 1* winner, and Brian all coming to see me and Sue Jenkins in panto! The front page read: "The Chelsea fan was in Liverpool last night to support Penny's stage debut in the Neptune's panto, *Jack and the Beanstalk.*" I was feeling really bewildered all the time, and I got very ill and rundown in Liverpool with about thirty ulcers in my mouth. At the walk-in clinic, they wanted me to go to the hospital, but I didn't want to let the show down. We had three shows a day; it was exhausting. I can remember all these schoolkids sitting in the front row, and I tried to say my lines with my mouth semi-closed, which I know is ridiculous, but all I could think about was that they might see my really disgusting ulcers, some of which were already full of pus. My mouth looked like it was full of furry green caterpillars. I think I was completely stressed out of my mind. I really did not know what I was going to do from February onward or who I could turn to for advice and help. While still in Liverpool, I met up with Atomic Kitten, and we did an anti-cancer campaign. We took part in this massive photo shoot with all of us hanging off railings in a factory somewhere in Liverpool. I also remember being out for lunch with my director and Heidi, and while we had lunch, Heidi's phone rang, telling her she was now part of the band the Sugababes. We were so excited for her! I did interviews for radio; I had a TV slot over Christmas; it was just nonstop.

Despite this, and because of this, I had a very lonely Christmas. I just seemed to shut down, disconnecting from everyone and myself, and pretending that everything was super. Being alone on days when everyone else is at work and going about their normal routines is dangerous, so I made new friends who were also free during the day in London. One of them came up to spend Christmas with me and went out; I just wanted to sleep. I realise now that these new "friends" were not helping me get myself together. You really need the oldest friends around you—the ones you can trust. Letting in hangers on was part of my downfall. No one knew how I was feeling. They all thought I was having the time of my life.

I also did a modelling shoot for *The Echo* newspaper and realised I was piling on the weight. *Big Breakfast* called and wanted me on their farewell New Year's show, but I couldn't go as I was in Liverpool. I had cards from my oldest friends in Australia, and I felt so far away from them mentally, as though we were on a motorway, but they were six lanes away and going in the other direction. *The Daily Mail* also called, wanting me to do a parachute jump. I did a question and answer for *The Times* Educational Supplement. I went on local radio with Little and Large to talk about panto. Duncan called again from Paris. Brian, the *Big Brother 2* winner, was hosting on SMTV with Cat Deeley. The Jules Holland band were on tour and called. Alan rang from Manchester as Steps had finished their tour, and I had kept in touch with him since Mardi Gras. I found out I was in the top one hundred moments of 2001 on TV; I was actually in the top ten!

But I was slipping down this vine of fame; I was in Jack and the Beanstalk, but all the gold of my life was out of my reach; I could not find my magic beans. The spotlight had turned into a flickering flame in a cold, damp room. The last week of the show, I sat with Sue Jenkins, wrapped in towels to keep warm, and drinking soup. Darling Gary (clap clap) from the Rupert Street Bar was there again, seeing the show, and turned up at the dressing room with a cup full of positivity and a lovely single red rose. His friendship has been a lifeline and amazing all these years. I love you, Gary, Ant, and Sebastian King Cat. I asked if he wanted to say anything that I could add to my book, and I was in such an emotional state when I read what he wrote. It came from his wonderful heart. Thank you, Gary.

These are his words and opinions, and his recollection of events as he remembers them:

"I first met Lisa around August 2001 at a bar I was running called Rupert Street in Soho. She came in with Brian Dowling, who had just won *Big Brother 2*, which was Chanel 4's second most watched programme, and that series of *BB2* was the most watched ever with nearly 14 million viewers for the final. I went over to congratulate him on winning the show, and he introduced me to Penny.

I remember that night so clearly even though it was 20 years ago, they were both swamped with well-wishers with the press outside the 2 bar entrances. Brian and Penny went to the office with me, where we had a gossip, and I looked at the CCTV and saw the fire exit was clear. Penny asked if it was OK for her to stay in the office a bit longer, and the two of us got chatting; a wonderful friendship grew and blossomed from that crazy night. It was a mad time for a while going to celebrity parties, charity balls, various exclusive restaurants, and nightclubs. One of my favourite moments was going to Liverpool and seeing Penny in *Jack and the Beanstalk*. We got into one of our chats in the dressing room after the show, leaving everyone else who had travelled to see her waiting for ages, oops! We seemed every week to be doing something wonderful, glamorous, and exciting. Penny was in magazines one minute and on Celebrity *Weakest Link* the next. I remember she paid for lots of things, but as her celebrity waned, people who had taken from her soon disappeared thick and fast, with a few like Peter, Ted, and myself remaining. Penny was (to me) unhappy, and I remember a turning point in our friendship when it was just the two of us sitting in Café Boheme in Old Compton Street in Soho, where we put the world to rights. We vowed to always be there for each other no matter what, and from then on in, we were, and she was Lisa to me. My affection and love have never waned; we have been at each other's weddings, called at the exact moment the other had absolutely needed it, and loved each other when we felt no one else did. I have seen most of Lisa's greatest highs and deepest lows, stood by both, and will continue doing so.

I love you, Lisa.

Gary."

His partner Ant wrote this for me to add to my book: "I have known Lisa for many years, nearly fifteen! I was a bit confused at first as we also called her Penny, so for a while I was using both names when talking about her. We share a passion for cats and always share updates and check in on WhatsApp regularly. We have been to each other's weddings, which were both magical, and we have shared so many happy memories. Here's to another fifteen and creating more memories together. I'm really proud to say that Penny, oops, Lisa is in my life, and really proud of her writing this book! Love you. 🖤 🖤 "

Thank you so much, Gary and Ant.

SCENE 5:
Losing it all.

Hope lost (A Poem)
When you realize the "fame" is over.

What are you looking for in there?
  As you dig into the very corners edge.
  There is a speck, and I will call it hope.
  But it is a shattered dream.
  I dig out the tiniest speck remaining.
  It is the courage to let go of it all
  This is what is left.

The End.

On getting back to London, my Liberty Radio job was over. I was back in my flat, devoid of any furniture or people. It was February 2002. There is a Getty photo of me from around this time that shows Narinder and I going to the after party of Julian McDonald's show at London Fashion Week, held at the National History Museum. No one knew how depressed I was. I kept it buried deep within me.

Paul, Donna, and Steve finally knocked on my door, insisting they help me. They would come over, and we would order takeaway while sitting on the floor of my living room, as I had no furniture. They carried me for a while, and I cannot thank them enough. I started seeing more of my oldest best friends, like Marie, and going over to Knightsbridge and having a meal in their local bar.

I really missed my normal life. I was talked into getting hair extensions that I had no idea how to care for and that just looked like swirls of twigs on my head when I saw Esther, who had put them in, about a month later. She had spent hours on my hair, and now she just had to cut them all out. It was the nodules of glue that I couldn't get on with; every time

I touched my hair, it felt full of insect eggs. I knew it was the glue, but I didn't like it. To thank her, I took her and her friend out to an event at Red Cube to watch Johnny Vegas. We had sat in this massive area of the club all night, wondering why no one was around. By the time we realised it had all been happening in a separate section of the club, it was all over! It was 1 a.m., and we left Red Cube and went to Balans in Compton Street, Soho. Our food arrived, and we ate it, but her friend slept while her plate of food went cold. As they were clearing the plates, her friend woke up and was really upset that her food had gone while she slept, as she was now starving. I knew Four Poofs and a Piano, the covers band, around that time, and I think I took her to meet them another time.

I participated in another charity event, *The Sunday Mirror Charity Challenge*. I literally went over the top of the Canary Wharf skyscraper, One Canada Square, in a cradle the size of a bucket. It took three separate days of rebooking the event for the wind speed to be safe and for me to finally do the challenge. It was for Barnardo's. In a thank you letter, the organiser said that out of all the challenges, mine was the most daring. It was terrifying but better than the idea of a parachute jump, which was their first option.

By March 2002, I was in a real mess, both emotionally and financially. Ironically, on 30 March a year earlier, a letter came through the door of my flat confirming I was in the second stage and was on my way to being on *Big Brother*. That must have been nine hundred out of two hundred and fifty thousand applicants who were interviewed. What can happen in a single year requires all of our strength. That has got to be the most famous towel in the world! Every part of my life under the umbrella of a towel dropping has been peeled, pricked, shredded, and violated.

On 6 April, I was invited to a club belonging to Dean in West Norwood. Dale had booked me, and I was judging a competition with the late June Brown (Dot Cotton in *EastEnders*). Dean decided he did not like me at first. But after all these years, we've remained lifelong best friends. It was a holiday in Cancun that sealed our friendship.

When we first met in 2001 at his club, he didn't think that much of me. By then I was so exhausted and full of low self-esteem that I was not at all my shiny, happy self that he has since gotten to know and love. We were thrown together as Dale didn't turn up at the airport for a two-week holiday to Cancun. I had become best friends with Dale, and he had invited me to join him and Dean and a whole group, including Dean's sons and their friends. I remember getting to the airport and just standing on my own while the rest of the group were getting into party mode. I had that cold, creeping fear come over me as I realised Dale was a no show. Dean had that look I had seen on the faces of people I had met, like when I sat in the VIP area and a famous pop group was sitting opposite me with that look of *what do you think you are doing here?* I thought I would go anyway and just sit on the beach and read my books. Instead, it turned into the most fantastic holiday full of joy and laughter and forever friendships. It was talked about for years as the best holiday all of us had ever had. It was made so poignant as we lost one of the young, beautiful boys later that year in a terrible accident. As I am writing this book now, there are so many gorgeous people I have met who are no longer with us; I feel blessed to have known them.

Since February 2002, despair and depression had been creeping in, and I was feeling more and more desperate. I had no idea about my money. I had become chaotic in all areas of my life. Unfortunately, there were still a few hangers-on that I allowed in my life, and they would lurk around licking the inside layer of my purse. I started to do aimless things instead of taking a good, sharp look at my reality. I stayed with Dean and Dale for a while, as I just didn't want to go home. They seemed to like me being around as I would cook them hearty, healthy dinners. Dale tried to help promote me and made-up photo cards I could send to people requesting autographs. He made a demo tape of my *Liberty Radio* show. He made another tape for me to send to casting directors. I ended up doing a show at their club in West Norwood; Dale called it "Pennies from Heaven." It was a game show, and it involved a lot of cabaret. I absolutely adored the drag queens and had such a laugh. But I had to face reality and sort out my home and finances. I had to go home.

Now the question was, *what do you do in the drizzly end of fame that created this reality?* I can understand now why maybe some stars have extreme beliefs because you do feel like you are somewhere and no one else can really understand where that is. The higher you climb, the greater the fall. The shiny bits started to drop off. Fear dominated my life. I tried to please a lot of people who, in the end, did not care for me at all. I became a puzzle even to myself, an unknown matter washed up on a beach. I was disconnected even from myself. I had to find the courage to keep going, to make a boat of all this driftwood, and immerse myself in the sea of challenges to find another shore. It has taken years for me to finally realise I have been (metaphorically speaking) wearing shoes that don't fit.

PENNY ELLIS

To Realize (A poem)
Leaving my flat in London.

Inside it all.
But you don't find the key of life until your inside.
How can this puzzle even be?
No beginning, no end but a centre from which you look out at it all.
As if projected thousands of miles in the air.
You can see the mindless journeys where nothing is at the end, but you don't know that until you too are there.
There is an unexplained peace reached by completely risking all and free falling.
Not knowing how or where or why once you fly into the unknown you discover a truth very few will rise in the dawn possessing.
Like a blind man playing in the dusk of the day with a smile he would never see.
He knew to live within, the beauty inside us all.
To let the dreams in their truest colours come out of all the blackest fears and sadness.
I had to learn to take the right colours into the realness of my life again.
A lot of people took up position inside the frame of my life, took a pose and then left. There is only enough oxygen for one.

The End.

So, I sat in my lonely flat with nothing to do. I knew I had to let my anchor of sanity fall somewhere, or I wasn't going to survive. The anchor had to plummet to the depths, to the dark unknowing of my soul, so it could rediscover the creativity and bring it up to the light in its entire colour. My life was now in a state of self-inflicted chaos, with bits of "has-been celebrity" thrown in. *How can I solve this problem?* is what I thought, but even to this day, I cannot begin to describe the overwhelming feelings. I felt tangled up in all those newspapers and their stories, their words like a grip, as if a net had been thrown over me, full of all the words ever written about me.

For all the friends who helped me survive. (A poem)

A moment is the uncurling, so hesitantly stretching into the filtered rays.
So gently I see through the bluest crocus petals eye.

I find a connection as our smiles meet as they used to.
The many frozen winters fear can melt past,
Now a torrent rushing towards a waterfall,
Cascading disjointed memories are tumbling,
So many suitcases breaking open in the sky.
All around the losses are evident yet springs sunshine follows the
lonely sweepers along the dawn street gutters.
Strength breaks through the set memories now fondly favoured.
I follow a lost scent into a maze and am awoken inside a dream, a
surprise, so deeply held within me as a cave found under the sea's ocean
bed of my mind.
It is glittering and dazzling.
So, summer will follow on from spring and my friends I will never
let go again of our summer days.
I swing softly on and on and my friends we can create a new
harmony a back and forth in time in tune in place at last.
The End.

Once you're not high profile anymore, about eighty per cent of your fame vanishes overnight.

The explosion of people in those first few months is incredible, like you're a new flavour of ice cream. They touch you as if you were made of gold leaf, and it gets peeled off like the prince in the Oscar Wilde story. I was free falling, as if I were playing poker but didn't even know the rules. I was looking for a way back into my own life, but the walls of the media, it seemed, kept me in a space they had built around me. I was disassembled like parts of a car. Life was desperate; it was like tiptoeing on a spider's web, so beautiful with the drips of dew, and becoming entangled in its brokenness. It was now April 2002, and I was back at the beginning, trying to walk through the same territory, but now on stilts; no one was up there with me, and the loneliness was crushing. I was at the end of myself. No job, no money—just a blank page. I had gotten rid of at least half the people that came around me. I had to shift the baggage of emotions I was left with. I had to find a way out of the chaos of debt, fluctuating weight, fears, and the loss of my dignity, reputation, character, and job, as well as one of my best friends.

PENNY ELLIS

Hope Found (A Poem)
For my family and best friends.

I saw a smile inside your hand as you reached out and took both of mine.
> And you filled them with light.
> The light stayed just surfacing.
> Although it didn't touch me.
> I felt the laughter reach my lips and give me hiccups.
>> The End.

I had absolutely no idea what I was going to do.

Everything and nothing (A Poem)
The life I lost.

When it becomes everything but nothing, except the darkness inside the night.
> The weight is felt, it is the memory. Unable to lift it you can only gaze on it and try to touch it.
> Like a photo is cold despite the warmth of the moment it was taken in.
> Inside captured in there is that moment.
> Somehow it will always return in a sound or colour to that space inside the beat of that time that can't be switched off.
> So real again for it has had its resurrection in you through you.
> It lives in the turning pages of a newspaper its power grows and takes on its own shapes
> Becomes a continent.
> Becomes the last ripples tip touch with the mouth of the ocean.
> Becomes another universe altogether.
> That you walked into because you did and now you must.
> It is time creating time and
> Everything now is as nothing can be what it was so that everything is possible.
>> The End.

It was the end of April 2002, and I was in despair. I was wearing a cloak of shame, fear, and embarrassment. I finally took it off in 2020.

ACT 3:
Meet me at the Mirror.

SCENE 1:
Going Home.

I shall call the final act of my *Big Brother* story *Meet me at the Mirror*, the title of my book. I hope my journey has inspired and encouraged you personally to be brave and believe in yourself, to know that whatever you face in life, you can find a way back to hope and sanity. Don't quit but get up and find that path that has your destiny on it. Walk through the mirror into a reality worth living.

This part of my story is about the enormous effect of being loved and the value of true family and friends. They are the breadcrumbs left by Hansel and Gretel to find their way back home. The people that don't shake or take from your hand, but instead hold it. A quote I say most days to my husband Mark is "It's a funny old world."

It was now 2002, the year the baby that was reality TV began to properly grow up. On 5 May 2002, the *Osbourne Show* made its debut. This was also the year of the first *American Idol*; reality TV went from crawling to walking.

What people may not realise is that once you have been on *Big Brother* and your time is understandably over, it doesn't stop. It didn't stop for me until March 2020. For the next year, and the year after that, and as *Big Brother* became bigger and better with each new show, and as social media platforms were born, and as adverts for the next *Big Brother* began and recaps from previous years of *Big Brother* were shown back on television and discussed in the papers and on social media platforms, you are once again in the public's mind every summer when the new *Big Brother* show begins.

In 2001, no one could have predicted the impact of social media or its growth. Now, on every phone, there you are: Penny Ellis from *Big Brother*.

To add to that stress of having to relive it all over again is the mockery of journalists as they write columns about "where are they now?" where journalists can discuss and comment on your life and give their own opinions, not just on what you did on TV but also on what you are doing in your private life years later.

They can easily mock your downfall from fame. I quote: "Bumbling Penny Ellis was known for being the English teacher that went wild and stripped off." My time was up. I can understand and accept that.

But I did things some people only dream of doing.

I was very naïve. I didn't build into something better, but I have learned my lesson. I am lucky I survived it. I am grateful to everyone who helped me. I am glad to have my faith. I have gotten wiser over the years, and I am a good person. What happens, though, is that none of that really matters, as the media will write what they want even if it is twenty years later. The world of a reality star is the life of a human being, not the latest trend of characters in a popular series. You're a real person, and if there is an interesting enough story ten or twenty years after your fame time, it will be written about. I have accepted that. I am only writing my views here as I see them. That is why I have shared my whole journey with you in my book. This is my whole life, what I did after *Big Brother*, and who I really am as a real person. After all that has been written about me, I now claim myself back and write about who I really am and where I really am now.

Another thing I've noticed is that once the next season of *Big Brother* begins, you become almost as identified with those people as if they were family relations. It is weird, but the more outrageous the behaviour got on the *Big Brother* shows, the more I would have difficulty trying to be back in a normal world of teaching. It was as if my towel dropping was just believed over and over again as the rest of my family on *Big Brother* conducted themselves in sexual and outrageous ways. It is a free world, and I certainly don't judge or criticise anyone, but *Big Brother* 2001 was simple and not glitzy; it was a very meagre place with chickens, and the tasks were simple.

The show became a bigger, glitzier, more daring version of itself over the years, but I was still identified with whatever went on in the *Big Brother* house every year, and it got more adventurous over the years. Many of the people I've met in schools and in the general public over the last twenty years (some of whom were not even born in 2001) believe it's a reality show where people will do anything for fame, and therefore believe that I must have dropped my towel as I was desperate for fame. It has been attached to my name, like a surname, for twenty years—all the good, the bad, the horrible, and the amazement.

The first night of *Big Brother 3* and the reunion night for the *Big Brother* 2001 contestants took place on 24 May 2002. Of course, the press had been alerted, and cameras flashed outside as we all met up in a restaurant. Someone had sent a cab with a TV so we could watch the new contestants go into the *Big Brother* house; the late Jade Goody was among them. I had felt vulnerable, and Dale said he would come with me to support me. The others embraced him warmly. I just felt really depressed. The group split into two camps, and I just didn't feel like I belonged with either one. There was pressure put on Brian to buy wine because he had won the money, and I remember Helen saying something to me in the cab because I made conversation with Paul; I wonder if she had read all the articles written about me and formed an opinion.

Later on, we went back to Josh's house, and I had to lie down. I lay on his bed with a massive migraine; it was a crushing headache, like the weight of a scaffold had been dropped on my head. I lay there like a frightened child, consumed by fear. My life seemed in such pieces, all with jagged edges; I just couldn't bear to face it. I felt fragmented and not part of this world, like I was in a black hole. The evening ended, and Dale had really enjoyed meeting everyone in person. He is a huge *Big Brother* fan.

My mother arrived at my flat in May and realised just what a mess I had gotten myself into. She sat in my empty living room, which the lovely Steve had repainted a subtle powder pink. I also had it carpeted and added a tiled area to put candles in as a feature; all of this is costing me money that I should have saved. I don't know why I did it. I remember carrying the paint pots home all the way from Angel Station. It was like I was pretending everything was OK. I just felt so desperate and alone. I bagged up all the dresses I had purchased for upcoming events. I always wonder if they recognised me in the charity shop and made some good money for charity from all my dresses. I didn't realise it at the time, but I could have probably sold my Eviction dress on the internet. I was desperate to just get back to the life I had known.

I think that is why I kept trying so hard to make it as a teacher all these years, as it held the memory of when life had been really quite nice. It was not until March 2020, when I was forced to leave teaching again as there was literally no work at all, that I finally realised I had been hoping to survive something that had already died the day I walked out of Sarah Bonnell.

My mother made me get all my direct debits, bills, and loans out of my file. We lay them all over the new carpet. She cried. It was awful. The following year, 2003, she even had to lend me £12,000 for my tax bill. What a mess. I had earned some good money, but I really don't know what I did with it all. I have learned to respect money now. If you don't respect it, it will dominate you and ruin your life. Be slightly afraid of it, as it can kill your hopes and dreams. It is hard to get out of a cycle of debt, and I had been in one since 1994, when I was with Adam. It is difficult to break those cycles, whether they are related to debt, OCD, or the need to please others. I happened to have all three addictions.

My mother said: "Always be true to the best of you and give it to God. Then you will be amazed at your life." I finally listened to her and did that in 2020.

I went back to my wonderful church, All Souls, Langham Place, once. Rico, a mighty man of God, had warned me not to go on *Big Brother*, and I hadn't listened because of that vice-like grip of compulsion—once I had something in my head, it would dominate me. He was talking at the service I was now attending and referred to *Pretty Woman*. It made me cry as he quoted what Julia Roberts says in the film: "It's easier to believe the bad stuff." After all the dreadful press that the church had to suffer, I am so thankful to the wonderful late Richard Bewes, who just said with such forgiveness, "God has thrown it in the sea of forgetfulness."

My friend Paul took me in hand. He helped sort out things in my flat and helped paint it, even straining his back—sorry, Paul! He said that I needed to sell it as I was in too deep with all my debt and had no job and no teaching certificate, which he was still fighting to get reinstated. I was now living with the consequences of my hasty decisions.

My best friends love me, but they also had to cope with lots of people coming up to us if we were out somewhere. There was lots of positive love from the public towards me; it was always positive. I signed autographs, with my friends smiling in the background. Once I was tired and in mid conversation with a dear friend, so I was a bit abrupt to someone running up to me with a piece of paper to sign. I realised then that you must keep your happy face on, as otherwise you really offend people. This person was angry and shouted, "Who do you think you are? " I really wanted to tell them that I really didn't know anymore, and I felt like complete and utter crap. That would have been a has been mess; I just said sorry instead.

I remember Paul being aghast at my finances; I was out and about with no job or future and a tonne of debt. He said to me on numerous occasions that I needed to face reality, but I just felt numb and as if I were travelling through space. I have never known depression like it. My mother and Paul took charge of sorting out my life. They saved me, and I thank them. I was in so much debt. I have really had to retrain my brain to view money differently. They have helped me so much. I must add in here that none of my other amazing and lovely best friends had any idea how I felt or the debt I was in. I was too ashamed to tell them. I know they would have helped me. They have been wonderful, and I thank them all for all the years of friendship. I did have to ask one of them just before I left London, and she immediately gave me all her savings and even said not to pay her back. I paid her back in full after a year of teaching in Hastings. It took a lot longer, but I also paid my mother back in full for paying my tax bill.

Inside the Mirror (A poem)
Believing in hope again instead of depression and fear.

It isn't what people think.
  It isn't what people say.
  It isn't their taking hand.
  Their critical eye.
  Their charming words.
  Their burning touch.
  Their abrupt walk, or their past regrets, their perception, their drowning sighs.
  Oh, fly through the storm.
  Your jigsaw is undone.
  But live life abundantly.
  Do you not realize you are fearfully and wonderfully made?
  The invisible is the grey weight enormity of the truth of life.
  A lime green maze passage.

Within which many think they can find the theory of life in all its equations.

So, of the lines of a Kandinsky and the efforts of architecture as linear abrasive fingers reaching skyward as an example of one field of reason that hopes to define an answer.

Yet confines itself as human limitations try to touch life's definition and all become too true in forms as completion.

Too much of the real reveals only a burning orange end against which we have no weapon.

Death is imminent black ink spills overall.

Oh, I gasp as velvet purple imagination swirls and inside our thoughts we cling to an essence.

Like an unborn child who stays buoyant in the citrene tranquil safety.

A cocoon on a leaf unaware the trees into self-self's imagine and see layers of reflection.

The truth faces self so open your paint box and agate, amethyst, aqua marine spills out overall.

The End.

I did start writing in May 2002. I was asked to write an article for *The Sunday Mirror* magazine. I had to interview Josh, Stuart, and Narinder. The front of the magazine had a huge photo of Pink, and in the corner was a headline about the article: "The *Big Brother* rich list. Can fifteen minutes of fame lead to a fortune?" It is interesting that the media were starting to question what impact reality stars were having and how much money they could make in 2002.

Nowadays, many reality TV stars are super wealthy. The article was called "Someone to watch over me" and was written just before the next group of contestants went into the *Big Brother* house. My advice to them read: "Be strong enough to handle the dual sense of reality that will hang over you like fine mist."

Josh added, "Once you're in there, try to be yourself because it isn't that easy with so many people watching."

We were all given outfits to wear; I had a white suit on. I was bloated and had put on a lot of weight. When the article came out, I shouldn't have been surprised that certain information had been added or exaggerated. I was so upset about it.

I was very proud of the article I wrote for the *New Statesman* that came out on 3 June 2002. The headline was: "How to get an identity crisis."

The answer? "You simply become a media-created commodity. Meeting the press on my eviction night was like being invaded by a vampire. My whole identity has undergone a radical reinterpretation in the media prism I am now trapped in. I have become what the public believe me to be, the personality the nation created. I am confronted every day with the task of undoing Penny who dropped her towel. I am no longer an educated, respected professional, a creative writing initiator, and a performance poet, but Penny, who dropped her towel. Overcoming this mantle confronts me every day as I try to re-enter the rat race. I walked into that house with a suitcase full of suppressed questions about myself that I was forced to confront. The experience has reaffirmed my passion and energy for inspiring others that I brought to my teaching. Finding myself metaphorically washed up and shipwrecked, my teaching career in tatters, has forced me to draw on my personal strengths. It is possible to begin life again, and after the media frenzy that was merciless this past year, to survive is to find a priceless reality. Beware the heady allure of fame. Strangers chat to me like a long-lost friend. Some even buy disposable cameras to take my photo. My feelings of isolation in the *Big Brother* house increased to such an extent over the two weeks as I was exhausted having to justify myself and my actions."

Under that was a headline: "Throwing in the towel. Penny Ellis, once a teacher, now a media commodity." The interview was on Page fourteen of the *New Statesman*, which is very bulky with sixty-three pages, so my interview was right at the front.

I also wrote the book review for *Sleb* by Andrew Holmes. On the blurb, it said, "Fifteen minutes can mean life." It was a satire about celebrities, fans, and the way the media attempts both to satisfy and inflame our obsession with success. In my review for the novel, I wrote, "An addictive read, intricately informative about the media. The author manipulates us as we sympathise with and gasp aloud at the unfolding of the protagonist's life. The protagonist is an alcoholic in denial and believes in what he believes is a celebrity lifestyle. He is in prison for a crime he did commit, and like the A list celebrities who are unable to be free to walk down the street or have their lives scrutinised and judged, he is living trapped in what he has become."

Ben Elton would also bring out a book inspired by *Big Brother* contestants from the first and second series called *Almost Famous*. He dedicated the book to us all from *Big Brother* 2000 and 2001, writing a thank you and listing all of our names at the front of his book, saying "it wouldn't have been written without us."

The whole idea of reality stars seemed to be weaving together in the public and media worlds. Writers, novelists, and the general public watched as these shows started to be born and became what, today, is our normal. *The Osbournes*, starting in 2002; *Punk'd*, beginning in 2003; *The Anna Nicole Show*, first airing in 2002; *Keeping Up with the Kardashians,* launching the KarJenners to stardom in 2007; *Joe Millionaire,* beginning in 2002; and *What Not to Wear*, starting in 2003.

I found over fifty-four reality TV shows dating from 2002 when I quickly googled reality shows, and I'm sure there have been even more!

By 2020, *I'm a celebrity, get me out of here!* had fourteen million viewers tuning in—a long way from 2000, when *Survivor* premiered in America.

Now, with Instagram (created in 2010) and Tiktok (created in 2016), we all have a chance of becoming reality stars. Tiktok was the most downloaded app from the app store in 2018, surpassing WhatsApp (created in 2009), Instagram, and YouTube (created in 2005).

May 2002 was also the month where I just didn't turn up to some very big events. I will deeply regret not turning up to a really massive charity event. It must have taken them months of planning. Looking back now, it must have caused a great deal of disappointment as so much work had gone into it. I just couldn't face anything; I felt so depressed that I lay in bed for days in the dark. I was overweight, crying all the time, and desperately afraid.

I also missed Purple in the Park and Birmingham Mardi Gras, where I was supposed to be one of the main hosts. I just couldn't face it. I remember just lying in bed with all these messages appearing on my phone to try to find out where I was. I finally had to answer the door as my mother came to find me and planned to take me home to Spain. She had come all the way from Spain again, knowing something was wrong, as only a mother would. I felt like I was on a glass floor, and I could see my life before beneath me, but I couldn't get back to it. I can only describe it as being lost inside out. I had lost the twinkle of hope and sanity, but I could keep the "costume" of who I was now, as faded as it had gotten. Only my truest friends and my family could help me unstitch it and let it blow away. But it had blown in so many directions. It was like standing under a rocket that had just been launched, with the pressure forcing down on me. I had nothing left. My life was running its own reality show under magnified circumstances and consequences. I was a runaway train.

Back to Find (A poem)
Finding my way out of despair.

I went back to find something I lost along the way.
And realized it had not been what I thought it was anyway.
So, I left it there lying in the road.
Repeatedly flattened already dry bones.
I can't begin to tell you what freedom is unless you can fully sense the impossible becoming possible.
To be utterly changed inside and out and to believe the best is real.
A can opened without a can opener in sight.
The End.

I put my flat on the market at the start of June 2002.

I needed to get my sanity back. It had to be there somewhere, like a beautiful dress still wrapped in warm, scented tissue paper. Some people only know me as Penny from *Big Brother;* others know me for who I really am; and some don't know me at all but have made up their minds about who they think I am. How does all that fold neatly together?

Paul called to say he had got my teaching certificate reinstated, so I could plan my return to teaching. Before I left for Spain, I went to watch my wonderful form 10A graduate back at Sarah Bonnell. They were leaving school for good, and I was leaving London and my home. I wept in the school toilets like a baby. All the memories came flooding back. I am very grateful to have eight of the girls as my best friends, as over the years I have been a support, a friend, and a listener, and they in turn have been there for me in ways they probably will never know. They are gorgeous, and I love them. They have given me some home truths, told me off, and poured their love on me. The journey we have been on would be a novel in itself!

I left straight after their graduation to fly to Spain. I know some of my friends decided to go home to live with their parents in Lockdown in 2020, taking the opportunity to spend time with their families. It seems to be only when you go home that there is that specific mix of ingredients that only your family has. It is like marmite; you either love it or hate it. When you get home, you drink it in and let it take its effect; it isn't called home truths for no reason.

When I got home, I realised just how crude and out of control I had been and how kind, gracious, and patient my parents have always been with me. They are the same as they always have been – wise and true. If only I had listened to my mother over the years and followed her guidance. Her walk of faith has never wavered. Her business mind, the fact that she had wanted to buy property with me in Islington, and her friendship—I had every opportunity to enrich our lives on so many levels. Why did I live so desperately, clinging to false hopes and chaos? There was always honour, truth, and nobility of character waiting for me. Why didn't I build? I realised when I got "home" that I loved them so much more than I had realised. Unlike the firework glitter of fame and the betrayal of wrong relationships I had invested so much of my life in, their consistent goodness despite my sheer negativity and stupidity is astounding. I had to face my fears, now in Spain while my whole London life dissolved. I had feared all these endings—the trepidation you feel as the endings come, and you wonder what you will find at the other end. What I feared the most had come true.

So, I swam in the secret bay on the cove beach they had found a short drive from their home; it was an aqua blue. I swam with all three dogs; they loved swimming and moved so fast in the water, a bit like the pace I lived at in London. There was white sand that was raked each morning by one of the locals; we drank tea from a flask; Bella, one of the dogs, would hide her stones, and we would pretend not to know where they were; I read books after not reading in years; we made lavender pouches and shelled almonds. Truth is a barrier breaker. Time is a healer. To be back with my family, I returned to a place I left unattended. I returned to myself, and elegance returned to me.

That was a time of freshly squeezed orange juice collected in sacks from the market and laughing at the dogs that swam back to shore like they were remote controlled toys that people take out on lakes. It was a time to relearn discernment and start unlearning things. Although, there would be a few more dreadful mistakes before I finally did land in sanity and wholeness in 2010. My mother would say to me, "Stop gushing out everything and telling everyone everything," and I realised I had trusted some people who really didn't care for me at all. We would sit in the dusk of the day on the balcony and read. My mum's saying has always been: "Alles Fenkt nach vorne an," which means: It all starts from the beginning.

We listened to *TWR*, a Christian radio station. The word Chicago always seems to pop up whenever I am going through a massive change in my life. I hear that it was rebuilt from total ruin in 1871; those numbers add up to seventeen, the age I was when I wrote my first fiction book. That is my OCD counting thought pattern: counting up to certain numbers that make me feel safe. We watched films in German, and my dad and I tried to follow along as best we could. Over the road is the village olive oil press; we call it the "oily doily," and we watched it do its thing magnificently. I reread *Forever Amber* and wept over what might have been.

The year before 2001 was like living in a pressure cooker. Being in Spain allowed me to let go of the catastrophe and all those chance decisions. Mum said that is what life is like, and if dad had been posted to Germany when we came to England when I was six years old, I would have probably been a swimmer because all that side of the family are swimmers. My granddad's brother won silver at the Berlin Olympics! There is always an "unborn" someone else within us. I have always written. I love writing, whether it is a shopping list, a letter, or a diary entry. I wrote my diary from the age of ten up until a few years ago. There was very little to say about 2012, as it was just one big ball of chaos trying to teach in the schools as well as juggle a lot of other awful episodes. I just kept hoping something sane and normal would happen. I developed a lot of character in those years, and I hope, like with my story, that all the pain and confusion, all the disappointments we have to face, can be of use and help someone else. It is then worth all that you have been through.

I spent the time in Spain reflecting, regretting, and reenergizing. I think of my granddad Percy, a butcher whom I never got to meet and who died so young. I think of my mum working in the top hairdressing salons in Düsseldorf and her glamorous days and lovely evenings going to dances. I remember the smell of my grandma's back garden in Southborough, with the woody, wet smell of the outside toilet and the heavy chain that you could never reach. I reread *The Thorn Birds*, a book that shocked me to my core when I read it at ten years old. Ironically, Catherine Cookson, who wrote it, resided in Hastings. Other famous people who lived in Hastings were David Hockney and Grey Owl. In a book called *The Idler Book of Crap Towns. The 50 worst places to live in the UK*, Hastings is listed as No. 39. The page reads: "Famous residents: the late Paula Yates and 'mad' Penny from *Big Brother*."

I have found Hastings to be a very creative town, and it really comes alive in the summer months.

One day at the beach in Spain with my mum and dad, we were relaxing, and there was this seriously dangerous fly with huge teeth. It didn't even look real, but rather like shiny plastic. It was real and bit us all! But we sat at the beach defiantly, knowing it would not make us flee, with a mixture of tranquillity and terror. We talked in the evening while I drank red wine; I continued to crawl out of this victim suit while mum came up with another of her sayings: "The tone creates the music." She told me about dancing in the Rheingold club in London and how they would play her tune as she entered the club. Then we found a mouse in my bedroom, and we all chased it around, throwing open the windows and landing on the bed laughing. One day we hunted for figs, and dad ate wild meat bought by a local. In this time, I had put polish back on again, like a veneer of protection and a sanity that shone out. My family became a protection kit, a first aid box. I needed to stay strong and not veer into another dramatic mess. As I left, my mum repeated to me to stop trusting everyone and telling them everything. On the plane flying back to London, I looked out of the window and saw what looked like the very outer edges of the world. The captain suddenly spoke over the speaker and announced, "We have Penny from *Big Brother* flying with us today." The whole plane claps and cheers. I am shocked and snapped out the safety of Spain with my family.

The Air (A poem)
On that happy plane journey.

I wrote a poem in the air.
   Miles above everyone I knew.
I flew.
And as the clouds broke like candy floss.
I knew as I flew.
How much I loved.
Because I saw the middle, bottom, top of a cloud.
And an eternal sky that was as real close up as far away.
             The End.

In July 2002, my flat sold immediately. While I was waiting to finish all the paperwork, I was on Claire's sofa, as now my home was gone for good. I didn't understand where some of the debts on my property had come from; who would have done that to me? Who would take so much from me? I filled envelopes at Mount View Theatre School for a bit of cash. I went on ITV2's *Britain's Sexiest Teachers*, a discussion group, but no one listened to me or my point of view. The other teachers on the panel seemed to look at me with utter disdain. I just felt so ashamed.

I even started to go to what is known as "the opening of an envelope." I was like a dead battery—perfectly intact but utterly useless. I let my outline be painted in the deepest, darkest colours. I don't want the unravelling of nightmares and confusion, that surreal feeling deep in your bone marrow, where you just can't adjust to the fact it is a sunny day and yet the snow is fixed, frozen on the ground. What had I neglected on the levels of duty, pleasure, and even existence? By neglecting it, have I allowed chaos to dominate? I was left with such desperate memories, some unplaced, some just vacant.

I needed to stay in the calmness, like that of a ladybird lumbering over a blade of grass. I was still trying to fill up my identity, where truth and purpose are highlighted. Like the stars that shine brighter in the darkest sky, I needed to navigate my mind, will, emotion, and heart. I ached at the waste and the pointlessness of it all. I needed to find an ebb and flow, get out of these illusions, and realise that this reality was anything but real. I had trapped myself in my own mirror.

I felt there was a challenge somewhere for me. I was in a trickling stream of longing and exclusion, too famous to get back to normal and not famous enough to reach for something else. I really wanted the nothing in my life to return. I wanted so much to get a package with my old life in it and to give this life back—the life that had become nothing and gave me nothing to hold on to. I wanted all the unplaced memories to go, as they now had a sell by date. I think about how timeless memory can be, but if it had been an actual taste, would it have filled me up or made me throw up? It was time to gut this life I have tried to live. I had sold, discarded, given, scraped, and discarded my whole life. We all hope that one day our dreams will fly out of us on trembling wings and take flight. I really had to face myself. What on earth had been my magnetic centre? Now, in the cold light of day, why did pain draw me in, mesmerising me? What habits did I have that kept me so separated from happiness? Was this real what I had allowed myself to become?

I stand at the mirror and start a monologue to myself.

"My feet dangle; they have become a compass. I am limp, which way

will they take me? I can kick, skip, jump. I dance backwards through all my nearly dreams. I am elsewhere in my direction, and my elsewhere heart needs to be at home. I need to go home. The clouds are the dust on our father's, God's, feet. Once I made that decision, it was like time itself sewed itself together and flew fast in front of me. I need to sew. Can the thread in my mind neatly pierce the pieces of my life and sew them back together? There will be a scar, of course; we can call it a seam, and it will run the length of who I am. We all have one; I just lengthened mine. It is always the chaos that seems to find me, in a job or a relationship, then the getting sewn up again. I do not know why I keep getting on the treadmill of self-destruction as easily as someone else gets into a car. I take myself apart like the parts of a car. In all that unsticking and in shedding all those layers, I need to really see myself, not just in a photo or in a birthday video, where you look at just one moment in your life and relive it. I seem to keep unsticking absolutely every area of my life. I do this U-turn inside, letting myself be all undone like an emptied-out cupboard or a car part. I must find a way to be together, oiled, labelled, in place, and sealed from damage or leakage. I am once again terrified."

All I have found is a new loneliness, when loneliness is almost tasted in the air around and within the silence that another person is imposing. What scars do we all have? If they weren't invisible, maybe it would help? Maybe our scars would make up the whole shape of the world if they could all be seen. Or maybe we would see a face of hope, whatever that might look like, if we all held our scars out together.

I think I was having a breakdown. I did feel suicidal. I drank the wine I brought back from Spain with Carolyn and Claire—faithful, beautiful friends. Many relationships were so fragmented, having been dropped, chipped, or shattered. A chain of support fluttered nearby, wanting to meet up, but I thought, *I will be gone soon. I will be far away. Everyone must get on with their lives. London is busy. It is a busy life. Not for me. I have no job, no home, and I have piled on weight. I have lost so much and surrendered so much so naively. I can hear the thud. It is the sound of the depths of the great below. I dropped it. I dropped myself.*

Once it is that bad, you can allow yourself to drop even further. The phone rang to go on a TV panel to give an interview, but instead I decided to clean Claire and Carolyn's flat and then travel to meet my sister on the pier in Hastings. It was now the end of August 2002. My sister was there for me; she always has been. I don't know why I didn't listen to her wisdom a long time ago. I still didn't listen to her in 2004 and made yet another disastrous, disturbing, and dangerous decision that nearly took my life. But I did listen to her in August 2002, with a cappuccino, the squawk of seagulls, and the sea pulling itself back into the ocean. I was glad to be pulled back home by her, my big sis Kristina, I love you.

I stayed on her sofa like her stray cat. They found him by a window, so they named him Fenster, which means window in German. He had been run over and was bruised and battered. We looked at each other with the same grateful understanding, snuggled in a home that loved us. My emotions went awry; I felt so desolate, and my mind was spinning out of control with fear. I managed to buy a flat in Hastings with the little money I had left. I just lay there, looking out the window of the framed view, and thought about what was in my immediate foreground. I had to hoist myself up onto a treadmill again. It would take so long to undo all the debt. I was bloated and overweight, trying to pick up normal, but it was like trying to find specific grains of sand on a beach during a storm when they all looked the same.

Supply teaching called and found me a job. It was strangely comforting, but as soon as I walked in, I knew it was not for me. The mayhem in the corridors, the unexpected unruly children bouncing off the ceiling, piles of marking like recycled waste, and the dread of what Year 8 will be like tomorrow. I was back to my famously ordinary life, yet I still felt like life hadn't found me yet, like I was on a long-haul flight.

Losing it (A poem)
Trying to teach again.

I could have told you that the world goes on and on,
    Or how I saw a sunset sky bleed red last night.
    I cry not for the beauty but the sadness at the end of every day.
    Collar upturned as if tombed safely in a familiar jacket.
    I must brace the world again.
    Why am I still in a world that rejected my dream yet lets time continue in this vein?
    How can I be normal whilst famous for such things and too famous to be allowed my normal to return like the dove to the ark?
    An onion once peeled is the unlayered heart of a cold world.
    That leaves me crying alone.
The End.

Back on my sister's sofa, it is a running joke every time we watch TV that I seem to have met absolutely everyone, whether I just simply met, worked with, chatted with, or saw them at an event. One day, I saw Brian on SMTV, and my reality blurred—the reality of TV reality and the reality of life's brutal reality. My survival kit boiled down to family, painkillers, home, friends, and my supply job. I started listening to Christian radio again. It kept saying, "Don't fight against the goads." It means stop kicking against the truth as you only hurt yourself. The "goad" would guide the oxen by prodding them. I was getting prodded to stay in the truth, but my OCD was completely out of control. I felt like I was swimming in a warm sea, but suddenly I came across a cold patch, and it got deep, and then on top of that, something brushed against my skin. Paul, who helped me get my teaching certificate back, sent me a lovely letter and a tape to help me with my OCD; I still read his letter and have his tape. I felt like I was going to split open, like I would implode, like I was derailing. The fame I had was already eroding the possibility of teaching. I waited for it to crumble, but I didn't want to get buried alive. The cracks were already appearing.

Then it comes.

I sat on my sister's sofa, and the phone rang. It was my supply teaching agency; they said they would pay me for the week, but I could not go back to the school because there were what seemed like over three hundred people and the press waiting at the school gates to get an autograph and a photo with me. It went into the local and national press that I was teaching in Hastings; the school had never seen anything like it.

I was now at the mercy of everyone, and I knew nothing about them. I was now a problem, a joke, and a liability. I was me but covered in labels, added notes, and an example of what is not accepted. It drowned me in my biggest fear: not being accepted. I returned once again to fear, loneliness, rejection, and being misunderstood. A place of bloating, debt, weight gain, tax bills, guilt; the guilt is always the heaviest to carry, heavier than heaviness itself. How can you weigh shame? Can you divide and ration horror? What was I creating except chaos?

In March 2020, we were all in lockdown. It was in February 2020 that I was sacked yet again from another school because of the YouTube video of me dancing at Bubbles' football-themed birthday party. It has been like a recurring nightmare for twenty years. As soon as I got a brilliant English or drama post, just when I would start to feel it had finally been forgotten about, it would rear its head. I was once escorted off the school grounds by security as if I were a criminal. One of my first jobs when I moved out of London was as Head of Drama, and I taught English and some German there too.

That job came to an end when one of the teachers printed off everything on the web about me, "Penny from *Big Brother*," and placed a massive pile of all my pictures and stories on the head's desk. I never found out just who might have told all of these different students over the years, but it would start with a student suddenly, out of the blue, saying, "You were in *Big Brother*." The dread would wash over me, as I knew how it would end. It always ended the same. I would have to leave that school.

Unlike in 2001, every child, in my opinion, now has almost a PhD in social media, and their phone is almost another extension of their hand. Their lives are spent inside social media more than in reality, and even as teachers, we have had training on the lack of empathy and resilience and the mental issues children suffer because of social media's influence over their lives. Like you, I am thinking, how would they know? Why would they be interested? They were not even born when I was on TV!

The problem, I believe, is caused by word association. Even if it was twenty years ago, the words reality star and celebrity dominates their lives now. So, it awakens that response. By the next day, it would have spread throughout the entire school, eliciting massive reactions. "Penny" would be screamed at me at least five hundred times a day while I tried to dismiss it. The variety of reactions would vary from "you were really funny," to laughing at me in packs, to shouting abuse at me. Sometimes they threw soggy paper at pictures they had printed of "Penny from *Big Brother*," scrunched up and dipped in water.

Anyway, the last job ended particularly nasty, with even some teachers shouting at me across the class that I should be in "prison" and that I was a "disgrace" and "disgusting" and a "paedophile."

That was at the beginning of 2020!

I had kept quiet for twenty years and worked hard. I have always been a brilliant teacher, but then there was no supply work to be had as the schools closed in March 2020. It made me sit back and reflect on what had happened all those years ago; it made me realise that I was in a form of lockdown for just fifteen days in 2001 in the *Big Brother* house.

The Supply Teacher (A Poem)

I babysit the bags of chaos.

Sometimes there is a moment in which I can place my hand inside the whirl of it all.
To draw out an unblemished unstained flower
Still intact
Still all its petals.
That I can replant in good soil.
A vision of a warm quiet place that is perfectly true.
The End.

My lovely Marie picked me up, and we drove to Hayley's birthday party. What a friend! She is always so kind and caring. We dressed up like we were in the 1920s and had as great a time as we always did. It is one of those friendships that stays so true whatever the circumstances; even when we saw each other at the Race for Life in London and I was in the Celebrity Area in 2003, it was still our wonderful friendship, and we gave a quick hello across the rope that divided us from each other. We got back and drank peppermint tea. The next day we went to the Royal Academy, as I was in London at her flat. She was renovating, and the flat was stripped back to absolutely nothing, and she said that was good as she could see the structure and the details of the joins, and by stripping it all back, you could visualise how you would make it whole. I smiled; I was so happy for her, and I thought, *this is what I have done to myself—I am stripped bare. Can I get whole?* We walked through St James's Park and followed her favourite yellow brick road trail. I treasure that memory. It was a much-needed act of kindness. Thank you, Marie.

So, I looked for work once again, and found a job in the job centre cleaning out beer cellars for £3.95 an hour as I couldn't teach. The supply desk was lovely and said they would keep trying to find me a teaching post. My mother called from Spain, saying I must send Dad some pork pies as he wouldn't stop talking about them. He had a real craving for them. He was like a "pregnant duck," said my mother, and we laughed.

I also needed to find a cocktail book as they had finished restoring their home in the village. They restored it back to its original features, and the whole village had come through the house to pay respect and thank my mum and dad for what they had done. They all brought a bottle, so now mum had a wine cellar the size of a small continent and dad wanted to experiment with cocktails as the variety of bottles was unbelievable. *Celebrity Big Brother* was back on; the *Big Brother* theme tune shot through me like an electric shock. It all floods back into your brain, and I felt like I was in a third dimension, like in *Quantum Leap* when he wakes up and must figure out where he is. My mother always says, as another of her sayings goes, "Take a Polaroid, as truly you would never believe it."

My head screamed, "How can I get back to teaching now that the show is on again?"

I moved into my flat in October 2002, and I started to run every day.

I ran along the promenade and walked in the sand as the tide went out so far; there was a wonderful stillness. The sunsets were amazing. At my feet, small waves rippled in and scattered starfish all over my feet. The beach was strewn with starfish. It was so beautiful.

Closer magazine also wanted an article on me, so I went to London. I had the same makeup artist that Davina McCall used. A costume fitter, a lunch, and a taxi were all laid on. My photo on the front of the magazine is a full-length picture of me in a Santa outfit, and the heading is "A special visit from the ghosts of Christmas past." Next to me are photos of Jamie Oliver and Hugh Grant, and to the side is a Christmas photo of Del boy and Rodney. They treated me like I was really famous, and I found it so surreal.

I flew to Spain for Christmas in December 2002. I packed a Christmas cake that I had made over the month and that has been talked about for years. I put my heart and soul into making it. I wanted to do something properly, something that, when finished, was beautiful. I also packed a tonne of dog biscuits. Dad cooked a turkey that was so big it resembled a large goat. We made decorations out of foil; it was just so lovely and warm that we even hung washing out on Christmas Day. The smell of the dusk of the day is so life affirming. Dad made potent cocktails; he was convinced they were martinis. He awaited the ham that Kristina was bringing over with her. The scene was like a painting I like by Holbein, *The Preparing of the Feast,* circa 1886. You never ever go hungry in our home. We wore silver crowns made from foil and drank cocktails while singing along to Elvis on a double CD Kristina bought for my mother. Dad made bread sauce, and Kristina packed three bottles of champagne, which made my mother worry that they would burst in the suitcase.

I started to feel as lonely as Christmas ended. Kristina went, and my mother and father and I watched home movies. Somewhere, someone might be watching the *Big Brother 2* VHS video; we watched the New Year come in on TV and saw the Edinburgh celebrations. Fireworks went off all over the village; they celebrated so extravagantly and with such joy and colour. It is such a quaint, untouched, and beautiful village. We had walked around the square full of live animals as they recreated the scene of Jesus in the manger surrounded by real animals. Father Christmas was there too. There was a service in the ancient church for blessing the animals, and crowds of villagers were crammed in holding animals of every kind. They welcomed my family in the village with so much love.

I flew back in January 2003, sat on my sofa, and started to cry.

Supply rang me again. They thought the dust had settled and there was a school that would take me permanently. I became Head of Drama. I also taught GCSE History, English, and German. The school was in "desperate measures," which means, in my opinion, it is a notch higher than complete chaos. I was blessed at Sarah Bonnell School. School, it appeared to me in 2002, was just uncontrollable noise. I was seen as not having behaviour under control, but how was I supposed to control a group of boys that ran in my room while I was marking, opened the filing cabinet, and pissed in it? Or the child who howls under the desk and then flips the tables and chairs? Or the boys that pin me up against the wall and hold a pair of scissors to my throat? Behaviour management was the entire trend, and we had meetings with "85 PowerPoints" explaining the tone of our voice and how to build the child's self-esteem. I was seen as not having what it takes. There were concerns with my ability that meant I now had the eyes of the senior management watching me, like shadows appearing at the door of my classroom and observing my every move. I was once again being watched. I felt sick to my stomach every day.

(A Stream of Conscious)

I am a puppet; everyone has a string. I am a puppet, tangled in a huge heap, all twisted up and around in all the wrong perceptions. I heard somewhere that if you stand on the table, you can touch the ceiling. I have got to get back to who I really am and let go of catastrophic thinking. How can I stop this rush? One kind is a rush of impetuous extremes. The other is the rush of terror and panic. Too much of my life is being lived on the frontiers of extreme chaos and bewilderment. Can I harness the extremes and come back to myself? Yet I must do it, walking through more rules I did not write. I live so far away from all my wonderful friends, whom I used to see so regularly. Kristina holds onto my credit cards to help me sort my money out. My mother calls, Bella the dog has her period, so she has put some knickers on her. I keep saying to myself that I will get a grip, but I just don't believe it yet. We wear makeup on the outside, but think about the colours inside. If we could see the shapes and colours in our mind, what colour are our thoughts, emotions, and feelings? Would it be a warm glitter of fairy lights in the dusk of an evening or a raging clash of light and shapes that just smash into each other?

I clashed with this teaching, charging between four and five rooms, carrying all the books with me. I waited for the weekend to try to get over the whole thing. I had lost all my confidence. They say life happens while you're living it, but I seemed to be in a bumper car smashing into chaos. Then Ted, like a guardian angel, and Ali came alongside me.

Ali was my teaching assistant and was just marvellous. She got the class in order so I could actually do some teaching. I wasn't surprised when she became a deputy head. She was one of the best teachers I'd ever had the pleasure of meeting. I am glad we still have a friendship to this day. Ted had been at the school for a long time and again had that superb level of authority. He was there in those chaotic lessons, helping me, not judging me. He would give me a lift to work each morning, ringing me to let me know he was on his way, and waiting patiently for me; he never judged my OCD, some days my counting as I shut the door of my flat could take ages. We would listen to his newest CD and count the roadkill on the narrow country road as we drove to the school.

There is coldness in schools and an air of isolation as everyone is trying to get their bit done. There is no time for warmth or to ask someone if they are OK. Ted and Ali made time and became my lifeline. I would get in at night and run along the seafront, numbing the pain of loneliness with toast and VHS videos.

People continued to call, including Michael from *Closer* magazine. I did go up to see him once, and we did go back to Shadow Lounge, but it seemed the friendship ended in 2003. When Tim got the job as producer on Chicago, he was ecstatic, and then those calls stopped too. Duncan from Blue called a couple of times, but then that was over. Liz from Atomic Kitten, as well as a few other people, called.

Then it all stopped completely. I wasn't in London. That is just the way it is.

However, the press still loitered outside the school and wrote about me. This meant there were more meetings about me and even more concerns. It was the start of a process to get me to go. I was just viewed as a liability. I must have "dropped my towel"; I am unfit to work with children after having exposed myself on national TV and wanting to have live sex on TV. This judgement and condemnation would repeat itself again and again in schools up until 2020. I now know it is not a failure to let go of something that absolutely does not work for you. I tried to stay unemotional at school, but my nerves were shredded.

I am so grateful I have kept so close to Lizzie, Heena, Kuljeet Suky, Zainab, and Emma. I kept them in my thoughts every day as I struggled through the expectations of the school I was now in. As I said earlier, they were in my form, my English class, or my drama group. We went away to theatre events and Christian camp; we had holidays in my flat; and we spent nights at the theatre. Their phone calls in 2003 kept my hope alive. Today, we are as close as we have always been. To have met them was like opening a treasure box. I reunited with Kerri and Kathleen at Suky's wedding in 2022.

To my surprise, I also found genuine love and support from some teachers at this school in 2003; they reminded me of the closeness of my colleagues like Mel at Sarah Bonnell School. The support of Ted and Ali kept me going through that year. I got invited to the wedding of another kind teacher who worked there called Donna. I felt bad as she really hoped I might invite Robbie Williams and he would sing *Angels*. I wish I could have made that come true for her, but my sell by date was up; my moment to stand with the famous was over. Donna, Ali, and Ted are lovely teachers and beautiful, creative people. They are a true asset to the teaching world. Thank you for your friendship.

I felt like a whole set (not just one plate) of crockery, all smashed up inside. I remember, as a child, making toffee with this nice old lady when we lived in Scotland. The best part was breaking it, smashing it into pieces, and finding a big chunk to chew on. It was fun then, but as you grow up, you realise whatever you break can never be totally put back together.

I was grasping for moments in my days that reminded me of pieces of my life that were happy. I was looking for those pieces in the schools I have worked in since 2003, but I never found them. I let go of things that were so precious to me (my form group, my church, my flat) and never found anything to fill that aching gap. I found teaching virtually impossible, and every day was filled with chaos and fear that ripped chunks off my fragile mind. I needed to be too full to be able to swallow sorrow.

I did start to feel that some of my stitching is being sewn up again. I got some support at work from Mr Smith, my deputy head from when

I was at school in Tunbridge Wells, aged fourteen. How surreal is that?

Then *Big Brother*, it seemed, and from what I remember, wanted me to go on *Big Brother 4*. I couldn't. I did not feel strong enough; probably another huge opportunity missed.

In March 2003, I got up and did a massive interview for *Now* Magazine, along with a whole bunch of *Big Brother* contestants: Darren from *Big Brother 1*, Alex from *Big Brother 3*, Nick Bateman, Narinder, Melanie Hill, PJ, Spencer, Helen, and me. I don't know if I talked to them about anything. It looked like it would be a positive article, and my school was fine with me doing it. They didn't know *Big Brother* wanted me back on *Big Brother 4*.

I was wise enough to know my mental framework wouldn't handle that life choice this time around. I was more excited that Will Young was next door, a few feet away in the next studio, just behind a door, as I got my makeup and hair done by a stylist. I would have loved to have met him. When the magazine came out, the headline was "*Big Brother* Disasters." Mine was listed first in bright pink: "Penny forced to quit her job" on the front of the magazine. I don't know why; I was not surprised, but it was disappointing as all the stories over the years, even in 2020, talk about my teaching and my towel. I felt like I had held a mini sparkler, but now it has burned out in my hand and just the grey stick is left.

I was starting to forget the joy and laughter I once knew. The London I loved was trickling away. Anne Kneller, the lovely lady at church who said, "God sees your heart, Penny," having deliberately watched me on *Big Brother*, died. I lost something so beautiful.

The Sunday papers started writing about me again. These were the years of "What happened to... Penny?" stories that elaborated on the fact that you are now a nobody but still want to be a somebody.

Students at school brought the *Now* magazine in for me to sign. Some were nice, saying, "Can you sign this for my mum? She loves you." Some brought in other clippings from newspapers and magazines or some *Big Brother 2* memorabilia for me to sign for one of their family members who was a *Big Brother* fan. When I went for a walk during my lunch break, builders ran across the road to get my autograph. They were nice moments.

Big Brother 4 launched. Cameron sings a Christian song under his breath: "This is my story." It is an old song called *Blessed Assurance*, written by a woman named Fanny who was blind but taught at a school, was married, wrote poetry, and knew her Saviour, Jesus. Dermot O'Leary wore a "What would Jesus do?" bracelet. I wonder if, had I gone back in the house, Cameron and I would have had some good conversations about our faith. Would it have been aired? Would it have been a topic I could have discussed with Dermot O'Leary? Maybe I was meant to go back in to show people the truth about my faith. But then again, would it have really come across like that? I am a mixture of contradictions and haven't trusted God the way I should have. My life hasn't been much of an example of what a Christian is. I learned a lot about how to finally walk in faith and go God's way over the years ahead as I came to the end of myself.

Big Brother told us to expect the unexpected, and that was exactly what life I was experiencing. I was trying to get away from this *Big Brother* negative oxygen I am forced to breathe, as it kept preventing me from living calmly and sanely. I had no idea I would still be the focus of so much attention in 2003.

I heard Paul Osbourne's voice on *Big Brother 4*. He is now one of their big producers for the show. He was my friend for a while in 2001.

By 8 June 2003, the anniversary of my eviction date, I was quite unwell and completely exhausted. School was just so difficult with so many classes and such disruptive students, and the negative response to my identity as "Penny from *Big Brother*" started to increase again. Like in that film, *Legends of the Fall*, the bear is finally quieted within; I just couldn't fight to explain myself anymore. I kept going right through the rest of 2003, exhausted, judged, and battling OCD. I am permanently terrified, so I write my prayer book, *A River through My Desert,* to try and find some balance. I felt like I was a spinning plate.

I met my mother in Barcelona in October 2003, and we tried on identical ball gowns in a changing room for no apparent reason. We walked around the city, and she told me of her adventures here when she was a teenager. My friends sent me a plane ticket to Australia for Christmas 2003, and I saw all my wonderful friends, which was lovely, but I still struggled on at school.

The papers continued writing about me, and the students were starting to get slightly hysterical. *I am again too famous to be normal, but too normal to be famous. Will this ever end?*

But by February 2004, I had trigeminal neuralgia and a middle ear infection. The left side of my face was almost paralysed. The pain is horrific. I was signed off work and was told to keep my head still. If any water got near my ear, it felt like burning oil. Then it came. I must leave the school. *Big Brother* stories, gossip, and reactions were all too much for me and the school.

Ironically, I tried to work there again as a supply teacher and did so for a few months but was asked to leave again in February 2020. The video of me dancing at Bubbles' birthday party in the *Big Brother* house, it seems, was on every student's phone in the school by 2020. In 2020, it appeared that there would be mass hysteria and even more mockery and vile comments. The tide of reactions that "Penny from *Big Brother*" is "my teacher" or "works at my school" had turned. I was drowning in 2004.

Piles of words (A poem)
Headlines written about me on interviews I never gave, plonked by a teacher on the Heads' desk at the school I am teaching at.

On which was written what could affect and make a heartbeat race.
 On which was written what could evict a family onto the street.
 On which was written what is explained another sudden disaster.
 On which was written what could express what cannot be spoken.
Now –
All clumped mashed into coffin like shapes.
A tumble of utter terror and confusion.
Recycled paper depot is my mind.
Again, I repeat as I look at the letter holding nothing.
    The End.

Once again, I was facing the unknown. I really did not know what to do. I didn't know this year would be one of the most deadly and dangerous ones I would ever have to face. In March 2004, I was slowly getting better from the dreadful ear infection. I had to meet with the union and the school to finalise an exit plan. It would mean I would get some pay and a reference. That was a relief, and despite the meetings that made me feel so worthless, the union helped me get both of these things sorted. I had no idea what I was going to do for a job once I used up the last pay slip from the school. It is unbearable when you can't bear the touch of your own thoughts.

I found myself running every day and also swimming when my ear infection cleared up. I had started to get to know Hastings, and there were a lot of lovely things going on. It does have a huge music scene and open mic nights. I found everything was within walking distance, which was a new experience after having to get the tube everywhere in London. In London, everything was a half hour tube ride away. Here I could walk over the west hill, known as The Top of the World, with its grand view, and down the old steps into the magical atmosphere of the old town, brimming with life. I would go out with my sister to listen to music, as Hastings is full of live bands. There were some really funny and quirky musicians, artists, and poets that we got to know as we would all turn up to the same events and festivals and then be invited to something they were involved with. Everyone was so genuine and kind.

They were lovely people; one of the beautiful artists became a friend and made me some 1970s CDs I still play today. She died of cancer very suddenly in 2019. It is still hard to believe she is gone. Emma Neville Towle, my friend who helped me with the wedding flowers at All Souls Church, would call at least twice a week. She would send cards, letters, and postcards. Every time I open a notebook or start writing, one of her cards falls out of the pages. I still feel like she is with me every day. This was the year she had to have an operation after finding out she had cancer. She moved home to be with her parents for all the treatment and recuperation. Her dad died suddenly of a heart attack, and to add to that sadness, I didn't know then that she would die in 2010. I wrote to her mother in 2011 and got a lovely letter back. In 2021, the phone rang, and this lovely old lady said she had to call me as she was clearing out some of the possessions of Emma's mother, who had died. She had found my letter and was moved enough to call me. Her mother had kept it. It was as if Emma were there saying to me, "Be beautiful and shine."

The opportunities we miss with the right people in our lives can be a blanket of sorrow some days. Paul, who helped me get my teaching certificate back, would come to Hastings a lot. I got to spend time with him and his partner, Alvaro. It was a lifeline to have them, and I still go over to Alvaro's flat for a catch-up with his homemade food, a bottle of bubbly, and chunks of cheese, followed by an herbal tea. I can't count the number of times I've been there, spilling out my sorrow and also making them laugh out loud at the absurdity of a situation I was going through because I was able to talk so openly and had their full support. They always made me feel like I had swallowed a sunbeam by the time I left them.

MEET ME AT THE MIRROR

How long is (A Poem)
Missing my teaching days in London at Sarah Bonnell.

How I ache for these days, with the plane flying in the Flam bards series.
Think of a scene you can only gasp at.
Days that weren't there but a hope was of them,
Only because it is so long, on and on and at the end of this string is
the ground.
Onto which I jump.
Looking up it is a multi-coloured kite that vanishes.
Melting into cloud sheets so fine yet able to hide.
How I ache, how I long.
It is the remembering such moments.
Like the silver we take out to polish, like the very old photos we turn
and turn on and on.
Then all retreats and there is at its centre truth spelt in the shape of
emptiness I am left with.

The End.

By May 2004, Lee from Mount View Theatre School was in touch. He had gotten me an offer in a pantomime. It was the same month that I found a church that reminded me of All Souls in its teaching and values. I started attending it and found it really healing. Unfortunately, it closed down in 2018 as nearly everyone had died. The preaching had been immense, as these were men in their eighties who had been through the war and had found their Christianity in dramatic ways. It was an inspiring place, full of their experiences and enthusiasm for God. I couldn't find another church after that, so I have my Bible study downstairs. The cats cuddle up; they know it is time for reading as I call them to join me.

Paul Bedsprings gave me an ornament steeple that I switch on. For the time being, it is my church. I was in touch with him as he lived a ten-minute train ride away and moved back to Bexhill in March 2004 from Edinburgh. It was a time of finding our friendship; there were so many calls and texts, and I remember telling him not to be a trampoline and have friends bounce on and off while he gave so much. I wish I had taken my own advice. I can remember meeting him for the very first time later in the year, before I left for pantomime.

I was to be second billing again, this time opposite Nigel Pivaro, Terry Duckworth in *Coronation Street*, who played Fleshcreep. I played

Katie Cucumber. It was in Wales, in Porthcawl, at the Grand Pavilion, and I didn't have a job, so I said yes. The show ran from 8 December 2004 to 9 January 2005. It was the same pantomime, *Jack and the Beanstalk*. Again, I had a photo shoot in my costume and wasn't sure about using a cucumber as my wand, but I went along with the innuendo. It was a time to learn lines and have something to look forward to.

In the newspapers, it said, "Penny, a real-life vegetarian, plays the part of an organic vegetable fairy in this festive offering." I met the most wonderful Dame, Greg Aston, and also a lovely young West End star, Gary Jordan. Everyone is just so kind again. To have a pantomime family is a very special experience. Even Nigel Pivaro wrote me a letter at the end, saying what a wonderful time we all had and how much I was loved by everyone. The dancers, other actors, and the stage set were all incredibly brilliant. I felt like I was in a West End show!

In *The Buddy,* a local paper, there was a huge article on me. It said, "*Big Brother* Penny, who also wrote a weekly review for the South Wales Echo on this year's *Big Brother* 5 contestants, will be playing Katy Cucumber, the organic vegetable fairy." It then listed a vegetable soup recipe, and there is a photo of me in my Katy Cucumber outfit in the kitchen making the soup. My "In the kitchen, out the kitchen" quote was chanted to me kindly on the streets of Porthcawl.

I say in the article: "I'm playing a vegetable in this year's panto, and I should be kind to all my vegetable friends, but on these cold winter nights I just love to sit in front of my TV and catch up on my favourite reality shows." I was asked how I would cope with Nigel as the villain.

I said, "As an organic fairy, I have special powers that will make sure our story has a happy ending. I also have a special cucumber wand that just keeps growing and growing. Cucumbers are for more than salads, you know!" I really don't remember making such a suggestive comment. I felt so embarrassed.

The photo of me in my gold cardigan was used in the programme, where they talked about my degree and teaching. They added what I had done since leaving: "Penny made sure she would not be forgotten by a few cheeky exploits." *Oh, dear,* I thought. What was true was the last sentence written about me: "She is thrilled to be back fighting giants and adding a touch of fairy magic to this year's pantomime in Porthcawl."

I had some lovely publicity cards Dale had made for me ages ago, in 2001, and could send them with my autograph on them; so many handwritten letters flooded into the theatre addressed to me. I have kept some as they are so full of love and encouragement, as well as requests for an autograph. I would meet people after the show, and the other actors were bemused by the crowds of all ages that gathered outside the stage door, waiting for me. I signed whatever scrap of paper or photo of myself they had, hugged them, and chatted for a while. I was given a beautiful ensuite room right near the theatre this time to live in, and I found the atmosphere of Porthcawl so beautiful. Before I went to Porthcawl, the rest of the year unfolded, still full of *Big Brother* for me as I was to be a columnist for *The South Wales Echo* for *Big Brother 5* and was back again in pantomime as "Penny from *Big Brother*."

In May 2004, Dale was in touch from West Norwood, where I had hosted an event with the late Dot Cotton. He was moving down from London to Brighton with Dean in a few months. I was ecstatic as, for the first time in ages, so many people I knew would be nearby. My dad came over from Spain for a Christian conference and stayed with my sister. She had bought the house from my mother and father when she left London in 2000. It seemed now that she wanted to move out and sell it. This threw up a lot of anxiety for me, as I loved that house. As children, we moved all over the world, and when we finally settled in England, we would move again and again as my mother, a wise businesswoman, bought and sold our homes. She recognised the opportunity to make a profit and move up on the property ladder. I wish I had her skill.

This house in Hastings was one we had when I was seventeen years old, and I wrote my first book there. The memories of family time were so real and precious to me. I felt sad to think it would be sold. My mother decided to buy it back from Kristina, and I sold my flat in Hastings so we could all live there together. While my dad was over, we had a chat about it, but my mother was distracted as one of her dogs, Bella, who loved to hide stones, died.

My friends in London kept in touch, but, as I said, life is always busy if you live in London. Claire made the effort to come down and stay at my flat. We went out to the only club in town and dressed up as it was a 70s night. She came down again later that year and brought Lizzie, as the bonfire nights and processions are something out of this world in East Sussex. She was buying a flat in London, so she was moving on from the flat where we had so many good times and where I stayed on her sofa when I was leaving London.

Marie came down to visit me a few times, and I went up to see her in July 2004, just before the birth of her first child. She has always been so faithful and loving. Her strength, encouragement, and love have been a lifeline for me over the years since *Big Brother*. She is just incredible, beautiful, and the most wonderful friend. I absolutely adore her. This is her account of events in June 2001:

"My dear friend, Penelope, contacted me a few weeks before my wedding, which was to take place on 6 May 2001, to inform me that she was desperately sorry that she would not be able to attend as she had landed a place in a new TV show. The gist of it was that she would be somewhere she couldn't leave, and she would not be able to contact me. I didn't quite understand what she meant, but I realised it was a big deal to her, so I gave her my blessing! I saw and heard nothing more as I was completely wrapped up in my wedding, so I went off on my honeymoon to Malaysia oblivious to the show. Two weeks later, I returned to Heathrow on the 10th of June 2001, absolutely astounded to see my friend on the front page of every Sunday newspaper—I thought I had travelled to a parallel universe! In that short space of time, she has gone from anonymity to stardom. Beyond crazy!!!"

After seeing Marie in July 2004, on the way back to the station to get my train to Hastings, I saw Marie from Friendly's, who had hosted my birthday party in 2001. She was sauntering up Old Compton Street in her Vivienne Westwood cloak and red boots. She insisted we go for a drink, and I only just made the last train back to Hastings.

I was starting to feel quite lost again; everyone I knew had something to do and someone by their side. I wanted time to stand still, like in the photos I would put in funky frames and place around me. I have always had lots of miniature and artsy frames with photos in them that date back years. I look at them fondly and know that was a beautiful memory that will never happen again. Even to this day, I hold London in my heart. Everywhere I go in London, I see a memory. I'm overcome with emotion as I walk through Leicester Square, past Red Cube, where we had our *Big Brother* 2 wrap party. Opposite the club was a restaurant that I used to go to every week when I was teaching before *Big Brother* and meet my dear friend Sue, who I have lost touch with.

It's funny how I was in that space years before I knew I'd be walking into Red Cube on the other side of the street as a reality star. I just love Soho and the South Bank too. Thousands of memories make my heart twinkle. I will always adore London. But now, in July 2004, I was back in Hastings, and I went and signed on at the dole office.

SCENE 2:
<u>Making sense of it all</u>.

It was around this time that I would chat with Brian, Bubble, Narinder, and Josh from *Big Brother 2*. We had some lovely chats over the years. They would phone, and I don't know why the phone calls stopped.

I watched and had to comment on *Big Brother 5* as I was writing for the *South Wales Echo* in Porthcawl, where I ended up starring in the pantomime the following December. I was very grateful for Dale's insight and help, as he was a super fan of the show – also, I was useless on the computer. I didn't have a computer, so he was emailing my article to the *South Wales Echo* every week from his computer. I dictated over the phone what I wanted to say. I was truly unaware of how to access anything on a computer. I knew how to make PowerPoints for my lessons in school when I had been allowed to teach, but honestly, I was totally ignorant and completely in the dark about anything about me on the internet or on the new social media platforms that had only just been invented.

Some of the comments that I am supposed to have written are: "We've been tantalised by a bit of bare flesh thanks to one of the contestants' naked lawn mowing antics. When I dropped my towel three years ago, the nation was in uproar, and I lost my job. Now, three years down the line, it's hilarious and has probably secured her place in the house for another week."

"First a food fight, then a water fight, then a full-on riot, which ended with security guards storming into the *Big Brother* house. Who said reality TV is dead?"

I talk a lot about all the contestants in my column, and re-reading them now, I see sadly that they are in a similar tone to the columns and comments written about me in 2001. I'm curious what those contestants thought, if they did read my column after they left the house. I do add in my last column, "This isn't panto" (as even Davina had compared some of their antics to a pantomime), and I continue by saying, "It is not panto but their reality. When they get out of the *Big Brother* house, they will see something about themselves and pretend to be OK with that". I think I was actually talking about myself.

I arrived in Brighton in August 2004 to see the end of *Big Brother* 5 with Dale, send the final column to Wales from his computer, and work for him and Dean at Gay Pride. I have never seen so many balloons cascade down the side of The Bulldog pub. Such different shapes and styles swirled all over the building. It was like there were walls of balloons; everyone loved it. I worked flat out over the weekend. It was quite thrilling, and joy was in the air. I also got quite good at serving drinks, and Dean warmed up to me a bit as he saw how hard I worked. When he checked the guns we use to swipe the drinks, I had worked the hardest and sold the most drinks. It was one massive street party. I called Lizzie to see how she got on with her A-level exams. I was exhausted! We hardly slept. Dean bought me a bottle of Benedictine and told me he would offer me a job if I wanted it. The forever friendship was sealed that weekend.

By 17 August, my mother, father, and I had bought the family home back. That weekend, I had to return to Brighton because Kitten from *Big Brother* 5 was getting married, and Dale had gotten the job of serving drinks at her wedding. We arrived as the bar staff and set up our area. We decorated and were in charge of serving all the drinks. I got on with serving the drinks but ended up being called over to meet Kitten, so I congratulated her and Lianda.

It was a beautiful venue set in the rolling hills of Brighton's Stammer Park. The whole place had been decorated, and a pink balloon arch was lined with pink feathers. There was a chill out area with red sofas and pink chiffon drapes. Housemate Becki Seddiki turned up. There was a bouncy castle outside, a barbeque, and a disco late into the night. The next thing I knew, I was being asked for a photograph. In *OK!* Magazine's September edition, there was a massive full-page photo of me standing with the happy couple. It quotes: "Penny was on hand as she was one of the bar staff at the nuptials." Going out in Brighton was eye-opening because Dale loved drag queen bars and karaoke. Every venue was full of such laughter and happiness. I met some really beautiful people. It was a few days later that Dale told me the photos of Kitten's wedding were in *The Sun* newspaper and that it might jeopardise her *OK!* deal. I just thought, *I know how that feels!*

MEET ME AT THE MIRROR

The Past (A poem)
How words written about me made me feel.

To look up and see-suddenly.
   So real, in fact -facing you.
   A disembowelled hung drawn and quartered part of your life.
   It returns as a moon from an eclipse.
   You are faced with the eye of truth formed within what you created.
   It looks.
   It is between you both and the loneliest is the ghost eye truth-as it wanders away.
   Unwanted and misunderstood.
   As you have hold of its voice.
   Between you pulling it in to two.
   For you now want a part of the remembering a comfort shed blanket barely covering your loneliness.
   The ghost shivers so, do you?
         The End.

I finally got a job in a jazz bar at the end of August. I had met Paul for a drink, the one who got my teaching certificate back. There was an advert in the window of the jazz bar in Hastings, and Paul said to go up and ask. In my opinion and from what I remember, there were a lot of tensions and energies between the owners, staff, and customers. It was always an overflowing place full of live music, with groups of builders and retail staff coming in just after finishing work for a drink covered in paint and dust and in their work clothes. In the evening, you would hardly recognise them; they had their smart starched shirts and fancy jeans on, their hair was gelled, and the place was full of their perfume and laughter. I was amazed. I had only worked in formal school environments, and now I was observing the nights out and the letting loose of inhibitions all over the place.

Looking (A poem)
About people who came in the jazz bar with different hopes and needs.

Aimless glance into the pupil of your eye I walk on.
   A peer into the circle of that bottle, they sit themselves on that grey block bench, group breath warm.

Into the TV set groups glaze glare.
Into the diary looks the single lonely girl.
Into, the empty purse.
Into the room goes the business man into the file it is his job.
What are we all looking for?
Looking at?
I look out the window.
Out the bus
I look out at you.
Why are the most sure things unseen?
Even as I look is what I see only how I think I see it?
Or can love be as real as death is? I change my glance to a look.
The End.

In the jazz bar, there were fights, tears, screams, and an air of celebration. I found it quite a relief from teaching and got really good at handling big drink orders and adding it all up in my head. I would come away from an evening with my bag full of tip money. It was a time to meet the real characters of Hastings, some of whom are sadly not with us anymore.

A few would sit at the bar and want to talk. Keith, a huge bloke who worked in London, would have a bottle of rioja and a Manchego cheese platter every night as he walked to the jazz bar from the station. He would tell me about the music events he was involved with. He died suddenly six years later. I had nicknames for them, like Red Wine Ben, with his briefcase, as he was fighting a case of some sort and rant about it for hours.

One of the regulars became my best friend for a while, Brian. We are still friends today, but we used to go out to music events, drink a lot, and then stagger home trying to eat chips covered in mayonnaise. He really looked after me and was such a gentleman. It felt good to listen to people's stories and their woes and help them. The owner's son, who was quite shouty and small but had such presence, was fancied by two of the staff members. The jealousy boiled up most nights to the point of explosion between those two. If they kicked off while changing barrels in the cellar just under our feet in the bar area, we would just slam the lid down and let them get on with it down in the cellar.

The owners, when they sold a few years later, opened a nudist bar somewhere abroad. I only knew that as I turned on the TV one night and there were the previous owners in their hotel abroad and in naked splendour! The girls who worked there were full of energy and absolutely stunning. But coming in for the morning shift, they would have a huge hangover, throw up in the sink as if it were a normal thing to do, and then do the whole day and night shifts again.

Chaos (A poem)
For all the people who shared their stories
with me across the bar.

I have seen a sunset so full, spilling over with multi layers of red and gold.
  A sky beset with diamonds.
  There are no words to tell you how I felt.
  Even if I tried they wouldn't match the roar of that lion like a black hole that has swallowed every minute sound and intake of breath.
  Even if I tried they wouldn't match what has suddenly stopped.
  Yet if I keep quiet I can again relive not just remember.
  There are no words to tell you how I felt.
  Even if I tried how my sounds can even attempt to be an echo of what I heard then?
                    The End.

Claire had come down for the weekend when they called me to do my first shift. I had to leave her in my flat while I hurried to my new job. The next day, we went to Camber Sands and saw the kite surfers and the dunes. Then into the old town to the Electric Cinema, which is a quaint red velvet little cinema so full of atmosphere. She told me to value myself. She likened our friendship to a snow globe, telling me to stay sealed in the right friendships, because if you get a bit shaky or neurotic, at least it is with true friends. Like when you turn a paperweight up and shake it, and the glitter or snow falls, she told me to do that with real friends. But I started to trust someone who talked to me across the bar, someone who was no good for me.

Love (A poem)
Dangerous love.

I wrote poems longing for love.
  Up until I found love.
  Then I wrote poems about the break and its pain.
                    The End.

At the start of September 2004, one of the customers at the jazz bar asked me out. My yes led me down a very dangerous road. Lizzie sent me another email as she has been living in Madrid, Paris, and Barcelona, congratulating me on finding happiness! It is the same week that I moved back in with my mum and dad to our family home, which I have known since I was seventeen years old.

My mother was helping me rebuild my life with her love, advice, and encouragement. It was also the same week I got a beautiful letter from the head of the school I had left in February 2004. She hoped I would do well with future projects, that I would have energy, enthusiasm, and creativity, and she thanked me for praying for her. She also offered to help me with anything I might be doing. I don't know why, over the years, I just didn't ask for help from friends or the amazing contacts I had made. My darling, kind mother left my dad in Spain so she could organise the builders to create the first floor of our home into a flat for me. Her and Dad would live downstairs and I had the opportunity to live with my wonderful parents, go to a lovely church, and meet up with good friends.

Ironically, my now writing room is the kitchen she had put in, so I write in a kitchen with a hob, sink and kitchen cuboards that I have decorated! I am "in the kitchen, out the kitchen" at home writing, and at work in Morrisons cafe, washing up.

But once again, I was side-tracked, and I allowed something unknown into my life. This man called and texted me so much, it got into my head! One of the girls I worked with became worried and hinted that he wouldn't be good for me, and my sister warned me about him too as she is friends with an ex of his. Everyone in my family now had to worry about me again.

Out of reach and reach out (A poem)
Allowing yourself to be someone else's punching bag

Like Nelsons column yet tall only in pride.
So- chiselled cold stone.
Even your eyes mind is somewhere else.
Which makes me follow the café skirting board to find an end, yet it comes to a corner.
My words may just as well be "Blah, Blah, Blah," for all they mean to you.

Until I mention how you treated me then you wake up the roar in you.
And shape them on my face.
How could I have ever let you know me?
I was in a bath of ice, a storm of broken branches and a day of
continual rain,
Until I left you
We part not even a handshake.
If only there was some depth sin which I could tread water
Only
Stagnant slime trod under unwanted slips between my toes and is
forgotten.
But to feel unwanted while unwanting is a sort of drowning .

The End.

It started with him immediately. The comments, the feeling that you have always done something wrong, the manipulation of your mind, implying things so you start to question your own sanity—I started to feel vulnerable, and I don't know why I allowed myself to be gripped once again by something so terrible. It was full of rows, blame, accusations, unexplainable suggestions, violence, and incessant phone calls and texts from the very start that unnerved me. I started to get completely manic and full of panic.

At a festival, I said something wrong, and he threw me over a steep cliff. I landed in a ball, jaded, bruised, and confused. He charged down the steep cliff to find me, still shouting in a justified shriek. He then takes a massive piss on the tree where I am lying. A man followed him down, shouting that he saw him try to kill me, and my partner tells him to "fuck off." When I did try to leave him, as I walked to work, a car swerved up onto the pavement, nearly hitting me. It was him, shouting and screaming. I paid off his debts and cooked him dinners while he went off with, I think, both other men and women. He locked me out of the house in the middle of a snowstorm; I froze! He did other things to me, things I am too ashamed to write down. It was one big broken mess from what I remember until 2006. I think I was having a breakdown; I was seriously mentally ill.

PENNY ELLIS

Thrown up against a wall (A poem)
Violent relationships.

I am throwing myself up against the wall of reason.
  Grazed, totally knocking myself out so the real is unreal.
  It makes me cry.
  It makes me dizzy and I can't breathe.
  In these limits that tie me that bungee jump me that elastic pull me
back and smacks me into the wall.
  So I try to get away but am yanked up and out of all reason.
  I try to cut it, it just reconnects and rebirths its head.
  I know I need to hold the right hand to pull me back over.
  There are days and days but slowly the days light will burn these
ropes.
  They will weaken; will show themselves up as the shadows they are.
  One day I will again be me and there will be nothing wrong with
that.
                        The End.

My script for the pantomime arrived, so I had to keep moving; I had
lines to learn. I had to go to London to do my photos and costume
fittings for the posters, leaflets, and theatre programme, and the
builders arrived at the family house to start renovating. My mother
was trying to rebuild my life, while at the very same time, I was tearing
it down again by letting this man into my life. I can't seem to get away
from him. One minute he is so cruel, and the next day, bouquets of
flowers the size of a small tree would arrive at my family's home. He
showered me with gifts he covered up not being able to afford, while
I covered up my bruised and swollen body.

The receipt (A poem)
What we buy to find happiness.

A bag of soft white hope.
  Two bunches of longing rising despite the thorns attached.
  A case of glittering delights cork exploding.
  A sealed magazine with a free gift.
  A bottle of bubbles expanding chaos.
  A packet of special offer just adds water.

What lists are we buying into?
At what cost?
Have we looked at our receipts?
 Are we buying into the truth or just living in frayed seams?
When did we forget to add the value of the cross?
                    The End.

By the time my birthday came around in October 2004 and tonnes of cards and presents spilled through the door from all my friends, I was once again lost somewhere in confusion, fear, and isolation. My mother had gone back to Spain, but on the phone, she said we all need to brace ourselves for total change. She didn't know what to do. I noticed that I couldn't stop crying. I felt like I wasn't allowed to see or call my friends, as the argument afterwards was exhausting and soul destroying. This man completely isolated me. It is amazing how wrong someone else can make you feel—mentally and emotionally, just all over the place.

Friends reached me by letter. I received a letter from Paul Bedsprings saying he was happy for me but to remember I have a book to write! While I lived my life on eggshells, Claire was diving in Zanzibar; she was on a beach with small crabs just after the morning rain, and she could hear someone working on a boat in the bay while monkeys swung on the mango trees. There were notes left around my house from my mother, who hardly saw me so had to write stuff down.

One I found a bit late was to empty the washing machine as she couldn't open the door, and her saying that she hoped she hadn't upset me and that she had eaten her fish and chips on her own. My poor mother. What was I doing to myself? My Emma, who helped me with the flowers at All Souls for the wedding, sent cards asking how I was and what I was doing. She told me she was staying strong in God despite her cancer diagnosis and the operation. Why did I not spend more time with her? She sent me a poem by John Smith called Summer Song and highlighted the line, "Know you are precious Eve's daughter. This knowing will see you through."

PENNY ELLIS

You had me on hello (A poem).
If only I had listened to the wisdom of my best friends.

When it isn't what you say, what you speak but the song that is found inside.
   Never heard before.
   As dew dripping off the dawns' chorus beak. This is my song.
   It's a penetrating tone that pierces my soul, unlike any bleep, shout or sigh.
   Carried on the notes I hear the words pale and hesitant is my faith.
   The whisper gets louder; it is for me you come.
   The realization is the petals blown off the strong stem.
   I am so weak; you are so strong.
   I see as I breathe, I catch them.
   "You had me on hello".
   Truth answers the door.
The End.

I was glad to get away to Wales to be again in the pantomime, *Jack and the Beanstalk*. I was so glad to be away from that terrible relationship and to have time to breathe without cowering in fear of getting beaten. I was now Katy Cucumber, the good fairy. Last time I had been Fairy Starlight. I don't think I had any starlight left in me. Ironically, I had a real situation I needed magic powers for at home, where I was getting more and more damaged mentally and physically. It can get to the point where you could get damaged to the point where you can't actually repair it, and that is when you know it has to end forever.

I was really proud of the write up of our *Jack and the Beanstalk* in *The Stage* newspaper. There was a big photo of me along with a write up about the show that said, "On a winner, Penny Ellis." That was the first headline that was positive without alluding to anything sexual.

Although, in the article, it says: "Penny Ellis from *Big Brother* striking an ecological, if unlikely, note as the organic vegetable fairy Katy Cucumber."

I was so chuffed to see my photo and such lovely comments in *The Stage* newspaper on 13 January 2005. I got to go to London for the end of panto season party at the Arts and Actors Club in Covent Garden. All the stars of pantomime were there. There was a photo of me again in *OK!* Magazine, amongst lots of photos of the pantomime stars. I have such happy memories of my time in Porthcawl. On New Year's Day 2005, I was out with most of the cast, and we sat in a playground on swings, eating chips and laughing.

SCENE 3:
Self-Destructing.

Arriving back home in January 2005, my life was filled with tension, destructive repeating cycles, and the on-and-off relationship with that man that I was controlled by. It was nothing short of horrendous.

The Meaning (A poem)
Made to feel like you are going mad by a controlling partner.

I wrote a long word down the other day.
  And listened to the sound it made rolling round my mouth.
  Baubles, in a loop or dried poppy seeds shaking in a pod.
  In a rattle- in a drum.
  There were only sounds to it.
  The word- that is.
  As I didn't understand what it should mean.
  I can play it in silence.
  You a seized frowned face staring away.
  I iron the creases out of your shirt, but your face stays the same.
  Until the time stopped feeling evaporates.
  I breathe in toxins filtering my blood and turning my very tears to
a dull red.
                    The End.

I was still working at the jazz bar, which was eventful in itself. Everyone seemed to let rip with their emotions, sitting on the floor completely drunk and crying; there were all sorts of emotional jealousies and fights. It was still a great place, and I met Kate. She was new to bar work too, and we both realised we were really good at it and worked brilliantly as a team.

Friends tried to contact me, and even people as far away as Australia were starting to get worried about me. I did manage to see Peter and meet him in Tunbridge Wells. He always has the ability to be positive and very reassuring. Even so, he was very worried about the choice I had made with this partner. Ted and Peter made the effort to come down to Hastings over the years, and I met them in London, where they have embraced the truest love of our friendship in meals and visits to places in London. They have always been full of joy, kindness, and laughter.

I asked them if they would like to add any thoughts and memories to this book as we lived through the journey together—I literally lived with them for six months.

Here are their thoughts and feelings based on what they can remember, their recollections of events, and their opinions:

"I remember you inviting me (Peter) to your school. You told me in front of your class that you were going on *Big Brother,* and I found it quite funny as no one was supposed to know. You were very adamant that you wanted us to be your friends and family when you went into the house. I did an interview on *Big Brother's Little Brother.* When I went into work the next day for my night shift, it was on cable TV, so not everyone could see it. But my workers and colleagues had seen it and took the mickey out of me and made me laugh. That must have been the first day or so, because the next thing I knew, you were plastered all over the newspapers and on the front pages. It was mixed emotions for Ted and me as we felt in our opinion you had been set up. We did discuss with the crew that it didn't seem like good publicity. However, you were so popular, and people at work and outside of work were talking about you. My colleagues at work were constantly asking me what you were like and, 'Are you sure she is for real?' and 'Is she that tall?' We started a scrapbook for you, and Ted taped all the shows on video. We went back to the *Big Brother* studio, but I (Peter) didn't do another interview for *Big Brother's Little Brother.*

"It was wonderful meeting Davina; I think I was backstage having a really good natter and a laugh with her, and Ted wondered where I had gone. We loved seeing your fantastic interview. Cathal and Declan, my best friends, whom you know really well, came to support you as well. I remember you staying at the Charlotte Street Hotel and doing an interview for *OK!* I also remember you getting quite upset when Bubble was evicted from the house after five weeks. Ted and I went to *BB2* Dean's wedding when we went to Birmingham to attend a charity event you couldn't go to. Ted went with you to *The Weakest Link,* and he also went up to Stratford upon

Avon with you. I came along to Mardi Gras and saw you introducing Steps onto the stage. You lived with us for six months and exposed us to one of the most amazing experiences of our lives. We were there at the wrap party, and it was funny as I was trying to get one of the contestants' attention, and Emma Bunton thought I wanted to talk to her. It shows how famous you all were. I had to say to her that I was trying to get someone else's attention! The book signing event was huge. When you moved to Hastings, I gave you two pouffes for Christmas, and we named them Peter and Ted. You are the only person who has lived with us, and it was wonderful. We got to know Gary (clap clap). We would be out in Balans and Soho on so many occasions. We gave you the tapes and scrapbook to remind you that you are famous, notorious, and bloody fantastic."

I had two scrapbooks, one from Donna and Steve and one from Peter and Ted. The kindness of true friendship.

Time with friends is like being on holiday. This poem is for you, Peter and Ted, thank you.

Holiday (A poem)
For Peter and Ted.

A gentle dusk setting across the plane.
   With a cock crow who wants the rays of the sun to stay.
   The curves of each bend on pebbles babbling so telling a multitude of untold stories turning the pages with kindness.
   It is simplicity like a warm hand greets you.
   I see our faces creased with tears in the connection.
   I look on with wonder hoping by gazing on the moment it will not vanish.
   It wouldn't matter if we reached nowhere or did nothing.
   The arch of friendship holds up the sky.
   There is no hard work only in the crash of the waves.
   Let us work for you the water says.
   I can lay down all I possess and let the tide pull away all that does not belong to me.
   The tide pulls it away and it is drawn up to heaven by the rays of a passing sun.
   You are just left to be.
   Yet a raincloud will spill out on a troubled world where I am too tired and too cold.
                    The End.

I couldn't really face up to it or talk about the weird chaos my life had become again. I remember wishing for so much when I lived in London; I loved walking across Waterloo Bridge and just being wrapped in the whole London experience. The view in the 1990s was so different from now. It just gave me a feeling of hope every time I walked over that bridge on my way home from Sarah Bonnell school. I couldn't believe that the person I used to be was now just a blur in my mind. I am now battered and bruised. I ended up in the hospital in July 2005, cut open and scarred. I now cannot have children.

Written on the Heart (A poem)
Trying to find my way out of this horror.

I couldn't believe it, yet true.
   Lips blue.
   Stopped my stork carrying hope flew-
   You- too.
   Single- solitary- note sound.
   Green line, so linear.
   A perfect colour (against the black).
   Now my second self-floats
   High above even me.
   Untouchable.
   So light. Air free yes alive, then skipping line pulls forces back.
   Alone yet into me again I rise up. Ruby lips smile in the beginning.
         The End.

A dirt road at rush hour on the tube (A poem)
Going to meet friends in the 90s' so carefree
yet wanting to find a partner.

I could have lasted the hustle and bustle if on a dry dust road.
   The "Mind the gap" in a promise of rain in the sound filled night of artificial lights all jam packed tight.
   Alone, entombed.
   Universe twinkles a manufactured brightness.
   In attitude inside a sun rises yet sets.
   Not with the day and yet how I rise when it bursts in rays.
   But in the coldness of dusks days' whispers

I sink beneath the horizon.
Alone,
So very alone.

The End.

By November 2005, I had started counselling after falling apart at the doctors. To begin with, she offered me six free sessions, but she soon scheduled six more for me. She thought my OCD was out of control and I had hypertension. I just felt, each day, that I was walking through a hall of mirrors, like those crazy mirrors that are supposed to make you laugh at a fun fair. I felt trapped in other people's distorted picture frames. I was broken mentally. I just didn't know how to step out of this chaos and began taking anti-depressants.

On the sinking (A poem)
Losing all sense of self-worth.

I could go back into that colour.
    (It isn't even grey).
    I like the colour grey.
    No it is indefinable (otherwise those psychologists would have the answer)
    I can feel it (that colour).
    Like a pregnancy test stick certainty seeping intently into that litmus paper.

    But then I think of a child and the dot to dot adding up the numbers into shapes.
    I pick up the crayons and begin to colour.
    Creating the action that will begin the play.
    The End.

I wrote an email to my friend in LA.

"It is a strange and mad time, as life grows older, we become more awake to what was true but too late to change. I have to find a way of living without this huge weight of dread that follows me around and drowns me in grief. I keep trying to find a way out of these cul-de-sacs but keep ending up in the same place. I want to be able to run along the road of life, freedom, and joy. I want to live in the energy, not in the struggles. I am so tired of others' limitations on my life."

All she wrote back was, "Failure is the back door to success."

I was trying to find my peace. Looking at the moonlight, I felt that it was the underside of the day. I felt uneasy, and untruths surrounded me. It was like faces were staring at me—people I just didn't know or trust. I was trying to get back to the stuff I was made of. Emma was cancer free and on an adventure in Mont Blanc, all smiles and happiness.

I had started working day shifts in a café owned by the same people that owned the jazz bar. That is when Madge walked in on 7 December 2005. She had moved to Hastings after her husband died suddenly, and she was grieving. We became best friends, and I have never met anyone with such a big heart of love and such a gorgeous sense of humour.

On what I thought of you (A poem)
For Madge.

Sitting there I didn't know what to think.
   That's how I knew.
   No words came into my mind,
   Just colours and light, so many lights switched on together.
   The colour purple is my favourite.
   Grand, private, flamboyant.
   A whole octave of sound and colour
   Swirling round your silver spoon in the coffee cup.
   As you pass the sugar to me.
          The End.

She seemed to know exactly what to say to me, and I seemed to know exactly what to say to her. We would sit in her flat drinking port, and I would take her out in the old town. For the first time in her elegant life, she actually embraced the type of life and people she had never encountered. We started a journey that day that is still going on today, and with her I was able to start taking tiny steps on the road of life I had been searching for. She got me out of a dreadful cul-de-sac of fear, pain, and despair, and somehow, I was able to lift some of her grief.

MEET ME AT THE MIRROR

The Wedding Trail (A poem)
For all who keep going like my friends Madge
and Brian from the Jazz bar.

I found it behind me and under me as I walked stridently and alone over the millions of feet taps to have hit their own rhythm on this our waterloo bridge.

It was at first a passing thought in which I looked back, that caught me in more than this moment.

A take in of breath, at last free of others ways back to my sight.

I had to stop and stare its flecked glitter, a silent dance a heaving pulse a slow waltz.

It was longer than I realized and so much weightier.

It couldn't be held and if taken out of itself all its glitter would dissolve.

A Cinderella time span held it.

Our moments are the crystals scattered so unplanned over its length till the close of day.

To know I could dive in yet like an idea would catch me.

Yet could I swim like the ducks do to shore who aren't wearing such things?

The End.

Other women started talking about their feelings in that café, and despite the turmoil I was in, it was a healing time. We would meet in a group, and it became quite regular. Then one day I stopped showing up. The women waited over four hours, hoping I would show up. It became a talking point for the owner, who was amazed by their devotion. He was also pleased at all the drinks they had consumed while waiting. Again, I was leaving good choices in the trash can. It was a dark time. I wept for the friends so far away, my church in London, and my school. All the framework of my life had broken off. I couldn't face anyone, not even myself.

SCENE 4:
Hope.

I managed to join a Christian theatre company, and by the beginning of January 2006, I prayed this year would be when I gave God a chance to be Lord of my life.

Sovereignty versus Solitude (A poem)
Asking for God to save me from despair and anxiety.

It is on the royal road that the dust falls like dried custard into the past.
The holy ambition loosens the golden medallions round my mind.
I have been down avenues, tried too many times to follow the loose gold coins.
No more dead ends but forward into the straight way.
I follow the Sovereignty and walk this holy ambition on the royal road.
The crown fits in the stillness and holy hush of the dawn. I place on the gold jewels of a prayer life in secret.
I find the golden light of sovereignty comes through in such solitude.
The End.

Mended Nets (A poem)
Asking God for the strength to find a
way out of suicidal thoughts.

"What again Lord?"
"But the storm is too great I might get sea sick.
Yet I go, into a boat with a paddle.
Out and in, blisters form on my hands, salt stings my eyes and grates my face like sandpaper.
I hear him say: "Here throw now ".
I lug and pull oh the smell seaweed sticky net over the edge.

I want to go in with it, to die in its slime and trinkets its strands of coloured string.

To let go of this life of flesh but the net falls over and in and is gone so deep in the swirl of dark violent waters.

I am changed in a second's second.

The weight of it all is rising.

Angels pull up and out so shiny, so light so full of every type of sea animal and shell.

Rising in the light of Gods design.

For God has mended each and every strand.

I never knew my net could hold so much beauty.

Or even be that shape.

How can it be that big?

It is and I realize I am on the shore.

Sure'

Enlarged in an enlarged space.

There is more than enough to fill and rebuild the life in its true blueprint.

It is rebuilt and safety is thrown over it.

I am caught by God at last.

The End.

Gary (clap clap) came back from Lapland, having won a holiday there, he wins everything he enters, it is magical; Marie was all excited about her newest addition, baby number two.

I heard from my Australian friends, Veronica and Vanessa, about home renovations and business ideas they are working on; all this is in letters and Christmas cards, as I had found that if I called them, I would just cry.

I eventually stumbled back into my church and listened to the truths I learned as a child. But I couldn't seem to get out of the tensions and dangers in my life. I started supply teaching again in January 2006, hoping that by then the students would have forgotten me as "*Big Brother* Penny."

I worked at a school in Eastbourne, the same school I worked at from 2015–2019, where I met Harry. It was full of such polite students; one was called Caleb, which reminds me of Caleb in the Bible. At eighty-five years of age, he fought against giants and impossibilities, and he had no fear. He believed in his God and said, "Let us go up at once, and possess it; for we are well able to overcome it."

He realised only God can give us the mountains in our lives, and he alone can remove them. I added that to my prayers. The teachers were inspiring and lovely, and I felt very safe when I was at work.

My family was getting more concerned about me in this relationship, but all I did was a lot of shouting and screaming at them on the phone. Being in Spain, they try to let me get on with it. Claire came down, and we drove up to London as Lizzie's foster mum was in hospital. We drove through Islington, and I remember being so sad to see the place where I was really happy and where life was normal before May 2001. I got Claire to stop the car as I saw my friend Rima from university, whom I lost in 2001. I ran towards her, and we started to cry. I took her number but never called, as life got quite frightening in 2006 and I was too ashamed for her to know what a mess I was in. If something is meant to be, it will come back to you. She did in 2020.

The supply agency was really happy with me and found me a permanent job as a Year 4 teacher. I had never taught in a primary school before and agreed to go meet the students. I visited my Year 4 class in June 2006 to have a meet and greet and take the class for the day. I wore a lovely yellow dress as it is my favourite colour, and despite it being a warm day, I wore a thin, long-sleeved cardigan to cover the evidence of the violence I was subjected to.

The day went really well, and the head teacher and students (so sweet and tiny) all seemed to love me. When we did circle time and all sat on the floor, they started to swarm towards me to hug me. It was completely overwhelming, and they seemed to absolutely adore me, but one of them pulled at my cardigan. The sleeves went up my arm, revealing a range of old and new bruises. I was horrified and so ashamed. I could not live with this shame if it became public in my workplace, let alone in my friendship group. It is amazing how much silent, secret pain we live with, too terrified to ask for help. One of the girls thought it was a tattoo (the small bit she had seen), so I quickly pulled my sleeve down. I could not hide this any longer.

That same month, I had a conversation with the doctor, who told me I couldn't be hit by anything on a part of my head again or it would kill me. My bruises being innocently exposed, and that conversation, made me have a revelation: I had to get out of this relationship before the term started in September 2006.

My friend Kate, in whom I finally confided, came in a van immediately to get me home on 2 August 2006, and my mother and father moved back from Spain to be with me permanently. His friends turned up at our front door in matrix-like leather coats, bearing knives, and threatening me and my dad for money. It was the first time I heard my dad swear with gusto and venom.

By the end of August, my parents and I were waiting for Holly, our new dog (also rescued), and as she came home, laughter filled the air. After one of the darkest times in my life, I had a month filled with birthday celebrations and rehearsals for the new show I was part of with the Christian theatre company. Hastings was full of atmosphere as we all celebrated Old Town week, and I went to Brighton to see Dean and Dale for the Gay Pride celebrations. I also started a job at a brilliant theatre school in Bexhill. Friends began to pop up again like spring flowers.

I got a lovely card from Paul Bedsprings, telling me to be kind to myself and that all will be well in its own time. Claire also wrote, asking if there was anything she could do, and Emma said in another of her regular cards that every cloud has a silver lining and reminds me that God's promise will renew my life. She told me to be encouraged: "You're still riding this wave of God's future and his promises." Her birthday card to me that year said, "It is symbolic of a new era of God's grace in your life." I wish she was here today to see her words and her spiritual guidance coming true in my life now. A postcard I received from her just before I went into the *Big Brother* house in 2001 said, "Ring me before you go in; I want you to be safe always."

I was finally at home. On Wednesday nights, I taught performance art at the theatre school until one of the pupils recognised me from *Big Brother*, at which point I lost yet another job. They claimed they "no longer required me." I was there for a few months before I gave another humiliating exit, in which I apologised for being on *Big Brother*! I gave so much, directing end-of-year performances and helping students prepare for theatrical exams. It was employing all of the talents I had learned in my theatre degree, and also what I probably would have done with the Royal Shakespeare Company if I hadn't veered off track with Adam after I graduated.

For half of the week, I was the Head of Drama at a secondary school, and the other half, I was a Year 4 teacher. The Jewish Society also commissioned me to write a play. It was a massive responsibility as it was the real life story of renowned surgeon Bruce Eaton, who lived in Hastings and escaped from Nazi Germany. During this time, I also wrote *River through My Desert,* which got published in 2020, and was also in a play. Friends were jubilant to hear from me and see me. I got the same advice from so many with regards to that relationship: "Run as fast as you can in the other direction."

It was good to have Holly the dog to care for and take my mind off things. I started to get out and watch some of the artistic things that go on in our town, including a dance troupe that performed in the open space in the dusk of the day and released all these white balloons into the sky against the most beautiful sunset. My dad baked bread most days, so the house was filled with warmth, sweetness, and the fragrance of wholesomeness—things I had not felt for a long time. We all watch God TV and study the Bible together, just like when I was a kid. I went to the christening of Marie's second child, and the Jewish play I was writing had its first reading; the committee reported back with comments like "very good" and "loved it," and talk of auditions being held for the play followed. Life sweetened.

I also spent a lot of time with Madge; it has always felt like we have known each other all our lives. We embraced the quirky, creative events and sights of Hastings, like two schoolgirls who were always giggling and doing something fun. There is an age gap, but I never noticed it. She just sparkles, even when we are sad and dealing with some awful pain. There were some terribly sad moments, but she has a strength that makes you believe you can get through anything. She is a truly amazing lady. Her son was one of my doctors when I was damaged and in the hospital at the end of July 2005—such a coincidence. When he died unexpectedly on Christmas Day 2011, it was such a shock; there are no words to describe such a tragic loss.

I worked really hard and seemed to have finally found balance and some sanity. Our home became a prayer filled home, full of peace. My parents went to a nearby Brethren church, while I went to my lovely old church in town. The teaching there was awesome and so encouraging. "God has not changed his mind. You may feel like you're in a prison, but it is the birthplace of God's promises and the day of small beginnings."

I love the fact that God likes the small beginning. I know if I let him, he will build the foundation. There were talks on being a true friend by being honest with our friends and confronting them with love when it looks like they are messing up. There was a talk about Joni Erickson Tada, whose story I have been in awe of since my teenage years. She became a quadriplegic after a diving accident as a teenager. She learned to paint while holding a brush in her mouth. When she was offered an art exhibition, each piece included a testimony about her relationship with Jesus. Now she has a ministry, a radio show, and is the author of over thirty books.

I couldn't believe it when I received the most beautiful letter from her in 2020. I had sent her my book, *A River through My Desert,* and a letter about what she meant to me. Her response was so encouraging and discerning. It is wonderful when those around you who really don't need to help you just do. It makes you think these are signs to say you're going the right way.

There were talks at my church on Jeremiah 29, a chapter in the Bible that declares God has a hope and a future for us—a message I have heard since I was a teenager. There were also talks on Nehemiah, who, against all odds, rebuilt the walls of Jerusalem in just fifty-two days. It showed me that once you find a passion, you will begin to see things as you have never seen them; that God will take your chapters of regret and write a story of grace. As you begin doing God's will, change the way you think, and start believing, "This is what I was made for," you will have your heart set alight by God's passion.

I listened to talks on making mistakes. The Leaning Tower of Pisa was built with just ten feet of weak foundation for its one hundred- and eighty-three-foot height, causing its famous lean, proving that everyone makes some sort of mistake and that an unstable foundation will not always result in ruin. These men of God at my church spoke the word of God with such conviction. Their lives and the lines on their faces showed that through all their years—more than eighty—God had shown himself to be true. I started standing up inside and gaining back my self-respect and confidence. There is an old Italian proverb that says, "Between saying and doing, a great many pairs of shoes are worn out."

I was happy for the first time in years; I didn't know I would have to leave teaching again in July 2007. I hoped that by 2011, students would not recognise me at all. Trying to teach 2011-2020 was just as impossible, if not more so. By 2011, social media use grew exponentially, and trying to go forward in an ordinary life that I had loved and longed to return to was ok for a week or month, until I was found on social media sites, and then my ordinary would be snatched away again. I had to leave about sixteen teaching jobs in those few years. I wanted to share some of my memories of trying to teach from 2011 to 2020 after being a *Big Brother* contestant and a figure in the media.

I wanted to add what happened to my life; so many tabloids have used the headline, "Where are they now?" Well, this is where I really was, and my version of events was all about perseverance and trying to overcome obstacles. I need you to see that I did strive to go back to the life that I had known and that I didn't cling to my fifteen minutes of fame like the tabloids have stated. If I had just been allowed to return to my normal and teach, then there would be no story to tell and this book wouldn't have been written. I only hope it is a story that can help and encourage others to be strong and begin again, no matter what anyone thinks of you.

As was customary, I was called in at the last minute for one supply job. I was up at 4 a.m. just to spend some time with my cats, have a nice coffee, and have my prayer time. It would be the only calm part of my day. I'd always ensure I was ready to walk out the front door by 7 a.m., as supply would call between 7 and 8.30 a.m. If they didn't ring by 8:30, you knew there was no work for that day, and you would undress and put your packed lunch in the fridge, hoping for work the next morning.

This particular morning I was asked to go to Hadlow College, which was a three mile walk from the bus stop to the college and about two hours of waiting for the return bus home. I took the job as I was desperately trying to find my feet in teaching again. All I found on arrival was a few sheep in a field. They were really apologetic, as I was actually there to teach maths, which is the only subject I can't teach. I walked past the sheep on the way to the bus shelter and asked them what they thought about Shakespeare.

At another school, parent's evenings were sometimes at 6 p.m., so you would hang around for two hours after school ended, absolutely exhausted. On this particular evening, it got to 9.30 pm, and I was shattered. I tried to answer the questions of a particularly intense parent, but she was disappointed in my answers.

The next day I was called into the head's office, this time confronted with an email from this parent, complaining that I was drunk at parent's evening when I was talking to her! I was getting so tired of explaining myself all the time. The students still liked to hide in cupboards like I did in the 1980s; some of the old disruptions in the classroom never go out of fashion, but some of the new trends were downright disgusting and bullying. They would take out the inside of a biro pen and feed bits of very small paper through the plastic shell. At first, you wouldn't notice, but you would be aware of the sniggering. Then a bit of soggy paper would hit your face, and there would be an almost silent cheer from the mass of students. You now had to figure out what they were doing while pretending you hadn't noticed, so you would wander around the classroom pretending to look at their work and suddenly see the plastic biro cover and realise there were hundreds of tiny gobbed bits of paper all over the whiteboard as they had quietly aimed for your face. As you transferred to different schools, you were now well-equipped with this knowledge because all of the students followed the trends. One time, I just ended the lesson and wiped the gobbed bits of paper off with the students' books as cleaning cloths.

My worst months for supply work or having a permanent teaching job were April to July 2011–2018, when the *Big Brother* theme music and show would begin, making my teaching days virtually impossible. As I've previously said, I had around six hundred internet articles removed in 2016. Google privacy in 2014 did help, as the European Court of Justice granted "the right to be forgotten." However, there were some sites I couldn't take down because of freedom of information or expression. "The right to be forgotten" was a positive shift in law and policy for cyberspace in 2014 because it did increase an individual's control over personal information and restored some balance between free speech and privacy in the digital world, but more still needs to be done.

Regardless of changes to online legislation, in real life, I was still escorted off the premises of a lovely private school after being offered a job in the English Department because I was recognised by one of the teachers, who told the head master. Security literally marched me to the front of the beautiful private school. I was devastated and had given such a brilliant interview. In that "right to be forgotten" year, I was also called a "paedophile" by a teacher for exposing myself on TV and was sacked. I wept on the phone to my mother, and all she could say was, "The tone creates the music." She always told me to create a harmony wherever I went.

But all I could hear in the schools was chaos, judgement, and condemnation. Students loved it anyway when they got a supply teacher, never mind one with an online presence. It was a free lesson for them. It was time to torture the fresh blood, to pretend to be someone else on the register, to cause havoc and confusion, and then if the supply teacher called for the "behaviour team," the students would just say that the reason it was all so chaotic was because "the supply teacher is shit."

The focus always falls on you; they just think you can't control a class. Not only did I experience lots of these incidents of being accused by a thirteen year-old that I couldn't teach, incidents played out deliberately by a nasty student whose sole purpose was to make the other students like him—I would also experience the chant, "And you dropped your towel," followed by a YouTube video or photo off the internet being played to the whole class, who would then reach for their phones and find my *Big Brother 2* clips. The power these students felt they had over me was appalling.

Trying to add in differentiation for a child with social anxiety, or who has arrived from abroad and can't understand English, or who is back from having a few months out for behaviour problems, was impossible if they were all in the same class that was full of disruptive students. The only saving grace was suddenly realising you're not needed for the last lesson of the day, so you could dash for a train that wouldn't have students on it shouting and swearing and filming you on their phones. Another couple of highlights were suddenly getting a polite child or actually getting decent cover work for that lesson. Most of the time, it was get them to draw a poster. Five lessons of posters, all just to be thrown in the bin.

In the newspapers on 13 November 2021, I was saddened to read: "TikTok abuse is pushing teachers over the edge.

"Dozens of teachers have reported harassment on social media in recent weeks; some have signed off sick. The posts students are putting up often feature footage from learning resources used by teachers during lockdown. The government plans to introduce laws to make social media companies more accountable, but what is being done in the meantime?"

In 2021, I got a lovely message on my Twitter account saying, "My son started his first day in year 10 yesterday, and I was reminiscing about my own school days and telling him about teachers that inspired me (which I must admit was a hard thing to do.) And there you were, at the TOP of my list."

Most of my supply teaching days were spent as fresh meat, and acorns would be thrown as I left the train and walked to the school amongst the students. Then I would hoist thirty text books and a box of their lesson books and stagger in the pouring rain to the outside hut. On arrival, the students would be jumping in the puddles and kicking water at the other students. To my horror, the hut would be locked, and no one knew where to get a key. I was not supposed to leave the students, so I would send someone I thought would actually go and get the key. By then, the noise is likened to putting your head inside a plane engine, and it is still only 9:10 a.m.

I found it even more stressful to just have a thirty-minute break for lunch as the breaks were shortened to diffuse bad behaviour, especially in a difficult school. But then that behaviour just poured into your next classroom. Supply teachers were mostly called out to "difficult" schools where teachers were off sick due to stress. One of the worst experiences was a child returning from a loo break and throwing a whole toilet roll covered in shit and piss at me.

Then there are the lessons where you have to implement a flash test on the very next subject these students will be learning about. So they sit for an hour-long test on a subject they know nothing about with a supply teacher, and I am supposed to get this class to take this test in silence. The drama room is the worst, as there are so many light switches. When they know they have a supply teacher, the room goes black immediately. The students scream with delight in the dark while you are desperately trying to find the light switch. It is an opportunity for a fight to break out, and you fear for their safety as well as your own. As YouTube videos of me begin to circulate, it is once again a school that does not want me back.

Most supply teachers I met up to 2020 were retraining as horse groomers or gardeners—anything other than teachers. A popular phrase would be, "Just get me out of here!" How do I take the register when the computer is facing away from the students and is wired in such a way that the PowerPoint screen is behind me rather than beside where I can stand in this classroom?

Trying to set a table plan to try and separate the gang of bullies who wanted to torment you and any nice students in that lesson who did want to learn. Once TikTok's trend of dancing videos took off in 2016, it was almost impossible to keep them in their seats. All students are believed, especially over a supply teacher. "This teacher teaches me nothing."

They are allowed to say exactly what they want: "My trainers cost more than you earned today" or "you're picking on me." I will always remember the teacher who came into a class to help me and said, while looking at me, in front of the whole class (who were all hysterical about realising I was Penny from *Big Brother*), "We have all done things we are ashamed of." You can probably imagine how little that helped settle the class.

Another time, "Maybe we could put some strategies in place to help you," was said.

During those years, I had a massive mental breakdown in those years and sat in the garden, painting stones from the garden and gnomes I bought in Pound Land yellow. When I finally left teaching in

2020, I had night terrors for five months. Six lessons per day, plus break and lunch duty. I remember going into a primary school as supply and being told to take a boy to the toilet and hold his willy for him, so he didn't piss all over himself. Sorry, I'm not doing that! The assistant who asked me to do that then reported me to the head, saying that I couldn't do my job. The sound that still fills me with shivers is that of the students deliberately scrunching empty water bottles.

My mother told me to be boring. I tried, but I've always been me. The students would bring a row from a previous class or from the playground, and the fight would continue in my lesson. They would stand up for no reason, slap rulers on their desks, throw their pens and try to get them to stick in the polystyrene ceiling. They would bring in food made in the lesson before and just start eating it. There would be that student who would get up to pick up their pen from the other side of the room eight times in one lesson, all so they could punch another student in the arm, whom you deliberately sat them away from because you knew they were bullying that student. Then you would be put on "appraisal" for 3 months and suffer the humiliation of being assessed, which means any senior management can observe any of your lessons at any time. Once a week, the senior teacher in charge of you informs you whether you received a red, yellow, or green sticker for progress, as if you were a child yourself. It was too stressful and humiliating for words.

By 2018, forty-five per cent of students were permanently online on their phones fifteen per cent were sexting, and thirty-two per cent were spreading false rumours. Social media pressure caused almost twelve deaths per one hundred thousand in fifteen- to nineteen-year-olds, compared to just eight deaths in 2000.

I heard, "She's got YouTube up; she's looking up how to teach us."

"Should have gone to Specsavers, miss."

"My friend said you were on drugs."

I just wish they could have realised that the pressure they were under, they also placed on me—that we are all just trying to keep afloat and that teachers are human too.

Some of these schools had lectures, so you literally could not sit down anywhere all day in the classroom. Then there was the trend of placing foil over their teeth. Their phones are glued to their hands; they live inside what they see through their phones. They loved using translation on their phones, so suddenly an automated voice would say, as loud as anything in your classroom, "So and so has a big cock."

Students thrown out of other lessons would wander in and sit down, increasing the chaotic atmosphere further. Some students would try to get in the way and say, "You tried to touch me."

"You haven't helped me; I'm going to report you."

"You're useless. You haven't explained anything."

It gets to break time. You're desperate for a wee, and some students would sense that and linger, saying, "You can't leave 'til we have all left the classroom." They draw a poster the next lesson with a face with a cock for its nose and say it's "dribbling." Such sexual connotations from small, young mouths. On certain days, schools would hire a speaker to inspire us all. It cost them about £800, and we got to take a day off from teaching to build a structure with furry wires.

By 2019, teenage suicide had doubled, and social media giants were told to bring in duty of care procedures, but online abuse is still causing self-harm and suicide among children, teenagers, and adults.

By 2020, thirty-eight reality stars had taken their lives around the world.

I keep remembering my former teacher in 1984, who told the papers in 2001, "Penny was a wonderful girl from an exceptional group of girls; I'm quite disturbed by what they are saying about her." I really mean it when I say I could have easily become another of those statistics at some moments in my life, another poor life taken by cruelty that began in the media and seeped into my real life.

In August 2022, in *The Guardian*, the headline read, "Can *Big Brother* distract us from our own reality show? The original titan of the genre transfixed audiences. In a more forgiving and less self-aware age, a comeback seems irrelevant."

I think of the students and young adults of today. How times have changed. In 2004, another newspaper article said, "With the majority of panto audiences tucked up in bed by the time *Big Brother* was shown, Penny is relieved youngsters will see her just as a good fairy rather than a TV celebrity."

That was no longer the case following the dawn of the age of social media. With the loss of my reputation year after year, I felt for those being threatened by an article published on 7 May 2020. It read: "*Big Brother* stars fear for their jobs as TV bosses decide whether to re-air the *Big Brother* raunchiest moments from the show in an anniversary special."

In 2010, there was another article along that vein. It read: "*Big Brother* Bombshells: reportedly fearing the prospect of some of their racist moments seeing the light of day on TV again, they have formed a WhatsApp group to try to prevent producers from re-airing their infamous appearance in the house."

There really is no escaping your past once it has been put in the media or shared online.

In 2001, there were three hundred thousand people subscribed to E4, which was, in those days, aimed at teenagers. Back then, *Big Brother* screened for twenty four hours, and viewers chose different camera angles like I have already explained, voted by remote control, and followed their favourite housemate with the camera angles chosen. In light of this, the article in 2001 continued with a campaign group called Family and Youth Concern. They said, "It is not the role of TV companies to push back the barriers. Their job is to entertain and hopefully educate."

The article links *Big Brother* "pushing back barriers" with the activity in the house in 2001, and of course I am mentioned again as wanting sex live on TV. Another article in *The Guardian* in May 2001 read, "The Naked Truth. A contestant on the TV show *Big Brother* could lose her job for appearing nude. But most parents couldn't care less what teachers do in their spare time."

In another article, I am supposed to have said: "My headmistress said to me not to come back to school if I start shagging."

There was even an article in *TES*, the paper found in almost every school staff room across the county, in 2008 saying, "Now Penny is teaching again, she is trying to live a low-profile life on the south coast. A Hillcrest school spokesperson said she was not currently working there. But Miss Ellis hasn't completely abandoned show business ways; her agent said she would do a phone interview with the *TES* for £1.00. We declined."

It is all lies, but teachers would have read this and believed it!

Another article in 2005 read: "Miss Ellis, known to millions of viewers as Penny, has left the spotlight and moved to East Sussex to be a supply teacher. Despite claiming that she is happy with her life, she has found it difficult to go back to her former career." Again, I never gave any of these interviews.

The phrases "standout moment" or "largest moment" have been a constant in newspapers over the years. Then, alongside these recycled phrases or headlines, there's the subject of me showering naked, and every year from 2005 through 2022, the newspapers repeat these exact words at the start of a new article!

The sentences in the newspapers are always the same: "School teacher Penny Ellis came under fire/was shot in the outside world, after she was seen showering in the nude on screen." Even though the actual newspaper story has nothing to do with me, such as Kate Lawler's reunion, this exact story, headline, and phrase continue to appear in 2022.

The same narrative about me showering naked was used at the beginning of the actual story about *Big Brother*'s 20th anniversary, with photographs of Davina and Rylan, and there it was again, next to a piece about Alison Hammond. Remember, all these stories and phrases stay online too, so the students read about me showering naked, the teachers read about it, and anyone else can see those stories online.

So many *Big Brother* stories online and in the media start with me being shot in the outside world after showering naked! My head screams as I didn't film myself showering! I didn't know I was being filmed taking a shower! No one has a shower with their clothes on. Everyone takes a shower naked. It is so humiliating, as sometimes the headline is "Where are they now?" Being perceived as purposefully showering naked, as well as people passing judgement on what I am doing with my life now, is a double blow.

In one story, it says I did a deal with the *Express* newspapers. My "well-placed soap suds" are highlighted, referring to the photo of my naked body covered in bath foam from my *OK!* Magazine photo shoot, where I felt powerless and desperately tried to cover myself with whatever I could. It continues, saying, "Penny told *Now* magazine she had become obsessed with fame but found the pressure of the celebrity circuit self-destructive."

I wonder why *Big Brother* didn't find my footage "offensive," as they say in their apology for showing my towel drop?

So many online quotes I'm alleged to have made have cast doubt on my ability to teach.

"Prim and proper teacher Penny has turned into a man-eater days after going into the *Big Brother* house."

"She told pals she is willing to have sex on TV to scoop the £70,000."

"Millions saw sexy smacker screened live on the website."

"Penny says, 'It is like diving off a high board and leaving everything else behind.'"

"Penny hungry for men."

"'Penny is a man-eater and will do anything it takes to win', said her best friend."

"Penny who gave 4 million startled viewers a full-frontal flash of her naked body in the shower, claims it is the fault of the cameramen."

These quotes and headlines are, once again, stories I never sold and things I never said.

In 2012, an article in the tabloid again quoted a member from one of the schools I have worked in in Hastings as saying, "She had trouble fitting into school life. The children recognise her, and it has made a difference to her working relationship with the students."

My question has always been, how did the students know who I was? I am teaching eleven- to fifteen-year-olds. It is 2012; these children were only about four years old in 2001. By 2012-2020, the worst ever years of my teaching life, how did students who hadn't even been born when I was on *Big Brother* even know about me or my other name; how would they recognise me when they had never seen me on TV?

Again and again, the same article has been in the tabloids over the last twenty years, just tweaked and with sarcasm added or a mocking tone. "Lisa Penny Ellis, the teacher who gained notoriety when she bore all on *BB2*, has returned to the classroom. The drama and English teacher was forced to leave her job at a London girls' school when her towel slipped and she exposed herself on Ch4 TV show *BB*."

The things I am supposed to have said are just so rude and inappropriate; I never would ever talk like that, and those articles that state, "Only exclusive interview," as if I gave the interview and was paid for it. Both of those are not true. Yet I am supposed to have said, "My headmistress said to me, do you expect me to let you strut around naked for two months on TV?" I am supposed to have told the papers that "the experience helped me clear out loads of emotional baggage."

All these exclusive interviews; I wonder how many teachers, students, parents, and members of the general public really did believe all these so-called interviews?

Closer magazine used the popular phrase "Where are they now?" again in 2005 to mock how low people had fallen and reveal all their failings, stating that "Even Penny Ellis, who dropped her towel on live TV, had managed to go back to teaching."

Another article with the same headline, "Where are they now?" talking about the cast of BB2, said, "Bumbling Penny, the English teacher, who went wild and stripped off after she bared all, had decided to go back to teaching after pantomime in Porthcawl," alongside a photo of me arriving at Emma Bunton's birthday party taken in 2001.

In 2006, "Following her eviction, Penny was fired from her job as she appeared nude in the house and has then hastily returned to teaching as a supply."

People I'd never met were saying whatever they wanted about me, as if they were my friends. Again, in 2011, in the "Where are they now?" segment, I am listed alongside pop bands, actors, and other reality stars, saying, "After a stint waitressing, she is now back teaching." I did try to teach 2011-2020, but how was I meant to be successful when article after article was published for all to see, reminding those reading of my naked body in the shower? I wanted so hopelessly to return to my old normal, to return to the career I once loved so much.

In 2011, I got a beautiful letter from my old student, Suky, telling me that "if someone doesn't grasp your character, they don't deserve you." She is glad I am teaching again, as she says, "It was the greatest gift you could have given me." All my girls are so happy when I am teaching, as their memory of me as their teacher is one of being inspired, happy, safe, and learning. My time as a teacher at Sarah Bonnell School was magnificent. I am glad they haven't seen the chaos and nastiness of my days in teaching since them.

Suky wrote what she remembered about those days and seeing me go into *Big Brother*. It is what she remembers, and it is her opinion and memories.

"In 2001, when you went into Big Brother, I was in year 11.

I believe it was quite near the end of the school term, so my time was coming to an end at the school. I recall you being very excited, and us being very excited for you. Back then, reality TV was so new, such a novelty, and felt like a genuine experiment.

I remember seeing you on screen for the first time and being confused as to why they were calling you Penny, but of course it all makes sense mow. It was incredibly surreal and exciting; to me, it felt like you were at the centre of it all. From the outside, all the hype was about you (even before the controversy), and you were one of, if not the most, interesting people in there. I think the school was excited that you were going in (I could be wrong). Perhaps they didn't understand what it all meant.

I recall when the controversy happened around the 'towel incident.' My initial and only thought has ever been, oh, it's an everyday accident. I honestly don't think it occupied more than a few moments of my time. I don't mean to minimise it, but I thought absolutely nothing of it, and I still don't understand how such a story was made out of it. I don't think I thought about it again until we met sometime later and I realised just how devastating an impact the media had had. I'm so sorry. I had assumed others, or most folks, had made the same assumption I had; I'm sure many had, though I hadn't paid attention to the media, which you were obviously at the centre of.

For personal reasons, I was unable to come see you when you came out of the house, though I recall many students did, and I remember them being really excited. I remember the hype afterwards; it felt like you were jet setting all over the place. Of course, I'm not sure what the reality may have been like for you, but from my perspective as a sixteen year-old, it looked very exciting. I think I had left school that summer, so I am not sure how the school dealt with it. I recall that some parents may have written to the school, but I cannot recall what they did, if anything.

We stayed in touch during my college years, and I think we met again just as I finished or came back to London for university. . . and then the rest is history. Obviously, our relationship was now able to evolve from teacher and student into friends.

I think I was taught by you from year 7, possibly. I remember thinking, this is not your ordinary teacher, but I loved it. Growing up in East London, it's incredibly important for young women to hear that, as you told us, 'These are all the doors, endless doors, available for you, and you can walk through any one of them.'

You were one of those who taught me exactly that; you have probably never realised how fundamental a lesson that was and how it would go on to shape my future and my life choices—I will be forever grateful. You are exactly what young people need—you showed us anything is possible—just give it a go—TRY (as per your poem). You made things simple to understand—'to accomplish great things, look straight ahead, and it is much simpler to get there,' you may have said this to me when we were lost somewhere in central London trying to get somewhere with the theatre company I was in that you had set up called Kinderwein (Voice of the Child). We eventually looked up to get our bearings. I wrote that sentence down; it became a personal mantra.

I loved Kinderwein, and personally, it was a lifesaver. It taught me confidence and started to open up opportunities... We did numerous performances in schools, community groups, and English-speaking debates; I recall a mock court trial. I had a script I had written and performed it, winning a Shining Through Award—such a geek!

You introduced the school to this award by sending our creative scripts and poems into this new programme that had started in Newham to promote and praise the talent of young people. After that first year, when I won along with Lizzie and others from your form and Kinderwein, the school got very involved as it was a really prestigious ceremony with high profile names giving out awards and life affirming speeches. Lots of other teachers from Sarah Bonnell then entered their students. I think it has grown and grown. Kathleen got into National Youth Theatre as well with your help.

Our theatre group had a write up after our first Easter workshops. It is sad to think the group was just really taking off in the community when you went into Big Brother. I know you thought, like us, you would be back after a few weeks and maybe have a contact for our theatre company from the experience.

The headline read: 'An EGG-cellent Idea from Drama Girls.'

The article said: 'A group of studious Newham schoolgirls gave up part of their Easter holiday to hold a series of creative drama workshops for local children. They held six-hour workshops which they devised themselves for the five- to twelve-year-olds. The fourteen-year-old school girls taught various drama skills, improvisations, and theme based work exploring a range of social issues.'

We had the opportunity to work with Play Development in North Woolwich, as the organisers were really impressed and said we could have gone back every year devising theatre projects for young people.

To others, you became Penny; for me, you are always Lisa.

If I had to try, though it probably doesn't do justice, I would describe you as: adventurous, talented, courageous, inspiring, daring, exciting, challenging, honest, human—never any pretence—wicked sense of humour, and that you grabbed life. Today you remain all of the above and still an amazing teacher (I find I'm always learning from you, your experiences, and wise reflections), and you are always a kind, caring, wonderful friend. Anyone who has had you in their life is very lucky.

You gave me a notebook for my fourteenth birthday, and it has been by my side these past twenty-two years as an inspiration ever since. Your poem is at the front, and the quote at the back."

PENNY ELLIS

A Wish for Each Day. (A Poem)
The Poem I wrote for Suky.

It is the first breath of the birds.
   That dawn yawns wide enough -
   For us to discover in the sameness-a newness.
   For days of hours, minutes, seconds is a flutter of wings
   Millions of words -
   Thousands of smiles on faces.
   Each day begin WITHIN your inner souls self.
   The knowing of what was TRY.
   The splendour of what could be.
   And fly.

The End.

In her journal I wrote: "To accomplish great things, look straight ahead and it is much simpler to get there."

I keep hoping I will find this nugget of gold again, and I hoped to have found it in the jobs I had at the moment. Paul Bedsprings came down for Christmas from Edinburgh, and we enjoyed the music and atmosphere of Hastings at Christmas. He again had wise words and said, "Instead of sitting in something you can't have, live in something you can do." I started to see friends I haven't seen for ages and caught up with Racheal, whom I met at university. I am so grateful for the friends that have stayed from years before and who are more like family now having known each other for so long. It is always surprising when new friendships become incredibly precious, and you feel blessed for meeting them; I'm sure we all have those moments. I found that to be true with Guy and Liz, whom I met through my husband—a most wonderful couple.

My mother and father decide to book a trip to Las Vegas for the New Year. On TV was a programme about a nudist hotel, and I recognised the owners standing there in all their glory in Portugal. It was the couple that owned the jazz bar I had worked in. I went to see Dean and Dale in Brighton over Christmas 2006 and then spent New Year's in London with Claire. I am crowded with kindness again.

It is pantomime season, and to celebrate, *Big Brother* actually filmed ten of the past housemates from different years living for eleven days in a house and enacting out the pantomime *Cinderella* from the 20 December

2004 until 5 January 2005. Over the next few years, a lot of *Big Brother* and *Celebrity Big Brother* contestants took part in panto. Once again, I missed that opportunity. I just can't seem to build towards anything.

By February 2007, I was really struggling with the teaching again. It was starting to get prickly. People started to recognise me again, and it is hard to avoid. There are comments from staff and students alike. The year 4 class, however, just love me. Every time I worked there, I got posters, pictures, and always a bunch of weed like flowers from tiny hands; there was always something on my desk.

They wrote things like, "You really heal my heart."

"You're good at art and sewing and knitting."

"You deserve everything."

When I observed their innocence and joy, I was astounded by their words and their little ways, which filled me with such emotion.

However, I was crying most mornings before I went off to teach at the secondary school. It was terrifying, and I couldn't seem to get a handle on behaviour. Dad became concerned, so he decided to start driving me in the mornings. He gave me a pep talk each morning and then just told me to stop doing this teaching thing to myself, as it had again made me a nervous wreck.

One morning we went to leave a little bit later than we usually did, and with that, we were just about to leave when we heard a massive crash upstairs. I ran up the stairs to find my mother not breathing and lying at the top of the stairs. I screamed for dad to call 999. He was in shock, and I repeated it again to him calmly before I tried to revive my mother. It took a few tries, and I was shaking and screaming at her while praying. I thumped my fist down on her chest and gave one more breath into her mouth, and she coughed.

The ambulance arrived, and she had to stay in the hospital the rest of the week. I always think, *what if we had left on time for school?* because we wouldn't have been there for her.

Paul Bedsprings sent chocolates from Edinburgh, and I made up the biggest flowery gift box full of memories, books, and all the creams, perfumes, and sweets she loves for Mother's Day. She was absolutely speechless, and I thought to myself what joy and surprise it gave her and why I hadn't done that before. All those years, I never built into our friendship or the value of my precious mummy.

I asked her to write a comment for my book, and my mummy wrote: *"Many years have gone by now since June 2001. I moved to Spain in 1999,* and to recall the Big Brother experience is quite vague as we didn't know Penny had gone into the show. Everything was done very secretly. My husband and I didn't have a TV in Spain, so we never watched Penny on the show. We heard from our other daughter that a journalist was parked outside her house, offering a lot of money for a story on Penny. He was there for days.

I didn't have a landline in Spain, just a small mobile phone I bought from a Spanish shop. However, my Spanish mobile kept ringing, and all sorts of people from the newspapers were on the other end. It was very bewildering. One of them told us that our granddaughter had died in a car crash, but I didn't have any grandchildren. It was most distressing.

When I travelled back to England for a brief visit near the end of 2001, I was shocked at how famous Penny was. We couldn't walk down the street without everybody screaming her name and wanting autographs. Penny was not herself at all; she was caught up in the whirl of it all and seemed very lost. She was hoping someone might help her, like a manager or someone, but didn't know how to go about sorting it out. She had a lot of low self-esteem still, and she said someone in the industry had said she was too old to get any sort of presenting job.

She wouldn't talk about how her teaching job had come to an end. I was worried about her state of mind. Her finances were in ruins. I realised later on that a lot of people used her and took advantage of her. A lot of things were said to the papers by people pretending to be friends of Penny. We as a family never sold a story to the papers, but in hindsight I wish we had, as we had a lot of lovely stories to share.

Penny was manic, and we couldn't give her any advice. The whole experience has left deep scars in her life. It had taken her till 2020 to finally talk about the experience. She has rediscovered her faith in Jesus, in whom we all as a family believe. We all gave our hearts to Jesus as a family when we lived in Cyprus in 1973. As a Christian, he has never let me down, and Jesus only wants the very best for us. I wish Penny all the best with this book.

She has a lot of support from her husband, Mark, who is a good man. I pray she will be used by God to talk to people and help them. She has a heart to help people overcome the challenges we all face at some time in our lives. I hope she can return to her church and give her testimony, and maybe some other churches too. She might have the opportunity to talk at the prison reading groups, and maybe she can go into their prison bible groups to share with them. Penny is a blessing to us and a beautiful person inside and out; our love has always been there and will be for ever. Mummy and Daddy x"

I wanted to share some of the incredible uniqueness and creative spirit of my Hastings. Living in Hastings is a pleasure; it is a beautiful place to live. Hastings' historic old town has a long-standing Easter tradition that has been performed for many years—the Easter procession. On the cobblestones of the narrow, historic streets that meander through the entire old town, the Easter story is dramatized. The closing sequence, which takes place on the arduous ancient steps that lead to the enormous west hill known as the Top of the World, is immensely poignant.

Brian, Claire, and Madge experience it with me. What Jesus has done for us is brought home when we watch the Easter story faithfully performed by these actors. I recognised the grace, experienced the guilt, and rejoiced in gratitude. I now always say, "The laugh of the amazed." My days were slowly becoming more amazing.

In March, I got to know Einaar, who works on the film I am making as part of the backdrop to the physical theatre production I have written and am directing for the Jewish society. He is a Christian, and we start working together for the next two years. In that time, we make visual poetry films, some with me acting in them (hanging off boats or running around a park), all of which tell a story of hope. We make a longer film about a young couple deciding to keep their baby. He also films the theatre production. I hope I can share the films I made one day.

It is the month my mother and dad go to Las Vegas, San Francisco, and other places (a sort of tour of different cities, including Vancouver, where one of her sisters' lives). They leave notes as usual around the house on scraps of paper, telling me the water is hot and there is fish to eat up in the freezer. I need to clean the fridges out, wash my dad's bedding, and remember to always unplug the TV if I am out. There is one terrifying moment when one of the planes they are travelling in has to crash land. The news filters through slowly, but then, to my relief, I find out all is well despite the crash landing.

May is another month for one of the biggest celebrations in Hastings—the Jack in the Green, full of music, dance, and storytelling. There is so much live music, the procession is full of drummers, and everyone wears their significant green costumes that they have worn for years; some are in cascading gowns and symbolic jewellery. Visitors to the town always watch in amazement. The Jack dances through the old town and goes up onto the West Hill. Once Jack is slain on the Top of the World, the bush is torn apart and all the branches are thrown into the crowds eagerly waiting with their arms stretched in the air. If you catch a branch, you will have fertility and prosperity. Again, over the years, all my friends have come along at least once just to experience this incredible festival with so many atmospheres. Everywhere is decorated with green branches, and all the restaurants and bars are decorated to the hilt with some putting on mini beer festivals. Everyone is very happy and quite drunk.

It is also the month my mother thinks I should write up my *Big Brother* story, which she calls "A hurricane in a plastic bag." It is also the month I see a play written and starring Bubble from *Big Brother 2* in London. It was in a pub theatre and was so powerful and poignant. I was so impressed by his acting skills and the subject he had written about. It was a strong message about the rights of absent fathers.

There is a massive spread in the London metro on how fabulous Hastings is and it says, "Travel round the world? Why bother when there are freshly harvested oysters right on your doorstep and fisherman's huts and festivals?"

But it is the saddest month as Robert dies at forty-six. I have not mentioned him yet, but I grew up with him at the Brethren church when we came to England at the age of ten. He was a lovely man of God. I saw him over the years, and when the Gospel Hall was turned into a primary school, I was at the final celebration service. He stood in the doorway on that last day and said, "What am I going to do now?" I looked around, and everyone was there. I wish we had stayed in that church like they all did; there is safety in consistency and a place that is full of love and truth. They were my years of learning so much about Jesus. Robert died of cancer. My mother and father went along to his funeral with me and met up with all those from our fellowship and church from when I was a teenager, and I will never forget him. He always said to me, "Go the narrow way." I wish I had done that earlier in my life.

By the end of May, I had to start taking antidepressants again; school was so challenging, and I was having panic attacks. I was suffering with facial neuralgia again too. I specifically remember spending more than forty minutes at the Boots clinic because the chemist was worried and had led me into one of the rooms to ask me, "Why are you suicidal?"

The value of family and friends is the most precious gift we must hold dear. We all need the people that draw around you when you are sinking and, like a golden net, pull you to the shore of sanity. Everyone needs the kindness of others. I remember Claire coming down, and we watched Eurovision with a picnic in my bedroom that Holly walked all over. I visited Dean and Dale's in Brighton and experienced one of their drag queen and karaoke events. It was so spectacular, bursting with colour, joy, and Benedictine. After an absolutely brilliant evening that lasted till 4 a.m., I made the decision the following morning to go to the church I had seen promoted on a flyer I had found in Brighton the day before; amongst all the celebrations, a little flyer lying in the street, as if it was placed there just for me to find.

There was a women's conference going on, and the speaker was from Australia. I was intrigued. I went along still dressed in my clothes from the night before, all a bit stinky. I felt so lost again. I was standing at the back of a hall that must have had a few thousand people in it. This lady is tall and beautiful and talks with such enthusiasm. Her name is Lisa McInnes-Smith. The next thing I knew, she took a pause and said that she had a message for someone there. I took no notice as I had a bit of a hangover and was still covered in booze stains.

Then she said, "That girl in yellow, come up on stage." Everyone turned to me. It took me a minute to register that she was calling me. She got me on stage and spoke God's words over me, telling me I was back to who I was meant to be all along. She seemed to know me. It must have been the discernment of the Holy Spirit. She put a tiara on my head and told me I was a child of God and valued. Then she gave me a £10 note and said, "You are still the same value as the day you were born." I have never experienced anything so specific. She gave me some of her books and calendars that I still use today.

It was when my first book was published in 2020 that I sent her a message on social media, and she responded. I couldn't believe it. We reconnected, as I always use her calendar for the week, and we got chatting via text. Out of the blue, she said in 2021, "You are one of God's miracles." She didn't have to do that. I thank her.

In June, I participated in the Race for Life again in Hastings. Emma now had bone cancer in addition to the initial cancer that had also come back. She couldn't see me. I didn't know what to do, but we continued to talk most days, and she sent me a study book, which I have read and reread in my reading every day since. She said, "Turn the earth of your mind over and stay on the other side."

I finally left the schools again in July 2007. I thought, *why did I put myself through it again?* but I was once again without a job. However, Dean was adamant to go on holiday and invited me to Cancun. I still paid my way, though, and it was the maddest holiday ever. In the middle of it, we braced ourselves for Hurricane Dean. (Of all the names for that year's hurricane.) The news was ripe in England; it was the main news on every channel, and my mother and father were beside themselves with terror as this was one of the worst hurricanes. I realised that Dean, myself, and a few others were the only English who hadn't flown back early. My family was frantically trying to contact me. We put our suitcases in the bath and started watching *Girl with a Pearl Earring*, but we never saw the end as the hurricane hit. The water poured in and smashed the glass windows. We were about four floors up. The whole hotel shook. The sound, which I have never heard since, reminded me of being right under the engine of a plane. That massive vibration and roar was deafening. We never saw the end of that film, not even to this day, despite saying we should every time we talk.

The hotel had unscrewed the outside lights and tied everything to the ground. We had a survival pack given to us with some coleslaw, crackers, and bread. Once the hurricane passed, we still had a glorious week left of our holiday, and the sun was burning hot. We swam with what must have been basking sharks. We went out on a small fishing boat with a few other tourists that had stayed and survived the hurricane. I had insisted Dean and I take a sickness tablet, and I am glad we did because the other tourists all started throwing up in abundance as the boat swung from side to side. The guide was determined to show off his skills and looked at Dean and me. We realised it was going to be just the three of us experiencing this tour.

Once in the water, we tried not to swallow the puke that floated around us. I couldn't believe the size of these sharks. The guide started talking rapidly with great enthusiasm. I just nodded, which I've learned you should never do if you don't know what someone just asked! With that, the guide dove down, grabbed my feet, and pulled me under water. He then pushed me right into the huge shark's mouth, right down his throat. Each shark was the size of a small building. The mouth was about 3 feet wide. I was glad he never let go of my feet, as I would have been swallowed. Even to this day, all of those who were on the trip say it was the best one they have ever been on, mixed with the sadness of one of the beautiful boys dying in a dreadful accident soon after we got back.

On my return, I really didn't know what to do. It was August 2007, and it would be my fortieth birthday in October. I sat in the garden at home and felt utterly lost again.

MEET ME AT THE MIRROR

It took a few days for me to type out my CV on my little typewriter, as I still didn't have or use a computer. I took it to the local newsagents and got it photocopied. I then decided to hand my CV into local restaurants in the Old Town of Hastings. I thought about the jazz café and how I had enjoyed that job. I turned up a bit sheepish at a tapas restaurant, and one of the girls took my CV off me. I was called by the owner the next day to go in and work a trial shift as a waitress. I found myself in the heart of the Old Town, which meant being in the pulse of all the good, bad, and creativity that makes Hastings so unique. I was really good and soon developed a steady flow of regular customers. I would know their names and what was going on in their lives. It became such a lovely atmosphere seeing some get engaged, then married, then bring in their first child. I worked there till 2010, and it was really like that scene in Notting Hill where Hugh Grant walks through the market place and the seasons change and the same people are having different experiences. I just love listening to people.

There was a lovely old couple who would have the same table every Friday. Keith, who knew me at the jazz bar, now came in for a drink at the bar on his way from London. Brian would come in. The owner questioned me about how I was using the bar area and my banter, but soon she let me get on with it as her business boomed. I took over as manager and developed my team; tips were higher than they had ever experienced, they put in a lot of effort, and we all treated one another with respect as I brought in new business. Customers were also pleased. It felt incredibly nice and meaningful to listen to customers and staff and to help them with their lives. But like with everything I have done, it was difficult at times. The rows were out of this world between the families who all worked there, sometimes in front of the customers. I would just say to the customers that we were filming a scene for *EastEnders*, and they loved it as they believed "Penny from *Big Brother*" was still as famous as they thought I was.

I would be shouted at too; if, for whatever reason, it was too loud, the owner would bash a wooden broom on the floorboards, as she lived upstairs, but it would just make us have a fit of the giggles. It was nothing compared to the dread I had felt in some of the schools. This was organised chaos, but I was in control and made it my own. It got so busy that tables were booked weeks in advance. It was a tiny restaurant, so we would have to rearrange the space like a theatre production every day and twice on Friday and Saturday. Sometime people had to just sit on top of each other, but they didn't care. I got the owner to make up jars of olives in gift boxes, which I sold in their masses.

Customers would say that I could "sell ice to Eskimos." It also meant I got to know the characters and other owners in the old town. John, the cobbler, with his banter, often held social gatherings in his shop that had a huge red velvet sofa outside; he always had someone there, chatting and having a drink. He became a good friend and was always amazed at how I survived in such a manic and crazy environment.

Monkey Dave, who used to have monkeys on the pier in the 1970s; I've always thought I must have seen him in the 1980s, when me and my family would drive to Hastings, and just before we would come over the hill, we would start to chant, "I can see the sea." He was very well known, and no one messed with him. When the owner's son would have a go at me, it was Monkey Dave who made sure no one had a go at me again. I had my own protection. The other owners of bars were quite intrigued and a bit dismayed that I was taking loads of their customers and building a must go to place. Their customers would come in and eat and chat with me, then go to the other venues, where the live music played.

I was respected and felt like I was doing something meaningful at last. On the festival days, we would cover the restaurant in green branches for Jack in the Green, create a romantic Valentine's, get involved in the window display competition for Old Town Week, and welcome the millions of bikers who would come down for the May bank holiday. It was almost impossibly busy some weeks. I could walk into any restaurant or bar in the Old Town and be welcomed with open arms; everyone had a story, and there was always drama, sadness, and celebration.

I had mornings at home to write and finished several books on A4 paper. On a Monday, my day off, I would see friends. It became a weekly ritual to visit Claire in London one Monday and Dean in Brighton the following week. It was quite magical. I loved my job; it was like being in a fairy tale. Ironically, my fairy tale came true in 2010 when Mark walked into the Tapas Restaurant, then later returned, and we married a year to the day he walked in.

In October, I turned forty. The old town decided to celebrate, and everyone got involved. It reminded me of my Soho birthday party in 2001. I got so many cards, flowers, and free drinks. I seem to have been given the same gifts over the years and have realised that these things are given to me with huge significance. It was after chats that have helped, healed, and strengthened friends that I have always gotten either a teddy bear, bracelet, key ring, or cup. Sitting on my little rocking chair in my writing room are teddy bears from Gary, Ted, Paul Bedsprings, Lizzie, and Veronica.

This year was no exception, and in the dusk of the evening in the old town, we all sat on the cobblestone street and on John the Cobbler's velvet sofa. The chip shop sent me a portion of chips with a birthday candle in it, and everyone sang Happy Birthday, along with the squawking seagulls. Paul Bedsprings' birthday card is addressed to "Penny One for the Road." This has become true over the years, as our catch ups always end with one for the road, which quickly turns into a few and leaves us in a stumbling mess. It is always a time full of laughter and stories. but even my husband Mark knows it is going to be a rather messy end, even though, before I go, I reassure him and myself that Paul and I will be totally civilised and just have one drink. It never does go that way.

Many of my Tapas Restaurant customers came down from London to celebrate, and one of the girls studying to be a doctor brought a specially created boob cake! They gave me key rings since they knew I had OCD about checking the door; I received cups with messages on them and bracelets; a customer gave me a bright blue hand knitted Teddy; and Peter and Ted sent me a bottle of champagne from Fortnum and Mason, which was very kind of them.

My mother, dad, and sister organised a dinner party for me a few days later, and I will always regret keeping them waiting, as the owner of the Tapas Restaurant wanted to have a celebratory drink with me that day after my shift, and I just couldn't get away. It made me realise how influenced I am and how I am not able to stand up for myself. I was too scared to tell her I had to go home.

My family celebrated my fortieth without me. I was being manic and irrational again. Suky wrote a letter and said that she had Mondays free after graduation as well and was afraid of making the wrong decisions, but she went to the theatre, and it reminded her of me. She wanted to jump up on stage and give Orlando Bloom a hug. My girls from Sarah Bonnell have grown up so fast and always seem to contact me, whether with a card or a letter, at just the right moment in my life, not just at birthdays. They always think I have helped them so much, but I know that over the years they have saved me from myself.

PENNY ELLIS

Am Built (A poem)
Rebuilding a life that is an absolute mess when you haven't got the energy or any self-confidence left.

No more under construction and rubble pile dust rising in the busyness of the days.

For now chaos leaves and the walls are built by Gods hands.

Up on a level of heights were eagles fly.

Where reaching up you touch and pull-down rainbows of dreams.

The Holy Spirit opens all the windows of your mind.

The walls are set with stones in fair colours and God has layered my foundation with gem stones.

The view is the field of opportunity I have bought and it is covered in flowers growing out of the fertilizer that was my life.

I move through the rooms and see you God have laid a table in the presence of my enemies. You have anointed my head with oil, my cup runneth over.

Even the forest up on the holy hill despite the stumps they will grow back and change the landscape.

I can take a walk to the dangerous pit and see what you pulled me out of, all the shards.

My phone line is connected, and it runs straight to you. The only connect and I can reach beyond my grasp to connect.

If you saw my home on a map it is indeed a Nazareth home.

God's fragrance is all around.

I look at my unfolded map and in this truest light I can see the journey and the thrill of the vision.

My wardrobe holds new clothes that are not made of shame, and nothing is frayed.

Each morning I can sit in the cornerstone, the cleft of the rock and worship God with awe.

My life is written ahead and I can step in his footsteps to see my white funeral.

He shows me life worth living.
The End.

When my mother and father returned to Spain to check on the house, she began writing me letters. She was proud of me for getting a job, but worried about how serious my OCD was and how bad my nerves were getting.

She said, "I have old letters from you on the same theme. I'm not sure when your problems began because you were a happy child. You have been to a psychiatrist and are intelligent enough to analyse things. Now you are forty, try to put it all behind you and go forward in the strength of the Lord. Why can't you trust him more? You are beautiful, so why let your mind rule your life? You have to stop the door checking and trust God to get the victory. You are so strong in many ways and so weak in others. Remember, not everyone is a true friend. Keep your own counsel. Stand alone with God." She also gave me a prayer, "Holy Spirit is with me when I walk the valleys and the mountains of my life. Let me rejoice over heights climbed and depths conquered."

My mother is a prayer warrior. I think about Charles Lamb, who was a clerk for thirty-three years, a writer, and had a sister who was insane. He always felt like he was writing inside the chaos, with a five hundred-foot drop on one side and a knife edge on the other; I related to that feeling, and I needed to fight my way out the other side.

So, I began to study my Bible again and read Joni Erickson Tada's quote from Hebrews 11v34, "Whose weakness was turned to strength." She says, "It is my prayer; you will discover the significance that has been yours all along as a child of the King. You may not know the full meaning of every event, but you can know that every event is meaningful, and you are significant." I also read Isaiah 61v7, "Instead of your shame you will receive a double portion, and instead of disgrace you will rejoice in your inheritance. And so, you will inherit a double portion in your land, and everlasting joy will be yours." I just didn't know why I couldn't get rid of this cloak of heaviness. In 2 Chronicles 31v21, it says, "He sought his God and worked wholeheartedly, so he prospered." God wants you to succeed, and most things fail because of a broken focus. It further advises to be cautious, to guard and prioritise your time, and to not rehearse your mistakes, as this only reinforces doubt. In Isaiah 41v10, God says, "So don't fear, for I am with you." God wants us to stop people pleasing. He wants to see that we actually grow through our failures. I kept writing and reading my Bible, and I kept believing I was going to get well.

Rehearsals were in full swing for the Jewish play about the life of Bruce Eaton. I combined film, physical theatre, and script. The actors stared at me some days as I tried to get them to be wallpaper, and I spent hours getting them to use a piece of red rope that symbolised Bruce's (the renowned surgeon's) blood and his life ebbing away. It was a bit artsy, as I tried to get them to move like "pieces of life." One of the actors even stormed out but did come back. We were using so many props and were part of the props ourselves, so we stood at the back of the stage when we were not in the action. It started to take form, and the film was dramatic with authentic black and white footage that placed the scenes in time. One example is when the train shoots through the station on this huge screen, as if arriving on the stage. It just worked so well with Bruce standing with a suitcase and steam being released all around his legs as if from the train.

The play was to be put on in January at St. Mary in the Castle, a splendid building in Hastings. The screen for the film was enormous and really added to the drama. In the last scene, it was full of his real-life friends, who were very elderly now but totally up for it. They had to time their arrival on stage with the play and get into position for the real-life final act because climbing that steep stage was difficult for them, but they were so excited to share their love and stories of Bruce in the final act of the play that they attended most rehearsals. I spent the next few weeks directing, adding to the script, and rewriting it, much to the dismay of the "storm out" actor, whom I still sometimes see around Hastings and who, I think, still hasn't forgiven me for this very complex theatre production where he had to play "life blood on a symbolic level."

The tech rehearsal in December had a mild hiccup when the young man helping Einaar electrocuted himself and turned off all the Christmas lights in the whole street outside. It seemed a miracle to me that he was OK. I had to go to the funeral of Bruce Eaton, who died on 17 December. I had interviewed him in his bed and written pages of his accounts of what he experienced. He saw me quite a few times, and despite being so frail, he was full of huge courage and incredible inner strength. He was so intelligent and just had an amazing presence about him. I was so honoured to have met him, and I felt very responsible to show what a wonderful man he was through my play. The Mayor of Hastings was to come and watch my play, along with dignitaries from Manchester and Bruce's family, his children, grandchildren, and great grandchildren, who were all driving down to see it.

The year 2007 ended with massive celebrations at the Tapas Restaurant. The decorations were like the inside of Santa's grotto! I put together the most fabulous New Year's party, which ended at 5 a.m., and all the customers turned up, from London and beyond. The regular customers who usually went on a cruise or to Barbados decided they would rather be at my New Year's party and said afterwards that it was the best New Year they had ever had. The owner gave me a Christmas card that read, "Thank you so much for all your extra help in this nut house. I couldn't have done it without you." Everyone was jolly, but I was fighting constant fears and OCD.

I was praying and believing that Jesus was the only one who could pull my dreams down from above. I began to search and reach for his love. I believe that addiction cycles can be broken and that any haunted or hounded mind can find peace. So, I looked into God's word. I was anxious as to when I would feel better. I wondered when I would be able to break free from some of the addictions that gripped my mind like fierce teeth.

I wanted my life to matter. I wanted to leave a legacy. I have lost so many people I have loved. I will never forget them.

Death is Nearer (A poem)
For everyone who has lost someone so
dear and is heartbroken.

1

I lost my cousin in a fire.

His body didn't burn his bedroom was a shrine.

A burnt out tree that was the rest of the top floor flat, its roof like broken teeth screaming into the sky.

Dragons' breath captured by newspaper news.

He is my cousin, his smooth skin asleep but never would be kissed awake again.

My last memory was the New Year fireworks in Bonn escaping Omi my mother's mother for a night. I loved him and always will. I brought her back pink sugar pigs on a stick in a bouquet of flowers.

2.

A phone call, my first boyfriend was Henry, from a distant voice; he had burnt to death too.

Wrapped his body round his child to save them. Unlike my cousin he was a burnt acorn.

His child died too.

I was supposed to be at his celebrations getting his flying awards and going to the ball. My mother didn't let me go at 16 years old.

3.

I had a dearest friend Emma Neville Towle, so many notes and letters that would fall out like petals whatever writing book I opened.

Her breadcrumbs led me to happiness.

She was gentle as a cloud resonating light; her last words were to me: Be beautiful and shine.

She was the ribbon that tied my life into beautiful. We had sat amongst the deer in Richmond Park and had picnic in the dusk of the day.

Cancer came and took her lovely long hair and fabulous breasts.

4.

Known since I was 10 years old. The small clear church in Southborough, full of sound biblical teaching. I didn't realize the value of a life at such peace then.

Robert had not known what to do when it closed. He dropped me off at the station after the final celebration service. He said to me: "Go the narrow way ". Yet I turned the wrong way and spiralled out of control.

5.

My Lizzies foster mum. More than a parent a most wonderful friend.

I had booked a trip to NY and take Lizzie with me from my form; we realized she needed a birth certificate and a passport. Ironically, she has never stopped travelling. Angela older but young in heart she was Peter and Teds' friend too. We were all at the funeral the same church Lizzie got married in.

6.

I met Madge in a coffee bar where I worked, she was dazed like a hit deer after the loss of her husband .Together we found a different rhythm to dance to.

7.

Norman a man of God who knew his Lord at the small church I found in Hastings that reminded me of my childhood Brethren church. Norman: a fighter pilot facing death many times. He had the laugh of someone who knew what pain and loss was. Hallelujah was his chorus shout. His prayers at church almost songs. He touched the lips of Jesus in his love.

Only once did I see fear, he saw my bruises and grabbed my coat and said: "Never let anyone do that to you again". He ran to the altar and poured the blessed oil on his head as he knew death was near. His eyes sparrow dark with the knowledge it was near the end.

8.

Monkey Dave. He was known by all. He did lots of things. He was full of eccentricities scarves flowed off him. There was a certain smell we never discussed. He protected me from those that tried to bully me. He was suddenly dead. Such an Old Town character.

9.

Broad accent, Cobbler John. Full of stories of the Old Town. Such a strong character brimming with personality. Parties were in full abundance despite it being a shoe repair shop. The welcome of the huge velvet sofa and a glass of wine. He had lived a life. In hot summer and dark winter we would chat; he was just over the cobblestone road from the tapas Restaurant. Then he was dead.

10.

There have been more entries of loss in my Birthday Book which used to just hold the dates of my friends' birthdays. It was a gift from a Canadian friend at University who would have Fortnum and Masons deliveries and drove a jaguar. Now my Art Deco Birthday Book is full of those who have died. It is just a breath away. It is inside us all. It is the direction which we cannot change. Some of us have a few miles to go. Others will stop in a layby to rest but never return. Some race ahead as if they can overtake it.

When it comes it takes the whole bloody lot.

The End.

My new Years' resolution 2007: I need to stop wasting my life in fear and chaos, in OCD and regret.

SCENE 5:
Meeting myself at the Mirror.

The year 2008 began with my mother and father returning from Spain and all of us living together. We went swimming, which is something we did every day before school in my teenage years in Tunbridge Wells. It was wonderful to be back in the comfort of childhood routines. There was something deeply nostalgic and restorative about it. My parents have always been so consistent, and now that they were back, an atmosphere of safety and peace returned. It fills my heart with sadness when I think about how many years, I spent not being with them, allowing myself to waste time with the wrong people. Such realisations are a blessing and a curse.

Work at the tapas restaurant involved developing a new Valentine's menu, which just caused even more strife and screaming fits. They were unbelievable and caused the customers to giggle into their napkins, but they made me feel like I was never going to get away from insanity. My dad continued to bake bread; the warm bread smell that shone in our home brought back such memories of days at "Appelcrotch olde Strase," our nickname for our first home in Tunbridge Wells when I was ten.

I had started swearing, and I couldn't seem to break the habit; all the shouting at work had planted itself in my brain. My mother got angry at this and demanded that I stop it at once. I felt I was improvising on God's instructions as this job was immersed in chaos, strife, and late nights. I was not sure what to do. Most nights, I finished at 2 a.m. I listened a lot to my staff and customers, and I saw a life I never knew existed. Their stories were heart-breaking and bewildering. The restaurant was overflowing every night, and so many sights and conversations were observed with surprise. I never knew this sort of life; I never went to a pub, and now I was in lock ins after work with all those conversations and people who were still drinking into the early hours. It was a strange life.

My mother was amazed that I always found my way home and never lost my handbag. She called me a "whiskey homing pigeon." She couldn't believe how much I drank. Looking back, I can see I was walking two paths. One was full of home, peace, God TV, bible readings, prayers, writing my Christian book, and my play. The other path was this job, drinking, manic moments, and strange experiences and people.

During rehearsals, I was incorporating more physical and symbolic action into the play, even wrapping one very old member of the cast in a carpet so that he could unroll from it at a pivotal moment. The cast finally understood my vision and recognised the point of being wallpaper and tearing themselves down.

I saw Dean regularly on my Monday day off; we always found something going on. One time, we went to Porters, a bar restaurant in the old town, and Liane Carroll, a famous jazz pianist, was practising and improvising on her set that she was to do at Carnegie Hall in New York. We sat through a wonderful performance; all her musicians played a different instrument and created a humorous and creative evening.

The play went on at St Mary in the Castle. It was a huge event as it was the Holocaust Memorial Service. I called it *Fingerprints and Footsteps*, and at the end of the play, one of the final scenes was a mountain of shoes in a huge mound that we carefully moved past. I was so honoured to have been trusted to capture the inspiration that is Bruce Eaton MBE, who said, "I always had a passion for mankind."

He was a fellow of the Royal College of Obstetricians and Gynaecologists and was honoured with the 1066 Award for his contributions to Jewish society, and he embraced musical theatre. He came from Berlin and had started medical training until rumours spread that he was a communist. On the advice of his headmaster, his parents sent him away at age eighteen to Switzerland. He then went to Milan and continued his studies as a doctor by doing so in Italian, but two months before he qualified, he had to leave and come to Manchester University, where he also had to redo some years of his study. When the war broke out in 1939, he was interned as an enemy alien and was one of the first to enter D-Day plus five into Belsen after completing his training in the Royal Medical Corps. His mother had died, but he was able to find his father, who had hidden in cemeteries to stay alive. The real time final scene, with his very old friends who had climbed the steep steps up into their position on the stage and expressed their devotion and admiration for the life of Bruce Eaton, was very moving, and there was a holy hush in the auditorium as the tradition of passing on the Jewish shawls took place, and the grandchildren received them.

I received a lovely good luck card from Paul Bedsprings, and my dad shook my hand and told me he was proud of me. I got an email from the theatre company Shades, who said thank you and that everyone found the play incredibly profound. There was a sentence added for the cast: "and thank you for all your hard work, especially the thirty-one hours spent rehearsing one scene." Even now, I cringe at the thought of trying to persuade the actors to be symbolic life blood.

By February 2008, I had to make copious drawings of the stage at work as the restaurant was so popular and I kept turning the tables for service, squashing everyone in. But I was still struggling with my OCD, spending ages checking the door of the restaurant when I locked up at 1 a.m. Zainab started to ring regularly, and she made so much sense when she told me to get a grip—without knowing it, she was keeping me grounded. When I saw Claire on one of our Mondays, while walking across Waterloo Bridge after a play at the National Theatre and a Wagamama's, she talked about the strife and screaming at my place of work in the tapas bar and told me to just get my coat and go.

Paul Bedsprings rang regularly too; sometimes we talked for over two hours, and I'd come out of my bedroom to my mother, who stared at me and said, "What have you got to talk about?" I made films and visual poems with Einaar, as well as working the lunch shift at the tapas restaurant, as the customers kept asking for me and the owner had to keep telling them, "This is not Penny's restaurant."

Madge and I spent a lot of time together too, helping each other through the sadness that fell on us both from past memories, while we drank port and other times had biscuits, cheese, and champagne and watched black and white films like *Rebecca*. Madge found a band of friendships at the charity shop where she volunteered, and she took a chance on new friends, I was so pleased for her and just wish I could have found some more confidence from somewhere to have done something like that, to have changed my path sooner.

She went to Spain and even went to Australia where my friend Veronica lives who always calls me regularly. We both have a love for Australia . My dearest friends ; Vanessa, Craig and Rohan and even Mel the one who lived in my flat in Islington and painted my living room blue lives there now too.

At home, I heard my mother's prayers as she prayed in her room and the living room, and there was always the TV on with a sermon or music from the God TV channel. But despite having so much love around me, I was dominated by OCD and a feeling of deep loneliness. I took courage from other men in the Bible whom God placed alone. He calls us to fight when we are alone. Daniel had to gaze at a great vision on his own; Elijah was alone in a cave; Moses had to meet God alone; and Jeremiah sat alone. I needed to stop wasting time and energy on things I couldn't change.

I started a leadership course at one of the new churches Einaar introduced me to. There was every opportunity to work with the church in the local community, be an encourager, and use my skills to develop projects to bring people to know Jesus. Unfortunately, there was strife, disagreements, and jealousies in that church, and the whole thing ended in nothing. But still, I sat and had Bible times with my mother, while Holly curled up and listened with a purple unicorn in her mouth and I would read out stuff I was writing. My mother would stop drinking her tea and say, "Why is your writing so dark?"

I tried to make her laugh by telling her that when I walked home so late at night from the tapas restaurant, there was a naked man who rode his bike regularly at night through Hastings and that I had seen him a few times in the quiet of the late night, where only the swish of his wheels and the scurry of foxes were heard. I told her that he almost floated past like a mirage. She just said to me, "Please stay in the right soil; stay unhooked from people's problems."

Following the performance, Bruce Eaton's wife called me because she wanted to set up an award at Manchester University and possibly put the play on again, and Einnar had managed to get a meeting with Meridian TV about our film, but nothing came of it. Instead, I was rushing around at work, so busy that when I cut my leg really badly trying to open a bottle, I just wrapped Sellotape around it and carried on. I even stood on a piece of glass and didn't notice until I took a really hot shower about a month later and wondered what the pain was in my foot, when I squeezed out a huge chunk of broken glass.

My parents and I drove to Tunbridge Wells in April 2008 to read the cards Robert had written forty-eight hours before his death. Whilst we were there, we dropped in to see Annie, a lifelong friend of my mother who is a dress designer, and the late Danny La Rue, who lived with her and was upstairs when we visited. On Good Friday, I went to the All Souls service with Claire, and as with every year, it was so wonderful to be back in such a strong, Christ-filled church. Someone wrote me a note and left it on the counter at the tapas restaurant, saying that God was pleased with me and was not looking for perfection. The note said that "he sees your faith in the things you do because of his influence in your life. It is important for you to know God is pleased with you. Your steps are ordered, prepared, established, and directed by him (Psalm 37v23)." I have absolutely no idea who left the note, maybe an angel?

Racing Cars (A poem)
To get up again and believe you can survive.

How could this happen, after such a win?
    I have cut the ribbon stepped up and into my prize.
    Raced away.
    Down the road.
    Far from the cull de sacs and no roadblocks.
    I am on the truth road. Promises unveiled in hopes' happiness.
    The joy of the Lord is my strength.
    Why use it again?
    Reuse what is a free gift?
    Get into debt, crash and burn all in a moment?
    What is hardly remembered?
    What stole in?
    Locked in and robbed you?
    Reprogrammed you, forced you to leave your first love.
    Your blueprint.
    What came in at such an invisible level and attacked with such force that uproots the very truth built so beautifully.
    Oh Lord again I cry that your gears are in place of my chaos.
    I speed into the sanctified sacred space that is now my life.
    Please lift me up again and don't let me crash.
    I see your starter flag.
    I can go round each sudden bend and sharp turn as they are cushioned in your favour.
    I race with a heart of excitement and win the prize waiting for me.
                The End.

I was starting to feel strong again. I was wrapped in my mother's prayers. I was, and still am, amazed when I think about the priests who held the Ark up in the Red Sea and stayed there until everyone had passed over to the other side. I wonder how they felt standing there with the entire sea on either side of them.

Through the Red Sea (A poem)
To walk to the other side of all you want to leave behind.

Either side- full of overwhelming temptations. Rise as if over and about to engulf me.

Yet it is perfectly parted and a clear dry path of sand timer grains warm my feet.

Despite these cold pressures intensely held either side of me
You outstretched on the cross you hold it back.
I can choose to drown in the delights of this world so easy to stop.
I can be covered by those waves and know no more.
The water slicing through all truth and laying me in layers.
In an instant I half wish for loss in the excitement and that loneliness and fears would be taken in the surge.
Why is it so hard to walk through this?
I lack trust that the walls of water will not flow in as your hope leads me to dry ground.
Only then do I see just what the life I left behind can do in its tumbling, falling, thrashing, and foaming.
The drowning time is over.
The End.

I think when you have been "dropped," you live in a broken space. Anyone who comes into your life finds there isn't room to breathe, and the volume is so intense. They will cut their feet and hearts on your glass.

In May, I got a letter from the AGM of Shades, the theatre group. The play about Bruce Eaton's life was "full of such depths of emotion and instant credible scenes and characterisations in a dramatic style never attempted before by Shades." I was over the moon with the response I received to my play. I was also sent a card from Claire that said, "Expect a move of God suddenly." It was a card full of encouragement, telling me God shows up just at the right time. It had the verse I was given so clearly in a church service at seventeen years of age in the card: "For I know the plans I have for you, declares the

Lord, plans to prosper you and not to harm you, plans to give you a hope and a future." By May, I was trying to follow my dreams, but there was still a lot of chaos around me.

My mother and father arrived back in Spain and ended up rescuing a St. Bernard dog who was wandering around the village, which took up all their energy and time; Holly was not happy. Bubble also called me. He was teaching and really successful at it, as well as writing another play. I even went back to Sarah Bonnell School with Zainab and Lizzie and sat in my old classroom. But I couldn't shift this ache of loneliness and fear. Friends were off on holiday, redecorating, falling in love, and doing life in a clear, steady, and sane way. I love them and all their phone calls, visits, and generosity. I just couldn't seem to find my normal. There was also the sudden death of one of the men at my church. At his funeral, the church was filled to the brim with boxers, as he had used his gym not just to train but to tell these men about the Lord. There were hundreds there, all listening to a proper hell and fire sermon declaring the word of God and how they needed to ask Jesus to save them.

Before she sadly passed away due to cancer, I continued to get my regular cards from Emma, who told me she was unpacking some wonky thinking with a counsellor and felt "empty" on the inside. It was just how I felt. She told me to stay tucked into the cloak of God's safety, but I just felt lost and confused. My mother wrote to me from Spain, telling me in capital letters, "DO NOT FEAR." Holly had their attention again as she was displaying a nose infection that could have landed her a part as a circus act. It involved bright green threads of spaghetti like substance oozing from her nose at a dramatic pace. They also managed to rehouse the St. Bernard dog.

By my birthday in October, one of the old men and his wife at church invited me to their home "anytime I needed to." He was a wonderful man and always asked me how I was and told me I was valued by God, especially that year when I had so many bruises. When he died, the church just seemed to end. It closed soon after his death in 2015, as if all of God's mighty men had died. I didn't take them up on the offer of going round for tea, as I didn't know which knot in my mind, I would be able to untie first. I just don't ask anyone for help.

By the end of the year, Lizzie was working at Sarah Bonnell, and Dean picked me up from the Tapas Restaurant, and we drove back to Brighton to his pub for Christmas. It was tradition to go down on Christmas Day and have drinks with the regulars. We got so involved in conversation, drinks, and laughter that we completely forgot where the turkey was and literally hunted in every cupboard, as we had left it somewhere to defrost in the flat above the pub.

I hoped not only to find the turkey but also for a sane calm 2009.

I read Isiah 43v18-19, "Do not dwell on the past. See I am doing a new thing," and think of people in the Bible: Peter, a fisherman with a terrible temper; Rahab, a prostitute who helped hide spies; Ruth, who had worshipped idols as a Moabite; Zacchaeus, an embezzler who has Jesus over for dinner. All these people were completely changed by God. Everyone has a past; I prayed that God would give me a new beginning.

I lay my hope in Psalm 92v14: "They shall bring forth fruit in old age." I knew deep down that God wasn't done with me yet. It does say in the Bible that he can get angry with us and turn his face and favour away for a time. But if we return to him, he will return to us. It does take a massive effort to learn and really understand the truth of God's promises, as I struggled with OCD and my nerves that were constantly shredded, I just tried to ignore the terror I felt.

Our Family (A poem)
Finally valuing my mum and dad and sister and Kerry and Harry Sausage and Sweetness.

I lived in a rage, a storm winds so loud I couldn't hear your kindness.
Holding onto bark for survival in unknown waters or direction.
I did not heed your wisdom.
No captain, no ship.
I found a shore and made a sandcastle into which I placed a flag and surrounded it with shells.
Whilst you had prepared a palace for me.
The waters lapped at its edges and filled the moat.
I laughed at the perfectly lovely sight.
But the next day it was washed away.
I rose early and walked to the roundabout at the bottom of my street.
And came home.

The End.

In January 2009, my hours were insane at the tapas restaurant. It snowed again, and the olive oil froze in my kitchen because I didn't bother with the heating as I was never home for long. I was grateful for my regular weekly catch-up with Alvaro at his flat; it was warm, and he cooked loads of lovely Italian food. It was the only time I ate properly. My mother flew back in February for my sister's wedding, which took place in the Old Town at a fantastic fish and chips restaurant that was super popular. It also meant I was five minutes away from where I worked, so I could get back on time. It was on Valentine's Day, and I was in charge of reading a poem I wrote for their wedding day. It is quite long; I worked on it at work on scraps of paper, trying to get it right while I was at work.

What are 2? (A Poem)
For my sister and her partner).

To love in leaps taken together.

To be just as you are together.

To entwine into a finishing of each other's sentences and smiles reaching the tip end of the other in a silent love look.

A mirror of each other circled in the pupil of the others eye.

To at last have found the tune to the song of each other's hearts.

Building a fire, red wine or cava, and strictly come dancing together, settling jess(the dog) ,together in phone calls, notes left pinned to the mirror and chats like glitter sprinkled as dusk falls.

Two whose passion understood the heights and depths.

Acceptance is two who create ribbons tied the yellow one of love.

A demonstrated affair becomes a whole, a unit of two is to be together to be recognized related as two is more than one.

To hold in both hands

To know the ocean of secret whispers , your truth inside the space of the rings reaching an horizon stretches and an arc of hope of light awakens as new colour bursts across the sky as it breathes in and gasps on this your day.

Two was me and my sister.

Two was my mother holding you.

Now two is the shape of you two as today is for you.

The End.

My mother left me notes to "put the big ladder in the living room," telling me the water was hot and to empty the dishwasher. I was working such long shifts that I missed her leaving to return to Spain; she left me a farewell note and told me to peg up her washing.

I did manage to get time off and go up to London for Peter's fortieth

Birthday, for a few hours at least. I also managed a quick visit to see Gary Clap Clap at his new flat, and he gave me a teddy bear. Emma from Sarah Bonnell wrote me a card that read, "If I had a single flower for every time I thought of you, I could walk forever in my garden." I got a lovely letter about the wedding of my pastor from All Souls Church. It meant a lot to me as my church was shrinking. Another lovely old man died, and at church we rejoiced that he was home in heaven.

Passing to Death. (A poem)
For the wonderful older generation I have met,
who have gone now to Heaven.

A blanket of all the words ever spoken, out of your mouth now the volume of the sounds of the breath carries you into death

Joy laughter love glee, extra turbo lifts and spins you faster there.

This is now your engine the fuel of all the good blends into forces to carry you gently a hum a unique tune only heard by the angels.

Summoned to greet you, there. Death that sound ends life here but for you is the beginning leaving us all walking running dancing towards it.

You have left such things as crawling, walking staggering limping

You now leap up and over limits and adjust your senses ,all replaced you take on a mantle unwrapped out of former self you are a piece placed in the fixtures of the universe

We peer up never seeing now till we meet again and blend our energies with yours

In the expanse a heavenly section perfectly fitted unique as ever you were is made more. Heaven is home.

The End.

I got a letter published in response to an article I read in *Women Alive* (a Christian magazine) about reality TV. The article spoke about how popular it was and that "putting people in front of a camera without a script offers flashes of insight into human relationships that will never be gleaned from contrived sitcoms."

It also stated that we were part of a generation that wanted to see extreme behaviour and titillation to hold our attention. I wrote, "I was brought out of my comfort zone; it broke me, but God has put the pieces back together. Please pray that reality stars would find the kind of freedom where God gets hold of them and makes them whole." I tried to live that as my reality, but I was still feeling so broken.

In July, I took part in an abseil for charity and went one hundred and twenty-eight feet down Ocean House in St Leonards. I made up little boxes and jars and placed them all over town in all the restaurants and pubs that now knew me. I managed to raise £592.07 for St Michael's Hospice. It was at 9 a.m. on a Sunday, so I missed church but could still get to work on time. I was getting really run down with all the stress at work and didn't know what to do. My other Emma now had liver cancer, and I didn't know what to say to her. Paul Bedsprings called and wrote to me a lot from Edinburgh. He said things in his letters that really touched my heart, like, "We should not be plagued with doubt or troubled by people who don't deserve us." I flew up to see him in August for the festival, and we went to see another play that Bubble had written and was performing in. I only had three days off and was so glad to get away despite being totally exhausted.

I filled my day off every week so I could feel normal. Monday had become the happiest day of my week, a time with friends. I even had to work on my birthday in October, but I was just happy that my mum and dad were coming back from Spain. It meant the house would be full of noise and the smell of bread. It would be warm and lived in. It would feel like home again. As I got home from work at 1 a.m., notes like "Bits of cheese and tomato quiche left in the fridge if you're hungry" would be left for me. There would be dinners with the famous prawn cocktail starters, a home filled with prayers, and God TV. We would go to the cinema and swim together. Holly would be back and embrace her white elephant toy as if she had just won the lottery.

Work got worse in the run up to Christmas, money kept going missing, and the tips were so good that the chefs demanded a cut of them. But I ran with glee and enthusiasm up to London to see the Norwegian Christmas tree in Trafalgar Square and to go quietly and on my own into my lovely All Souls Church and reflect on all the amazing experiences and people I have known there. I celebrated with Peter and Gary. There was an eight-foot-tall cross on the fourth plinth in Trafalgar Square; it was like a sign to look to God—he alone has the answers. There was also snow, which added to the magical atmosphere of Christmas time. I have always loved that time of year, and I still do. It also meant we had a family Christmas, all of us together with my sister and her partner; it was full of so much food and lots of chats. It was a beautiful time, wrapped in safety and love. I was so happy, and my mother remained my lighthouse.

January 2010 arrived—the month Mark walked back into the restaurant. We got married a year to the day we met, on 17 January. Emma appeared to be recovering from cancer in 2010. The snow lasted. Mark had been to the Tapas Restaurant with friends in October, and I just thought what a lovely man he was. I had already met his best friend when he started as a first-year student at my school in Tunbridge Wells in the 1980s. I had welcomed the New Year group and had given him a hug, being a fourth-year student at the time in 1980. He had never forgotten it, and he also knew Peter from school as well. It is funny how years, like invisible threads, suddenly appear again and are brought into the now of reality. They never go away and just wait in the wings until it is time for them to come back out into the light. I believe in God, and he will give things back that were not finished properly or discarded the first time, even if it is many years later.

Veronica and Peter have been such significant, life changing friends; they have been there for huge events in my life, and I believe it is symbolic that their birthdays and Mark's all fall a day after each other in this month. I take comfort in the fact that my February friends, including Mel, are loyal, fierce, wise, strong, and able to see a way through any confusion. They are consistent and have a bottomless ability to love, and you can feel that love like a furnace. In 2010, I just hoped that Mark was like them.

It is terrifying to allow yourself to trust again. I took Mark to my church, and he sat by the small electric heater. The sermon was full of hell and brimstone—how God would save you from your sins and from hell itself. The passionate old war veteran shouts his joy of the Lord. How, when he was in hospital in the war for eighteen months, all twenty of the injured men in the same ward along with him found their salvation. Mark was being burned by the electric fire to his right and being told about hell on his left.

He came round for a birthday meal that dad and I prepared from scratch; we made sauces, marinated meat, and I baked a cheesecake. I used rice to keep the pastry flat, so when we all had a slice, there was a lot of crunching as the raw, hard rice had mixed itself into the base. *But it went well*, I thought.

We tried to catch up as much as we could, but that usually involved seeing Mark after I finished work. Our courtship involved chats on the wishing chair sofa in his flat until 3 a.m., and we managed it somehow, despite Mark getting hardly any sleep as his work started around 7 a.m. It was still snowing, and he walked me home but slipped one early morning on the ice and snow, bashing his head on the street.

I spent my mornings writing before work and filming with Einaar. Paul Bedsprings had typed up one of my books in Edinburgh; it took him ages, and I sent it to Emma to look at. I didn't have the courage to send it to publishers; in 2010, I still didn't own a computer and wrote everything by hand without sending it out. I still felt so neurotic, and the chaos of work just exaggerated my emotions. I tried to help the people that came into the tapas restaurant: one was going through a heroin detox, another was trying to get out of a violent relationship, and another had lost her home because her partner had cheated on her.

Everyone was really surprised I had a boyfriend, and when they met Mark, they warned him: "She is hard work. Are you sure?"

We went to Alvaro's for lunch, and he graciously said, "He is lucky to have you."

Mel turned forty, and Lizzie started an MA in Anthropology. One of my old staff at the Tapas Restaurant also turned up for a job; he had been gone for nearly a year and said he went to Australia to be with his new boyfriend, but when he got there, this man locked him in a cellar, and he has only just escaped and gotten back home. I didn't know what to say, but I gave him his job back.

I went to one of Mark's food shows in London with Peter, who was delighted by the artisan bread we could take for free and the goody bag. He liked Mark. In fact, all my friends liked him when they met him. They were relieved, especially Claire and Gary, that I had met someone strong, funny, and completely normal. They were hesitant when I first told them, as they knew how hurt I had been by wrong choices and bad men.

My mother and dad sat quietly eating their porridge while I had outbursts and crying fits. My mother said, "How is Mark going to cope with your moods?" and told me not to "take it out on those who really care."

I planned to make another film with Einaar, which I had written, while we continued filming Alpha. I tried to make time for church, my women's group, seeing Madge, and I even booked a flight to Florence to reuite with Veronica. Dean met me and Mark on a Monday; he was flying to Cuba for a holiday, as our Mexico holidays were over. Alvaro was establishing himself as an artist, selling all over the world. I was burning the candle at both ends. My days were full, work was utterly chaotic, and then I caught up with Mark. I had no idea how to fit it all in.

On 5 April, I walked out of the tapas restaurant because I couldn't take it anymore. I had no idea what to do. I decided to call supply teaching again. They were overjoyed to hear from me and believed that enough time had passed for me to go into schools and be free of all *Big Brother* recognition and reactions. I believed them. While I waited for all my documents to be in order, I worked at the pub up the road from the tapas restaurant. It was a completely different atmosphere; there was no shouting, and everyone was kind to each other. The owner was generous and funny. Unfortunately, he got cancer and died. The cobbler found out he had cancer too, and Monkey Dave died suddenly. Paul Bedspring suffered the worst, most heart-breaking, desperate loss in August. Dear boy.

My insecurities that I had not dealt with kept floating to the top. But, on 11 May, Mark asked me to marry him. He had asked my dad for my hand in marriage—a very gallant thing to do. We were in his flat, and as he proposed, Gary clap clap was on TV in a show. It was unbelievable. I could hear Gary in the background, and this wonderful man, Mark, was proposing to me. I say yes!

I got a job with Einaar, in his carpet shop, but I am absolutely useless at Maths and had no idea what I was being asked by customers. I was still fighting my OCD and manic outbursts that leave me drained, confused, and exhausted. My friends know how much pain I have been through and have started to get worried about me again. I went to see an exhibition in London of Peter; he had been chosen and had a portrait of his face all over Westminster. It was very impressive. My mother and father flew back to Spain in June and packed a huge number of boxes as they were selling the house to us. It was very emotional for us all.

Mark came to Florence with me, and I reunited with Veronica. Mark and I walk around the city and climb up some steps to a lovely plateau with a fantastic, iconic view of Florence. We sat there for a while, taking it all in. Suddenly, a group of people arrived, all dressed in 1950s outfits and holding tiny brown suitcases. They unfolded tables, opened their suitcases, and inside was a record player, which they put a record on, and then they did this amazing dance, so elegant and stunning in the dusk of the Florence evening. We were thrilled. We realised we were really good at bimbling, just seeing what we saw and finding things as we went along. We walked down a little street and found a small pizza place full of atmosphere and got a pizza the size of a house really cheap.

Mark started leaving me little notes on the same note paper my mother used. It is uncanny. He says more romantic things like "Happy 100th day, darling." We got involved in the film festival in Hastings, and we filmed in the house with Einaar editing it. We had such a laugh making it. Unfortunately, we felt a lot of coldness when I took Mark to Einaar's church, as we hoped it might be a place we could worship. They just ignored us when we said we didn't feel comfortable doing the marriage course; it was quite heart-breaking for me, and we didn't go back. Our bans were read out in July, and as of the 17th of July, we were six months into our relationship. Before we left the church, Zainab came down for the weekend and came to church. Ironically, the whole service was about an Olympian and being who you are truly meant to be. She was amazed, as if the sermon had been written just for her. We left that church, and the sermon on that particular Sunday said, "Be manure and scatter your fertiliser." That was enough for us.

I now have a home with Mark that is growing in beauty, peace, and hope. Life is not easy, but to love and be loved is a gift.

The Missing Link (A poem)
For Mark.

I could never find that missing piece.
    For years what was it again?
    So, the jigsaw hung there with a gap
    Gaping
    It spoke of a loss much deeper than the game of a puzzle.
    Unsolved indeed it stayed for years.
    Until you came.
    "What's this wedged into your sanded floorboards?"
    Your eyes shining and mouth soft smile.
    I reframed it and hung it in the bedroom where your eyes reflected
on the glass and smiled.
                   The End.

By my birthday in October 2010, my mother was planning to buy another house in Hastings. My sister collected her massive dining room table from our house, which she has had since her twenties. It was a time of change for everyone. Emma sent me a story that she wrote and hoped to publish. She had a dog called Charlie and had to say goodbye to him in one of her phone calls to me a few weeks before her death. She

291

was happy she had found him a new home. I talked to her for an hour before she died in October 2011. She was just fifty years old.

2010 was a year of huge changes that would last a lifetime.

Promises were made, and plans were remade. It took the year 2020 to finally face myself at the mirror. I have written from my heart to hopefully make you laugh and find your own true self. I invite you to meet me at the mirror. I took a long, hard look at myself in the year of lockdown, a year of changes and sadness, in mirrors that show you all sides of yourself. I hope we can all move forward on the right path and not limit ourselves to small mirrors or keep looking with regret and shame in the rear-view mirror.

As a teacher, I have always used my first name, Lisa, and when I got married, I was known as Mrs Lisa Wickens in any school I have worked in. I had one wonderful job at Cavendish School in Eastbourne from 2015–2019, and it was the only school where I could be the teacher I used to be before *Big Brother*. The warmth, respect, and friendship from the staff for all my hard work gave me back my confidence and belief in myself. I met Julia, a teacher who loved and guided me, a lovely student called Lillie, and I met another student there called Harry, who reminded me of the wonderful students I had known in London. He was full of respect for me as his teacher and had a fantastic perspective on life. I keep in touch with him through his father, John, and am so proud of how he is building his life. He wanted to say some words for my book. He wrote: "Oh, Mrs Wickens, how can I begin to thank such a lovely supply teacher? It didn't matter what lesson we had; whenever we walked into our class and saw her sitting in the teacher's seat, that lesson would become 1,000 times better. She is so nice, has such a beautiful personality, and she could make you smile on the darkest of days. She would push you to follow your dreams and live life to the fullest. So here is to Mrs Wickens, the reason I made it through school!"

Harry was so encouraging, and in one lesson in 2018, I was scribbling a letter to one of my oldest friends. The students, all so polite, were working quietly. I had lost the friendship in 2001, as I was in a whirl of fame after *Big Brother*. I had been heartbroken about it for years. Harry told me to send the letter, and although I was afraid, I sent it anyway.

In 2020, Rima, my estranged friend, responded out of the blue by phoning me. The letter had sat in her pigeonhole at work, and she had found it by chance while clearing it out. Our friendship began again shortly after, as if no time had passed. She means the world to me.

PENNY ELLIS

Rima (A poem)

On the shapes only you see within the shadows.
   A shade across the sun makes you shiver, yet—
   You alone draw truth, dawn red around you.
   For it is you making from nature's free gift, a laugh of life.
   You have been given strides of strength that allow you to leap across
others crevices hardened as life's experiences fossilize.
   Yours is a new dawn.
   As delicate as a butterfly's breath.
   As well as the fresh crisp wind in amongst the leaves that is in you.
   You make me realise and hear its call.
   Being is the most difficult lesson we learn.
                   The End.

I used to pray as I walked to Cavendish School that God would keep me safe and sane, that I could just get on with life and teach, and everything would be normal. I would take the shortcut through a graveyard, praying I could write a book to help others and also get my friend Rima back. Both of these prayers came true. I left the Cavendish School in 2019 just as my first book, *A River through My Desert*, was in the process of getting published. I know my faith has saved me. It is what I personally believe. When the world has you dancing on a pinprick and there is a hurricane in your mind and a cloak of fear around your heart, it is in those moments that Jesus has helped me. An interview I had given to *Premier Magazine* in 2020 was found online in *OK! Magazine* in 2021, along with a photo of my cat. It was a personal photo I had put up on my Facebook page. Under the photo of my cat, it read: "Penny had a fondness for cats and has gone back to her faith," both of which are true facts, but what an invasion of privacy!

"Without whom this novel would not have been written," Ben Elton said of *Big Brother 1* and *2* contestants when he published his book in 2001. I will end my story with some of the emails I have treasured since 2001 and echo what Ben Elton said. I thank you all from the bottom of my heart for your love and acceptance and for watching *Big Brother 2* in 2001, or maybe you found it years later on social media? Without your support, there would have been no show.

For anyone twenty years along like me, life will take its toll, but no one can take away the experiences we felt in the summer of 2001 and that we shared together. What an experience it was! It will always be a forever memory in our hearts. Thank you all, in your thousands of emails, for your words of love and kindness.

You said in your emails from 2001:

"Hi there, Penny, I just want to say that I think you were really good in that house. And I have watched the live coverage every day from my study, when I was meant to be studying. I thought that out of all the people there, you were the nicest and most thoughtful."

"Thank you for the entertainment and brief view into your life, however removed it may have seemed from your usual life."

"Thank you for entertaining the nation. I work in the aerospace industry, where we are constantly trying to do the strange and wacky in an environment of restrictions. It is OK to be different; don't take it personally."

"Well done. We think you did really well and also think you should have stayed in the house. Never mind, though, it will be an experience you will never forget".

Finally, I would just like to say:

It has been wonderful meeting you at the mirror.

Thank you for sharing my journey.

I wish you a life full of peace, kindness, love, and acceptance. I hold you in my heart.